SYRACUSE UNIVERSITY 15219956
Cities of our past and present,

SO-AAG-005

DATE DUE

inst.coll. DEC 1 5 1980   NOV 1 6 1980 S/RT

MAR 1 9 1981 inst.coll.   SEP 4 1981 S/RT

JAN 1 5 1992 BIRD   DEC 1 3 1991

Cities of Our Past and Present

Cities of Our Past and Present

A Descriptive Reader

Edited by *Wilson Smith*

The Johns Hopkins University

John Wiley & Sons, Inc., New York · London · Sydney

Copyright © 1964 by John Wiley & Sons, Inc.

All Rights Reserved
This book or any part thereof
must not be reproduced in any form
without the written permission of the publisher.

Library of Congress Catalog Card Number: 64-15001
Printed in the United States of America

HT
123
S59
C.2.

To Philip and Mabel Reed

Preface

American urban history is more than ever a rich, intriguing, and open field for inquiry. Like all Americans within the past few decades, historians have been witnessing the creation of a metropolitan civilization. This is the immediate reason for a revival of their interest in our urban life. They are, in increasing numbers, turning to the study of our cities, bringing their common curiosity about the past and a desire to report their findings. In urban studies, moreover, historians are finding the special appeal of a wide and little used avenue into understanding the American past. We have only recently become an urban nation in terms of where our people reside, but towns and cities have been with us since colonial days. The few dozen significant studies listed in the Bibliography to this book reveal the magnitude and variety of themes in urban history. But there is a great deal more to be done. There are, of course, the same dangers of single-mindedness in an entirely urban interpretation of American history that have been overlooked at times in an exclusively frontier interpretation or a narrowly political or a close economic reading of our past. The history of cities, nevertheless, invites a new and important weaving of many separate strands of our national experience.

Nowadays urban historians have strong allies and co-workers, frequently their predecessors in the field. They are indebted to sociologists, economists, and political scientists, city planners and architects, students of public welfare and private philanthropy, housing experts, criminologists, and civic engineers under many labels. To these students and designers of city life belongs much of the credit for shaping intellectual order out of the vast social disorder, the tensions, and the complexities within our cities. The challenge to the urban historian is not only to extend into the past the special points of view and techniques of these experts on city life. It is also to overcome specialization and to provide an encompassing view of cities in our past and present, one that through its breadth of outlook can help us to gauge the pace and quality of urban growth.

At present there is nowhere available a convenient and inexpensive book of contemporaneous descriptions of cities in our past. Doubtless it will not be long before large and comprehensive documentary urban histories appear that are organized along topical lines, that have a "problem approach" to urban history, and that include analytical and critical, as well as descriptive pieces. One collection of this kind has recently been published; such books are needed and will be welcomed. But I think all who trace broad currents in American history will also be taught by, as they will surely enjoy, unpretentious and forthright general descriptions of cities in our past. Writings of this nature constitute much of our urban literature. They have generally been omitted from American documentary histories. Many of them make good reading; some of them are outstanding pieces of contemporary observation.

The appearance of a compact book of readings from this literature, containing pieces that describe how cities looked and what their cultural atmosphere was like, is long overdue. With this collection I have tried to begin to remedy the situation. It is of course only a beginning. As more historians publish in this field, the special problems of urban history will be increasingly documented and such matters as the development of urban health or sanitation or finance or transportation or cultural facilities will be given a hearing. Since my own interests lie in general social history I have sought for this book portraits of our cities at various stages of their development. The face of a city admittedly is seen differently by each viewer; and a city has many faces. In this sense each of these readings, like most witnessed history, is an impression. Yet I have tried to select pieces that speak to the entire condition of a city, particularly to the condition of its people, or that reveal its overall stature at an important moment of its development, or that describe some particular aspect of city life which we now recognize as having been representative, or significant, in other cities of that time.

Because our large cities incorporate most of the problems or characteristics of our smaller cities, and because the literature on our larger cities is more plentiful, these selections describe some two dozen of our large cities. There are incidentally more pieces on New York City than on any other single city simply because the literature on New York life is ampler and more varied.

The headnote preceding each selection is meant to place the reading briefly in a factual historical context, with a short biographical identification of the author of the piece and with references to the pertinent historical literature for that city. In the hope that the student may want to purchase inexpensive books, the paperback edition of a book, when available, is listed in these references and in the Bibliography.

For their help in gathering these readings I wish to thank Willie Lee Rose, Linda Grant DePauw, and Elizabeth Studley. And my thanks go again to Lilly Lavarello for her typing.

WILSON SMITH

Baltimore, Maryland
January 1964

Contents

Part One

The Colonial Towns

1   Boston in 1663 and in 1740

Although they have few exact figures to use, colonial historians have estimated our urban population before the Revolution as follows:

Date	Boston	Philadelphia	New York
1690	7000	4000	3900
1730	13,000	11,500	8600
1750	15,700	13,400	13,300
1775	16,000	40,000	25,000

Until the middle of the eighteenth century Boston was the largest town in North America. In the first of these two descriptions of colonial Boston John Josselyn (fl. 1638–1675), an English traveler and writer who twice visited this continent, briefly depicts Boston as a flourishing seaport in 1663. When he first had visited Boston in 1638, only eight years after its settlement, it was a village with only about 20 or 30 houses. Josselyn was devoted to natural philosophy, and in his book, published at London in 1673 and dedicated to the Fellows of the Royal Society, he recorded his botanical observations in New England. See Fulmer Mood, "Notes on John Josselyn, Gent.," *Transactions of the Colonial Society of Massachusetts*, vol. 28 (1930–1933), pp. 24–36.

The town where all streets led down to the sea was described again in the summer of 1740 by another English visitor, Joseph Bennett. Although Bennett stressed its commercial prosperity, he emphasized that Boston had lost few of its seventeenth century Puritan ways. See

3

J. G. Palfrey, *History of New England*, vol. V (Boston, 1890), 44n.

For colonial Boston see Samuel E. Morison, *The Maritime History of Massachusetts, 1763–1860* (Boston: Sentry Books, 1961), chs. 1–10; Walter Muir Whitehill, *Boston: A Topographical History* (Cambridge, 1959), chs. 1–2; Justin Winsor (ed.), *The Memorial History of Boston*, vols. I–II (Boston, 1880–1881).

Carl Bridenbaugh's classic accounts of our urban colonial history will interest all readers. They are *Cities in the Wilderness: The First Century of Urban Life in America, 1625–1742* (New York, 1955) and *Cities in Revolt: Urban Life in America, 1743–1776* (New York, 1955).

TWO MILES NORTHEAST FROM *Roxbury,* and Forty miles from *New-Plimouth,* in the latitude of 42 or 43 degrees and 10 minutes, in the bottom of *Massachusetts-Bay* is *Boston* (whose longitude is 315 degrees, or as others will, 322 degrees and 30 seconds.) So called from a Town in *Lincolnshire,* which in the *Saxons* time bare the name of St. *Botolph,* and is the Metropolis of this Colony, or rather of the whole Countrey, situated upon a *Peninsula,* about four miles in compass, almost square, and invironed with the Sea, saving one small *Isthmus* which gives access to other Towns by land on the South-side. The Town hath two hills of equal height on the frontire part thereof next the Sea, the one well fortified on the superficies with some Artillery mounted, commanding any Ship as she sails into the Harbour within the still *Bay;* the other hill hath a very strong battery built of whole Timber and fill'd with earth, at the descent of the hill in the extreamest part thereof, betwixt these two strong Arms, lyes a large *Cove* or *Bay,* on which the chiefest part of the Town is built. To the Northwest is a high mountain that out-tops all, with its three little rising hills on the summit, called *Tramount,*

JOHN JOSSELYN, *An Account of Two Voyages to New-England, Made During the Years 1638, 1663* (Boston, 1865), 124–126.

this is furnished with a Beacon and great Guns, from hence you may overlook all the Islands in the *Bay*, and descry such Ships as are upon the Coast: the houses are for the most part raised on the Sea-banks and wharfed out with great industry and cost, many of them standing upon piles, close together on each side the streets as in *London*, and furnished with many fair shops, their materials are Brick, Stone, Lime, handsomely contrived, with three meeting Houses or Churches, and a Town-house built upon pillars where the Merchants may confer, in the Chambers above they keep their monethly Courts. Their streets are many and large, paved with pebble stone, and the South-side adorned with Gardens and Orchards. The Town is rich and very populous, much frequented by strangers, here is the dwelling of their Governour. On the North-west and North-east two constant Fairs are kept for daily Traffick thereunto. On the South there is a small, but pleasant Common where the Gallants a little before Sun-set walk with their *Marmalet*-Madams, as we do in *Morefields*, &c. till the nine a clock Bell rings them home to their respective habitations, when presently the Constables walk their rounds to see good orders kept, and to take up loose people. Two miles from the town, at a place called *Muddy-River*, the Inhabitants have Farms, to which belong rich arable grounds and meadows where they keep their Cattle in the Summer, and bring them to *Boston* in the Winter; the Harbour before the Town is filled with Ships and other Vessels for most part of the year.

::::::::::::::::

THIS TOWN STANDS ON A PENINSULA, or almost island, about four miles in circumference, at the bottom of a fine bay of the sea. At the entrance of the bay there are several rocks of great magnitude, the tops of which appeared considerably above the surface of the water at the time of our passing by them. There are also about a dozen little islands all in view as we approach the town, some of which are as fine farms as any in the whole country.

JOSEPH BENNETT, "The History of New England," *Proceedings of the Massachusetts Historical Society*, V (January, 1861), 108–117, 123–126.

This town has a good natural security, in my opinion; for there is great plenty of rocks and shoals, which are not easy to be avoided by strangers to the coasts; and there is but one safe channel to approach the harbor, and that so narrow that three ships can hardly sail through abreast: but, within the harbor, there is room enough for five hundred sail to lie at an anchor.

The entrance to the harbor is defended by a strong castle, which they call Fort William, on which there are mounted a hundred guns, twenty of which lie on a platform level with the water, to prevent an enemy passing the castle; which is a quarry surrounded by a covered way, joined with two lines of communication to the main battery. This battery is situated so near the channel, that all ships going up to town must sail within musket-shot of it. They have always one company of soldiers doing duty in the castle, even in time of peace; but in time of war they are said to have five hundred: and so I was taught to believe they had now, till I saw the contrary. But there is such a number of men, who are excused all other military duty, on purpose to attend the service of the castle if need require it, whom they say they can call together in an hour's time.

About two leagues distant from the castle, on a rock, stands an exceeding fine light-house, at which there is a guard constantly attending to prevent surprise; from whence they make signals to the castle when any ships come in sight, whether friend or foe: for no ship is permitted to pass the castle without examination, for fear they should bring any sort of epidemical sickness into the town; and the captain is obliged to certify for all on board his ship before he can pass, and is liable to such fine and imprisonment as they shall think proper if he conceals any disease that is on board the ship. And in this they are extremely exact, and will not suffer any sick persons to come on shore, nor even any of the goods, until they have performed quarantine.

But when a signal is made from off the light-house to the castle of the approach of an enemy, if there be more than four or five ships, then the castle thereupon gives a signal to the town; and those of the town alarm the country by firing of a beacon. And for that purpose they have a very famous one on the north-west side of the town, erected on a hill. . . .

At the bottom of the bay there is a fine wharf, about a mile in length, on the north side of which are built many warehouses for the storing of merchants' goods: this they call the Long Wharf, to distinguish it from others of lesser note. And, to this wharf, ships of the greatest burthen come up so close as to unload their cargo without the assistance of boats.

From the end of the Long Wharf, which lies east from the town, the buildings rise gradually with an easy ascent westward about a mile. There are a great many good houses, and several fine streets, little inferior to some of our best in London, the principal of which is King's Street: it runs upon a line from the end of the Long Wharf, about a quarter of a mile; and at the upper end of it stands the Town House, or Guild Hall, where the Governor meets the Council, and House of Representatives; and the several Courts of Justice are held there also. And there are likewise walks for the merchants, where they meet every day at one o'clock, in imitation of the Exchange at London, which they call by the name of Royal Exchange too, round which there are several booksellers' shops; and there are four or five printing-houses, which have full employment in printing and reprinting books, of one sort or other, that are brought from England and other parts of Europe.

This town was not built after any regular plan, but has been enlarged from time to time as the inhabitants increased; and is now, from north to south, something more than two miles in length, and in the widest part about one mile and a half in breadth. . . . There are three Episcopal churches, one of which is called the King's Chapel, and has a handsome organ, and a magnificent seat for the Governor, who goes to this place when of the Church of England; and there are nine Independent meeting-houses, one Anabaptist meeting, one Quakers' meeting, and one French Church. There are sixty streets, forty-one lanes, and eighteen alleys, besides squares, courts, &c. The streets are well paved, and lying upon a descent. The town is, for the generality, as dry and clean as any I ever remember to have seen. When we were upon the sea, that part of the town which lies about the harbor appeared to us in the form of a crescent, or half-moon; and the country, rising gradually from it, afforded us a pleasant prospect of the neighboring fields and woods.

Boston is said to be not only the principal town of trade in

New England, but also of any in all the British-American Colonies. They employ annually between three and four hundred ships, great and small; and they also build abundance of shipping for the English and other European nations. They have likewise a whale and several cod fisheries, which are very considerable; which, with their ship-building, is the chief support of the country. They trade to the Carolinas, and also to Jamaica and Barbadoes, and all the other West-India islands and plantations in general; with whom they exchange their beef, pork, fish, and other provisions, and also what they call lumber (such as deal-boards, pipe and hogshead staves, shingles, and such like commodities), for rice, pitch, tar, rum and sugar, and spices and logwood. Great part of the last-mentioned commodities they send to England in return for almost all sorts of English goods, but more especially clothing for men, women, and children. They have paper manufactured here, and some coarse woollen cloths; but workmen's wages are so high in this part of the world, that they find it cheaper to import them from London. . . .

Boston being the capital of New England, as London is of Old England, the country people find their account in bringing of their choicest provisions to this town; by means of which, this place is well served with all sorts of eatables the country affords, many of which, as to the kind of them, are much the same as those we have in London. . . . Their beef, mutton, and lamb are as good as ever I desire to eat. Poultry are exceeding cheap [and fish]. . . . They sell a fine fresh cod that will weigh a dozen pound or more, just taken out of the sea, which are generally alive, for about twopence sterling. . . . Salmon they have, too, in great plenty, which is as fine as any I ever eat of, anywhere in my life; and those they will sell for about a shilling a piece, which, will weigh fourteen or fifteen pounds. . . . And they have, likewise, plenty of oysters . . . Lobsters are plenty, and very good and cheap, here . . . Bread is something cheaper here than in London, but is not near so good in common. Butter is very fine, and cheaper than ever I bought any at London; the best is sold all the summer long for about threepence per pound: but as for cheese, 'tis neither good nor cheap. Milk is sold here for much about the same price as at London; only here they give full measure.

As to drink, they have no good beer in this country: Madeïra wines, rum-punch, are the liquors they drink in common. With their victuals, the generality of the people drink cider. But there are several brewers in the town that brew for the shipping, and serve some private families with table-beer, which is very cheap, —less than half the price we pay at London. But cider being cheap likewise, and the people used to it, they don't encourage malt liquors. They pay about three shillings sterling a barrel for cider.

Their fuel is altogether wood, and is one of the most expensive articles of housekeeping in Boston; but, up in the country, they have it for cutting. . . .

Their observation of the sabbath (which they rather choose to call by the name of the Lord's Day, whensoever they have occasion to mention it)—it is the strictest kept that ever I yet saw anywhere. On that day, no man, woman, or child is permitted to go out of town on any pretence whatsoever; nor can any that are out of town come in on the Lord's Day. . . . And as they will by no means admit of trading on Sundays, so they are equally tenacious about preserving good order in the town on the Lord's Day: and they will not suffer any one to walk down to the water-side, though some of the houses are adjoining to the several wharfs; nor, even in the hottest days of summer, will they admit of any one to take the air on the Common. . . . But that which is the most extraordinary is, that they commence the sabbath from the setting of the sun on the Saturday evening; and in conformity to that, all trade and business ceases, and every shop in the town is shut up: even a barber is finable for shaving after that time. Nor are any of the taverns permitted to entertain company; for, in that case, not only the house, but every person found therein, is finable. . . .

As to their ministers, there is no compulsory tax upon the people for their support, but every one contributes according to their inclination or ability. . . . Yet they are not left to depend entirely upon the uncertainty of what people shall happen to give, but have a certain sum paid them every Monday morning, whether so much happens to be collected or not; and no one of them has less than a hundred pounds sterling per annum, which is a comfortable support in this part of the world. . . .

They also provide very well for their poor, and are very tender of exposing those that have lived in a handsome manner; and therefore give them good relief in so private a manner, that it is seldom known to any of their neighbors. And for the meaner sort they have a place built on purpose, which is called the Town Alms-house, where they are kept in a decent manner, and are, as I think, taken care of in every respect suitable to their circumstances in life; and, for the generality, there are above a hundred poor persons in this house; and there is no such thing to be seen in town nor country as a strolling beggar. And it is a rare thing to meet with any drunken people, or to hear an oath sworn, in their streets. . . .

As to money, they have no sort of coin among them,—nothing but paper bills, which are issued by the Governor and Council; but, being made current, they answer the same end as money among themselves. And the people in common had much rather take those bills for any thing they sell than gold or silver, notwithstanding many of them are so miserably fractured, that, in passing from one to another, they often fall into three or four pieces; and many of them are joined together in several places, and are so obliterated with their being often handled, that they are difficult to be understood by those that are unused to them. But, upon application to the treasury, they change them without any expense. The discount between those bills and sterling is four hundred and fifty cents at present; that is, five hundred and fifty pounds of this currency is equal to one hundred pound sterling. But they are variable; being governed by the rise and fall of bills of exchange. Some of those bills are so low as threepence; which is something more than a penny sterling. English half-pence are much used here for change, and are very valuable here. They pass current here at threepence apiece; which is twopence in every shilling sterling above the common course of exchange. I have made inquiry among the merchants of the reason of their being without a coin; and they say the balance of trade with England is so much against them, that they cannot keep any money amongst them: of which they have had the experience, having once had a coin of their own, but were soon stripped of it, so that they had not enough left for their necessary uses; and that obliged them to have recourse to this method of making bills. There is still a great deal of both English and foreign gold and silver in the hands of the merchants; but they use it only as merchandise, and buy and sell it only by weight, to send to England in return for goods. . . .

There are several families in Boston that keep a coach, and pair of horses, and some few drive with four horses; but for chaises and saddle-horses, considering the bulk of the place, they outdo London. . . . The common draught-horses used in carts about the town are very small and poor, and seldom have their fill of any thing but labor. The country carts and wagons are generally drawn by oxen, from two to six, according to the distance of place, or burden they are laden with. When the ladies ride out to take the air, it is generally in a chaise or chair, and then but a single horse; and they have a negro servant to drive them. The gentlemen ride out here as in England, some in chairs, and others on horseback, with their negroes to attend them. They travel in much the same manner on business as for pleasure, and are attended in both by their black equipages. Their roads, though they have no turnpikes, are exceeding good in summer; and it is safe travelling night or day, for they have no highway robbers to interrupt them. . . .

For their domestic amusements, every afternoon, after drinking tea, the gentlemen and ladies walk the Mall, and from thence adjourn to one another's houses to spend the evening,—those that are not disposed to attend the evening lecture; which they may do, if they please, six nights in seven, the year round. What they call the Mall is a walk on a fine green Common adjoining to the south-west side of the town. It is near half a mile over, with two rows of young trees planted opposite to each other, with a fine footway between, in imitation of St. James's Park.

The government being in the hands of dissenters, they don't admit of plays or music-houses; but, of late, they have set up an assembly, to which some of the ladies resort. But they are looked upon to be none of the nicest in regard to their reputation; and it is thought it will soon be suppressed, for it is much taken notice of and exploded by the religious and sober part of the people. But, notwithstanding plays and such like diversions do not obtain here, they don't seem to be dispirited nor moped for want of them; for both the ladies and gentlemen dress and appear as gay, in common, as courtiers in England on a coronation or birthday.

And the ladies here visit, drink tea, and indulge every little piece
of gentility, to the height of the mode; and neglect the affairs of
their families with as good a grace as the finest ladies in London.

<hr />

2   William Penn's Philadelphia, 1680's

Like John Josselyn (Reading 1), Gabriel Thomas (1661–
1714) wrote his description of Pennsylvania to attract
European settlers to the new world. Thomas, a Welshman who sailed for Pennsylvania in his twenty-first year,
was a birthright Quaker and early admirer of William
Penn, to whom he dedicated his volume. His account
was the fullest description of the new colony that had
appeared, surpassing Penn's own accounts of 1681 and
1685, upon which Thomas obviously patterned his book.
The annotations to this selection are retained from Meyers' edition of the *Account*.

See Albert C. Meyers' introduction to Thomas's *Account* in his edition of *Narratives of Early Pennsylvania
. . .* (New York, 1912), pp. 309–312. For early Philadelphia see J. Thomas Scharf and Thompson Westcott, *History of Philadelphia, 1609–1884*, vol. I (Philadelphia,
1884), Ellis P. Oberholtzer, *Philadelphia, A History of
the City and It's People*, vol. I (Philadelphia, 1912), and
Frederick B. Tolles, *Meeting House and Counting House:
The Quaker Merchants of Colonial Philadelphia, 1682–
1763* (Chapel Hill, 1948).

<hr />

I T REMAIN'D WITH VERY LITTLE IMPROVEMENT TILL THE YEAR
1681, in which William Penn Esq; had the Country given him
by King Charles the Second, in lieu of Money that was due to

GABRIEL THOMAS, *An Historical and Geographical Account
of Pensilvania and of West-New-Jersey* (London, 1698)
in Albert C. Meyers (ed.), *Narratives of Early Pennsylvania . . .* (New York, 1912), 317–318, 329–332.

(and signal Service done by) his Father, Sir William Penn, and from him bore the Name of Pensilvania.

Since that time, the Industrious (nay Indefatigable) Inhabitants have built a Noble and Beautiful City, and called it Philadelphia, which contains above two thousand Houses, all Inhabited; and most of them Stately, and of Brick, generally three Stories high, after the Mode in London, and as many several Families in each. There are very many Lanes and Alleys, as first, Huttons-Lane,[1] Morris-Lane,[2] Jones's-Lane,[3] wherein are very good Buildings; Shorters-Alley,[4] Towers-Lane,[5] Wallers-Alley,[6] Turners-Lane,[7] Sikes-Alley,[8] and Flowers-Alley.[9] All these Alleys and Lanes extend from the Front Street to the Second Street. There is another Alley in the Second Street, called Carters-Alley.[10] There are also besides these Alleys and Lanes, several fine Squares and Courts within this Magnificent City, (for so I may justly call it). As for the particular Names of the several Streets contained therein, the Principal are as follows, viz, Walnut-Street, Vine-Street, Mulberry-Street,[11] Chesnut-Street, Sassafras-Street,[12] taking their Names from the abundance of those Trees that formerly grew there; High-Street,[13] Broad-Street, Delaware-Street, Front-Street, with several of less Note, too tedious to insert here.

It hath in it Three Fairs every Year, and Two Markets every

[1] *The second alley above Walnut Street, Thomas Hooton being owner of an adjacent lot.*

[2] *Possibly opposite the bank lot of Anthony Morris (1654–1721), the emigrant, a rich Quaker brewer, mayor and provincial councillor.*

[3] *The first alley above High (now Market) Street, running from Front to Second Street, adjoining a lot of Griffith Jones (d. 1712), a Welshman, one of the wealthiest citizens.*

[4] *Not located, but Elizabeth Shorter owned a lot above Chestnut Street.*

[5] *Ewers Lane, above Chestnut Street, adjoining Robert Ewer's lot.*

[6] *Not located.*

[7] *The first below Mulberry (now Arch) Street, adjoining Robert Turner's property.*

[8] *May have been opposite the bank lot of Nathaniel Sykes, below Chestnut Street.*

[9] *Doubtless named for Enoch Flower, Quaker, who taught the first school in Philadelphia, in 1683.*

[10] *The first below Chestnut Street, William Carter owning an adjoining lot on Second Street.*

[11] *Now Arch.*

[12] *Now Race.*

[13] *Now Market.*

Week, They kill above Twenty Fat Bullocks every Week, in the hottest time in Summer, for their present spending in that City, besides many Sheep, Calves, and Hogs.

This City is Situated between Schoolkill-River and the great River Delaware,[1] which derives its Name from Captain Delaware, who came there pretty early: Ships of Two or Three Hundred Tuns may come up to this City, by either of these two Rivers. Moreover, in this Province are Four Great Market-Towns, *viz,* Chester, the German Town, New-Castle, and Lewis-Town,[2] which are mightily Enlarged in this latter Improvement. Between these Towns, the Water-Men constantly Ply their Wherries;[3] likewise all those Towns have Fairs kept in them, besides there are several Country Villages, *viz.* Dublin,[4] Harford,[5] Merioneth,[6] and Radnor in Cambry;[7] all which Towns, Villages and Rivers, took their Names from the several Countries whence the present Inhabitants came.

The Air here is very delicate, pleasant, and wholesom; the Heavens serene, rarely overcast, bearing mighty resemblance to the better part of France; after Rain they have commonly a very clear Sky, the Climate is something Colder in the depth of Winter and Hotter in the height of Summer; (the cause of which is its being a Main Land or Continent; the Days also are two Hours longer in the shortest Day in Winter, and shorter by two Hours in the long Day of Summer) than here in England, which makes the Fruit so good, and the Earth so fertil. . . .

It is now time to return to the City of Brotherly-Love (for so

---

[1] *So named by one of the Virginia adventurers, Captain Samuel Argall, who visited the Bay in 1610, in honor of the then Governor of Virginia, Thomas West, Lord de la Warr, of whose alleged visit there no evidence is known.*

[2] *Lewes, in Sussex County, Delaware.*

[3] *Light boats used on rivers.*

[4] *Now Ogontz, Montgomery County, Pennsylvania.*

[5] *Haverford.*

[6] *Merion.*

[7] *Cambria, i.e., the Welsh Tract, that area extending northwesterly from Schuylkill River and embracing at that time the townships of Merion, Haverford, and Radnor, occupied by Welsh people, many of them from the northern counties of Wales—principally Merioneth, Denbigh, Montgomery, and Flint.*

much the Greek Word or Name Philadelphia imports) which though at present so obscure, that neither the Map-Makers, nor Geographers have taken the least notice of her, tho she far exceeds her Namesake of Lydia,[1] (having above Two Thousand [2] Noble Houses for her Five Hundred Ordinary) or Celisia, or Cælesyria; yet in a very short space of time she will, in all probability, make a fine Figure in the World, and be a most Celebrated Emporeum. Here is lately built a Noble Town-House or Guild-Hall, also a Handsom Market-House, and a convenient Prison.[3] The Number of Christians both Old and Young Inhabiting in that Countrey, are by a Modest Computation, adjudged to amount to above Twenty Thousand.[4]

The Laws of this Countrey, are the same with those in England; our Constitution being on the same Foot: Many Disputes and Differences are determined and composed by Arbitration; and all Causes are decided with great Care and Expedition, being concluded (generally) at furthest at the Second Court, unless they happen to be very Nice and Difficult Cases; under Forty Shillings any one Justice of the Peace has Power to Try the Cause. Thieves of all sorts, are oblig'd to restore four fold after they have been Whipt and Imprison'd, according to the Nature of their Crime; and if they be not of Ability to restore four fold, they must be in Servitude till 'tis satisfied. They have Curious Wharfs as also several large and fine Timber-Yards, both at Philadelphia, and New-Castle, especially at the Metropolis, before Robert Turner's Great and Famous House, where are built Ships of considerable Burthen; they Cart their Goods from that Wharf into the City of Philadelphia, under an Arch, over which part of the Street is built, which is called Chesnut-Street-Wharf,[5] besides other Wharfs, as High-Street Wharf, Mulberry Street Wharf, and Vine-Street Wharf, and all those are Common

---

[1] *Philadelphia in Lydia, Asia Minor. A marginal note in the original reads: "Three German Miles from Smyrna."*

[2] *This number doubtless is an exaggeration.*

[3] *The prison was in the centre of High (now Market) Street, a short distance east of Second Street. "The Cage," a small jail, built in 1683, was still standing at the intersection of High and Second streets.*

[4] *Probably an excessive estimate for that period.*

[5] *An error; Robert Turner's wharf was at Mulberry (now Arch) Street.*

Wharfs; and likewise there are very pleasant Stairs, as Trus [1] and
Carpenter-Stairs,[2] besides several others. There are above Thirty
Carts belonging to that City, Four or Five Horses to each. There
is likewise a very convenient Wharf called Carpenter's Wharf,
which hath a fine necessary Crain belonging to it, with suitable
Granaries, and Store-Houses. A Ship of Two Hundred Tun may
load and unload by the side of it, and there are other Wharfs
(with Magazines and Ware-Houses) which front the City all
along the River, as also a Curious and Commodious Dock [3] with
a Draw-Bridge to it, for the convenient Reception of Vessels;
where have been built some Ships of Two or Three Hundred
Tuns each: They have very Stately Oaks to build Ships with,
some of which are between Fifty and Sixty Foot long, and clear
from Knots, being very straight and well Grain'd. In this famous
City of Philadelphia there are several Rope-Makers, who have
large and curious Rope-Walks especially one Joseph Wilcox.[4]
Also Three or Four Spacious Malt-Houses, as many large Brew-
Houses, and many handsom Bake-Houses for Publick Use.

In the said City are several good Schools of Learning for Youth,
in order to the Attainment of Arts and Sciences, as also Reading,
Writing, etc. Here is to be had on any Day in the Week, Tarts,.
Pies, Cakes, etc. We have also several Cooks-Shops, both Roasting
and Boyling, as in the City of London; Bread, Beer, Beef, and
Pork, are sold at any time much cheaper than in England (which
arises from their Plenty) our Wheat is very white and clear from
Tares, making as good and white Bread as any in Europe. Happy
Blessings, for which we owe the highest Gratitude to our Plenti-
ful Provider, the great Creator of Heaven and Earth. The Water-
Mills far exceed those in England, both for quickness and grinding
good Meal, their being great choice of good Timber, and earlier
Corn than in the aforesaid Place, they are made by one Peter

---

[1] *Tresse's Stairs, built by Thomas Tresse from the bank or bluff of Front
Street down to King Street, between High (now Market) and Mulberry
(now Arch) streets.*

[2] *Carpenter's Stairs, built by Samuel Carpenter from Front to King Street,
between Chestnut and Walnut streets.*

[3] *Id est, Dock Creek.*

[4] *Joseph Wilcox, previously mentioned as having succeeded to his father's
rope-walk at the north end of the town. He was mayor in 1706.*

Deal,[1] a Famous and Ingenious Workman, especially for inventing such like Machines.

All sorts of very good Paper are made in the German-Town; as also very fine German Linen, such as no Person of Quality need be asham'd to wear; and in several places they make very good Druggets, Crapes, Camblets, and Serges, besides other Woollen Cloathes, the Manufacture of all which daily improves: And in most parts of the Countrey there are many Curious and Spacious Buildings, which several of the Gentry have erected for their Country-Houses. As for the Fruit-Trees they Plant, they arrive at such Perfection, that they bear in a little more than half the time that they commonly do in England. . . .

What I have deliver'd concerning this Province, is indisputably true, I was an Eye-Witness to it all, for I went in the first Ship that was bound from England for that Countrey, since it received The Name of Pensilvania, which was in the Year 1681. The Ship's Name was the *John and Sarah* of London, Henry Smith Commander.[2] I have declin'd giving any Account of several things which I have only heard others speak of, because I did not see them my self, for I never held that way infallible, to make Reports from Hear-say. I saw the first Cellar when it was digging for the use of our Governour Will. Penn.[3]

[1] *Peter Daile (d. 1703) of Pennypack Mills in 1703.*

[2] *Of 100 tons burden. She departed from London in October, 1681, and arrived in Pennsylvania before December 15.*

[3] *Governor William Penn's house, built in 1682 in the centre of a large lot between Front, High (Market), and Second streets, patented in 1701 to his daughter Laetitia. After his first visit (1682–1684) the house was occupied by some of the provincial offices for several years, the council meeting there. Robert Turner's letter of 1685 . . . stating that his house, built the year previously, was the first brick house erected in Philadelphia, would seem to discredit the generally accepted view that the so-called Laetitia House, the brick structure in Fairmount Park, removed thither from the above lot some years ago, is the house built for Penn in 1682.*

3   Williamsburg,
The Tobacco Planters' Capital

The first account has been a standard description of eighteenth-century Williamsburg ever since its publication in London in 1724. Hugh Jones (c. 1670–1760) witnessed life in the colonial capital as professor of Natural Philosophy and Mathematics in the College of William and Mary and as chaplain of the General Assembly.

The next selection is from the brief journal of an anonymous French traveler who visited Williamsburg in 1765. It reminds us that Williamsburg lost its otherwise sleepy appearance when the colonial courts and the General Assembly were in session.

On Colonial Williamsburg, see Carl Bridenbaugh, *Seat of Empire: The Political Role of Eighteenth-Century Williamsburg* (Williamsburg, 1950); Thomas Jefferson Wertenbaker, *The Golden Age of Colonial Culture* (Ithaca, New York: Great Seal Books, 1959), ch. VI; and Richard L. Morton, *Colonial Virginia*, vol. II (Chapel Hill, 1960), ch. 9.

HERE [GOVERNOR NICHOLSON] LAID OUT THE CITY OF WILLIAMSBURGH (in the form of a cypher, made of W. and M.) on a ridge at the head springs of two great creeks, one running into James, and the other into York River, which are each navigable

HUGH JONES, *The Present State of Virginia* . . . (New York, 1865), 25–32. The style of this selection has been modernized in accordance with Richard L. Morton's edition (Chapel Hill, 1956), 66–71.

for sloops, within a mile of the town; at the head of which creeks are good landings, and lots laid out, and dwelling houses and ware houses built; so that this town is most conveniently situated, in the middle of the lower part of Virginia, commanding two noble rivers, not above four miles from either, and is much more commodious and healthful, than if built upon a river.

Publick buildings here of note, are the College, the Capitol, the Governor's House, and the Church. The latitude of the College at Williamsburgh, to the best of my observation, is 37°.21′. north.

The front which looks due east is double, and is 136 foot long. It is a lofty pile of brick building adorned with a cupola. At the north end runs back a large wing, which is a handsome hall, answerable to which the chapel is to be built; and there is a spacious piazza on the west side, from one wing to the other. It is approached by a good walk, and a grand entrance by steps, with good courts and gardens about it, with a good house and apartments for the Indian Master and his scholars, and out-houses; and a large pasture enclosed like a park with about 150 acres of land adjoining, for occasional uses.

The building is beautiful and commodious, being first modelled by Sir Christopher Wren, adapted to the nature of the country by the gentlemen there; and since it was burnt down, it has been rebuilt, and nicely contrived, altered and adorned by the ingenious direction of Governor Spotswood; and is not altogether unlike Chelsea Hospital. . . .

The nature of the country scarce yet admits of a possibility of reducing the collegians to the nice methods of life and study observed in Oxford and Cambridge; though by degrees they may copy from thence many useful customs and constitutions. . . .

Fronting the College at near its whole breadth, is extended a noble street mathematically streight (for the first design of the town's form is changed to a much better) just three quarters of a mile in length: at the other end of which stands the Capitol, a noble, beautiful, and commodious pile as any of its kind, built at the cost of the late Queen, and by the direction of the Governor.

In this is the Secretary's office with all the courts of justice and law, held in the same form, and near the same manner, as in England; except the ecclesiastical courts.

Here the governor and twelve counsellors sit as judges, at the General Courts in April and October, whither trials and causes are removed from courts, held at the court-houses monthly in every county by a bench of justices and a county clerk.

Here are also held the Oyer and Terminer courts, one in summer, and the other in winter, added by the charity of the late Queen, for the prevention of prisoners lying in goal above a quarter of a year before their trial.

Here are also courts martial, by judges appointed on purpose, for the trial of pyrates; likewise courts of admiralty, for the trial of ships for illegal trade.

The building is in the form of an H nearly; the Secretary's Office, and the General Court taking up one side below stairs; the middle being an handsom portico leading to the clerk of the Assembly's office, and the House of Burgesses on the other side; which last is not unlike the House of Commons.

In each wing is a good stair case, one leading to the council chamber, where the governor and Council sit in very great state, in imitation of the King and Council, or the Lord Chancellor and House of Lords.

Over the portico is a large room where conferences are held, and prayers are read by the chaplain to the General Assembly; which office I have had the honour for some years to perform. At one end of this is a lobby, and near it is the Clerk of the Council's office; and at the other end are several chambers for the committees of claims, privileges, and elections; and over all these are several good offices for the receiver general, for the auditor, treasurer, etc. and upon the middle is raised a lofty cupola with a large clock.

The whole is surrounded with a neat area, encompassed with a good wall, and near it is a strong sweet prison for criminals; and on the other side of an open court another for debtors, when any are removed thither from other prisons in each county; but such prisoners are very rare, the creditors being there generally very merciful, and the laws so favourable for debtors, that some esteem them too indulgent.

The cause of my being so particular in describing the Capitol is, because it is the best and most commodious pile of its kind that I have seen or heard of.

Because the State House, James Town, and the College have been burnt down, therefore is prohibited in the Capitol the use of fire, candles and tobacco.

Parallel to the main street mentioned is a street on each side of it, but neither quite so long nor broad; and at proper distances are small cross streets, for the convenience of communication.

Near the middle stands the Church, which is a large strong piece of brickwork in the form of a cross, nicely regular and convenient, and adorned as the best churches in London. This from the parish is called Bruton Church, where I had the favour of being lecturer.

Near this is a large octogon tower, which is the magazine or repository of arms and ammunition, standing far from any house except James Town Court-House; for the town is half in James Town County, and half in York County.

Not far from hence is a large area for a market place; near which is a play house and good bowling green.

From the Church runs a street northward called Palace Street; at the other end of which stands the Palace or Governor's House, a magnificent structure, built at the publick expence, finished and beautified with gates, fine gardens, offices, walks, a fine canal, orchards, etc. with a great number of the best arms nicely posited, by the ingenious contrivance of the most accomplished Colonel Spotswood.

This likewise has the ornamental addition of a good cupola or lanthorn, illuminated with most of the town, upon birth-nights, and other nights of occasional rejoicings.

At the Capitol, at publick times, may be seen a great number of handsom, well-dressed, compleat gentlemen. And at the Governor's House upon birth-nights, and at balls and assemblies, I have seen as fine an appearance, as good diversion, and as splendid entertainments in Governor Spotswood's time as I have seen any where else.

These buildings here described are justly reputed the best in all the English America, and are exceeded by few of their kind in England.

In every part of this town are excellent springs of good water, or else may be made good wells; and the ground falling on both sides, conveys the water and rain by small channels into the creeks;

but to make the main street exactly level, the Assembly lately gave a considerable sum, which was expended in removing earth in some places, and building a bridge over a low channel; so that it is now a pleasant, long dry walk, broad, and almost level from the College to the Capitol.

Williamsburgh is now incorporated and made a market town, and governed by a mayor and alderman; and is well stocked with rich stores, of all sorts of goods, and well furnished with the best provisions and liquors.

Here dwell several very good families, and more reside here in their own houses at publick times.

They live in the same neat manner, dress after the same modes, and behave themselves exactly as the gentry in London; most families of any note having a coach, chariot, berlin, or chaise.

The number of artificers is here daily augmented; as are the convenient ordinaries or inns for accommodation of strangers.

The servants here, as in other parts of the country, are English, Scotch, Irish, or Negroes.

The town is laid out regularly in lots or square portions, sufficient each for a house and garden; so that they don't build contiguous, whereby may be prevented the spreading danger of fire; and this also affords a free passage for the air, which is very grateful in violent hot weather.

Here, as in other parts, they build with brick, but most commonly with timber lined with cieling, and cased with feather-edged plank, painted with white lead and oil, covered with shingles of cedar, etc. tarred over at first; with a passage generally through the middle of the house for an air-draught in summer.

Thus their houses are lasting, dry, and warm in winter, and cool in summer; especially if there be windows enough to draw the air.

Thus they dwell comfortably, genteely, pleasantly, and plentifully in this delightful, healthful, and (I hope) thriving city of Williamsburgh.

WE CAME BACK TO WILLIAMSBURG; there was a great number of people from all parts of the province and also the adjoining provinces, for this is time for Carying on business and setling maters with Correspondents. I supose there might be 5 or 6000 people here Dureing the Courts. it is Computed that the province Contains at present 130,000 taxables, from 16 to 60, that is to say the white men and slaves, the white men amount to 60,000 which is the militia body. they are mustered four times yearly. those that are absent from the generall musters without a leagal Cause are fined 10 shs., from private musters 5 shs. these are the laws but seldom put in Execution. never was a more Disagreable place than this at present. In the Day time people hurying back and forwards from the Capitoll to the taverns, and at night, Carousing and Drinking In one Chamber and box and Dice in another, which Continues till morning Commonly. there is not a publick house in virginia but have their tables all baterd with the boxes, which shews the Extravagant Disposition of the planters; there are many of them who have very great Estates, but are mostly at loss for Cash. they live very well haveing all the necessaries on their Estates in great plenty. Madeira wine and punch made with Jamaica rum Is their Chief Drink. there are no large towns in this province, by reason of the Conveniency of its many navaiguable rivers, by which ships go up to all parts of it to the planters Doors: the Chief of those reside Mostely on the borders of James and York rivers which is the best soil for tobaco Especially the Sweet sented which is so much Esteemed in England, where they keep it for their own use, or what they Call home Consumption. the other sort Called aranoacke, is Exported to holland, Denmark, Sweden, and Germany.

the Common way of traffic here, is by bartering one Commodity for another, for which reason Coin is scarce. their Common Currency is paper, which it has in Common with the other provinces.

> "Journal of a French Traveller in the Colonies, 1765," *American Historical Review*, vol. XXVI (July, 1921), 742–743.

Part Two

Cities for
a New Nation

4   The People of New York
in 1788 and 1794

Our first great peacetime parades came after the ratifica-
tion of the federal Constitution. Boston and Charleston
rejoiced with triumphal processions in honor of the
"New Roof" over the "Federal Mansion." Philadelphia
held its parade on July 4, 1788, and 3000 people were in
the line of march. Restless over the slowness of the state
convention at Poughkeepsie to ratify the Constitution
and impatient because ten states had already sanctioned
our new government, New Yorkers, who have always
loved a parade, saluted the Constitution with their parade
of 5000 people on July 23, 1788. Three days later the
Constitution was ratified by New York state.

Although these readings are not meant to emphasize
events in cities, this description of the Federal Procession
in Manhattan is included chiefly because it suggests how
the 30,000 people of our second largest city in 1788 made
their living. The Federal Procession in Philadelphia was
similarly arranged by occupational groups and is described by Francis Hopkinson in J. T. Scharf and T.
Westcott, *History of Philadelphia*, I (Philadelphia, 1884),
447–452. See also Whitfield J. Bell, Jr., "The Federal Processions of 1788," *The New York Historical Society
Quarterly*, vol. 46 (January, 1962), 5–39.

William Alexander Duer (1780–1858) was a New York
City lawyer, state Assemblyman, jurist, and president of
Columbia College (1829–1842). He remembered seeing

the parade as a boy of eight. See the *Dictionary of American Biography*.

Henry Wansey (1752 or 1753–1827), writer of the second selection, was an English clothier who visited Boston, New York, and Philadelphia in 1794. From his business trip to an early cotton mill near New York City, he foretold that industry would increasingly be situated as close to large cities as water power would permit. His account of free public labor by the men of New York City conveys the sense of civic unity and pride that made even our largest cities retain a small-town character into the nineteenth century. On Wansey see Allan Nevins, *America through British Eyes* (New York, 1948), 35–47.

For New York City at this time see J. G. Wilson (ed.), *Memorial History of the City of New York,* vol. III (New York, 1893); Sydney Pomerantz, *New York an American City, 1783–1803* (New York, 1938); Thomas E. V. Smith, *The City of New York in . . . 1789* (New York, 1889); and Bayrd Still, *Mirror for Gotham: New York as Seen by Contemporaries* (New York, 1956), ch. 4.

AT TEN O'CLOCK IN THE MORNING OF THE DAY APPOINTED [July 23, 1788], a salute of thirteen guns was fired by the federal ship "Hamilton," as a signal for the procession to move. This ship was built for the occasion, and presented by our patriotic ship carpenters. She was equipped as a frigate of 32 guns, twenty-seven feet keel, and ten beam, with everything complete in proportion, both in hull and rigging, manned with upwards of thirty seamen and marines, with a full complement of officers and uniforms, under the command of the veteran Commodore James Nicholson. After firing the salute, she got under way from the "Fields," and proceeded to her station in the centre of the procession, the various bodies composing it, having been collected there from their

WILLIAM ALEXANDER DUER, *Reminiscences of an Old Yorker* (New York, 1867), 51–65. First printed in the New York *American Mail,* July 24, 31, 1847.

different places of rendezvous. After forming, it proceeded down Broadway to Great Dock (now Pearl) street, thence through Hanover Square, Queen (now also Pearl), Chatham, Division, Arundel (now Clinton), and Bullock (now Broome) streets, to Alderman Bayard's orchard, between the Bowery and Broadway, under the direction of Colonel [Richard] Platt, as Grand Marshal, and Colonels Morgan Lewis, Nicholas Firth, and Aquila Giles, and Majors James Fairlie, William Popham, and Abijah Hammond as Assistants.

First came an escort, consisting of Captain Stake's light horse, preceded by trumpeters, and Captain Van Dyke's Artillery, with a field piece.

The remainder of the procession was marshaled in ten Divisions, each of which was preceded by a white flag, in honor of the ten States which had acceded to the Constitution.

First Division

Foresters with axes . . . Arms of the United States . . . Gardeners . . . Tailors . . . Measurers of Grain . . . Brewers. . . .

Second Division

Coopers . . . Butchers . . . Tanners and Curriers . . . Skinners, Leather-breeches makers and Glovers . . . .

Third Division

Cordwainers. . . .

Fourth Division

Carpenters . . . Furriers . . . Hatters . . . Peruke-makers, and Hair-dressers . . . Artificial Florists. . . .

Fifth Division

Whitesmiths . . . Cutlers . . . Confectioners . . . Stone Masons . . . Bricklayers . . . Painters and Glaziers . . . Cabinet-

makers . . . Chair-makers . . . Ivory Turners and Musical In-
strument-makers . . . Upholsterers . . . Lace and Fringe Weavers . . . Paper Stainers . . . Civil Engineers. . . .

Sixth Division

Shipwrights . . . Blacksmiths and Nailors . . . Ship-joiners . . .
Boat-builders . . . Block and Pump-makers . . . Sail-makers . . .
Riggers. . . .

Seventh Division

The Federal Ship Hamilton, under way, with her top sails a
trip and courses in the brails. When abreast of Beaver street, she
made the proper signal for a pilot. The pilot boat made sail from
her harbor, in Beaver street, and appeared on the ship's weather
quarter, when the latter threw her main-topsail to the mast, and
received a pilot on board. She then filled away and made sail to
the fort, opposite Bowling Green, where she discovered the President, and members of Congress, and immediately brought to, and
fired a salute of thirteen guns, followed by three cheers, which
were returned by the members of Congress. The procession then
moved on, and when the ship came opposite to William Consta-
ble's, in Dock (now Pearl) street, she was presented by Mrs.
Logan with a suit of colors—after securing which, the crew gave
three cheers. When she arrived abreast of Old Slip, she was saluted by thirteen guns from his Catholic Majesty's packet, which
was duly returned. She then made sail again, through Queen (now
Pearl) street to her station, opposite the dining tents on Bayard's
farm, near the present corner of Broome and Mott streets. She
clued up her topsails and came to anchor in close order, with the
rest of the procession, and the Commodore and his officers went
on shore to dine. At four, P.M., she gave the signal for marching,
by the discharge of thirteen guns, and the procession moved by
the lower road (now Broadway). At half past five, P.M., the ship
arrived at her moorings, abreast of the Bowling Green, amidst the
acclamations of thousands; and the different branches of the procession, as soon as they were dismissed, greeted her with three
cheers.

Pilot Boat drawn on a wagon . . . Marine Society . . . Printers, Book binders and Stationers. . . .

Eighth Division

Cartmen . . . Horse Doctor . . . Mathematical Instrument Makers . . . Carvers and Engravers . . . Coach and Harness Makers . . . Copper Smiths . . . Tin-plate Workers . . . Pewterers . . . Gold and Silver Smiths . . . Potters . . . Chocolate Makers . . . Tobacconists . . . Dyers . . . Brush Makers . . . Tallow Chandlers . . . Saddlers, Harness, and Whip Makers. . . .

Ninth Division

The Gentlemen of the Bar . . . The Philological Society . . . Columbia College . . . Merchants and Traders. . . .

Tenth Division

Clergymen, Physicians, Citizens and Strangers. . . .

The rear of the procession was brought up by a detachment of artillery with a field piece. The line extended upwards of a mile and a half, and contained more than five thousand people. The doors and windows of the houses before which it passed were thronged, especially by the fair, whose smiles and animated gestures contributed to complete the general joy. As this interesting exhibition moved along, an unexpected silence reigned throughout the city, which gave a solemnity to the ceremony suitable to its importance. No noise was heard but the rumbling of the carriage wheels, and the necessary salutes and signals. The whole body having arrived at Bayard's farm, was wheeled into line and reviewed by the marshal and his assistants, after which the *insignia* of the procession being left upon the ground, the bodies composing it were conducted to their respective dining tables, where they were honored by the company of Congress, the foreign ministers and other strangers of distinction.

NEW YORK IS MUCH MORE LIKE A CITY THAN BOSTON [May 17, 1794], having broad footways paved, with a curb to separate them from the road. The streets are wider, and the houses in a better style. Boston is the Bristol, New York the Liverpool, and Philadelphia the London of America. The Tontine tavern and coffee-house is a handsome large brick building; you ascend six or eight steps under a portico, into a large public room, which is the Stock Exchange of New York, where all bargains are made. Here are two books kept, as at Lloyd's, of every ship's arrival and clearing out. This house was built for the accommodation of the merchants, by Tontine shares of two hundred pounds each. It is kept by Mr. Hyde, formerly a woollen draper in London. You can lodge and board there at a common table, and you pay ten shillings currency a day, whether you dine out or not. No appearance of shop windows as in London; only stores, which make no shew till you enter the houses. House rent is very dear; a hundred pounds sterling a year is a very usual price for a common store-keeper.

. . . . In the evening called on Mr. Jay, brother to the Embassador, and took a walk with him and Mr. Armstrong, to the Belvidere, about two miles out of New York towards the Sound—an elegant tea drinking house, encircled with a gallery, at one story high, where company can walk round the building and enjoy the fine prospect of New York harbour and shipping. You have a delightful sea view from thence, commanding Staten, Long Island and Governor's Island, Paulus Hook, Brooklyn and the Sound, names very familiar to us during the American war. There were also formerly fine orchards on the land side, but these were entirely cut down by the troops for winter firing.

From hence we crossed the Boston road, to another tea drinking house and garden, the Indian Queen. This place was filled by Frenchmen with their families. Here they all wear the tricoloured cockade, I observed, whether aristocrats or democrats.

Monday, May 19. Dined with Mr. Jay, and in the evening went to the theatre with Mrs. Sands and her two daughters. Mrs. Cow-

HENRY WANSEY, *The Journal of an Excursion to the United States of North America in the Summer of 1794* (Salisbury, 1796), 73–75, 81, 83–84.

ley's play, A Bold Stroke for a Husband, with the farce of Hob in the Well; the actors mostly from England: price of admittance to the boxes, one dollar. A very bad theatre; a new one is going to be built by subscription, under the direction of Hodgkinson, the present manager. Mrs. Wrighten, who used to sing at Vaux-hall twenty years ago, and was afterwards an actress at Bristol, is one of their principal female performers; her voice is as clear and shrill as ever. I think them altogether far inferior to the Boston company.

In 1740, there was but one printing press in New York; now there are near twenty, and some map engravers. . . .

.   .   .   .

Saturday, May 24, 1794. As I was getting up in the morning, I heard drums beating and fifes playing. I ran to the window, and saw a large body of people on the other side of the Governor's House, with flags flying, and marching two and two towards the water-side. What, thought I, can the meaning of this be? The peaceful Americans with the ensigns of war? What! have the Americans a standing army too in time of peace? The sound of the drum is what I have not heard since I left England. I hastened down stairs, and the mystery was soon explained: it was a pro-cession of young tradesmen going in boats to Governor's Island, to give the state a day's work. Fortifications are there erecting for strengthening the entrance to New York Harbour; it is a patriotic and general resolution of the inhabitants of this city, to work a day gratis, without any distinction of rank or condition, for the public advantage, on these fortifications. To-day, the whole trade of carpenters and joiners; yesterday, the body of masons; before this, the grocers, school-masters, coopers, and barbers; next Mon-day, all the attorneys and men concerned in the law, handle the mattock and shovel, the whole day, and carry their provisions with them. How noble is this! How it cherishes unanimity and love for their country! How much does it tend to unite all ranks of people, and render the social compact firm and united!

.   .   .   .

May 31. Went with a party to see Dickson's cotton manufac-tory at Hell Gates, about five miles from New York. It is worked by a breast water wheel, twenty feet diameter. There are two large buildings four story high, and eighty feet long. In one shop I saw twenty-six looms at work, weaving fustians, calicoes, nankeens, nankinets, dimities, &c. and there are ten other looms in the neighbourhood. They have the new-invented spring shuttle. They also spin by water, using all the new improvements of Arkwright and others. Twelve or fourteen workmen from Manchester. All the machinery in wood, steel, and brass, were made on the spot from models brought from England and Scotland. They are training up women and children to the business, of whom I saw twenty or thirty at work; they give the women two dollars a week, and find them in board and lodging; the children are bound apprentice till twenty-one years of age, with an engagement to board, clothe and educate them. They have the machine called the mule, at which they have spun cotton yarn so fine as twenty-one hundred scains to the pound, and they purpose making muslins. My observations on the undertaking are;—the situation is not well chosen; they have sunk a vast deal of money in buildings and machinery unnecessarily, which is a heavy tax on the undertaking, so that the interest of the money will eat up almost all the profit; they are so deficient in water in summer time to keep the wheel going, that to remedy this, a thousand pounds more is to be laid out, to erect in the sea another large wheel to work by the ebb and flow of the tide, to raise water into the reservoir, to supply this deficiency. The English workmen are dissatisfied, and ready to leave the factory as soon as they have saved up a few pounds, in order to become landholders up the country, and arrive at independence. The company also try at too many things, and the goods they make are very inferior to what they get from us.

---

5   Yellow Fever in Philadelphia, 1793

The spread of disease, like the spread of fire, periodically terrorized city dwellers throughout western history until epidemics were gradually brought under control in the nineteenth century by public medicine and the passage of public health laws. Next to a great fire (see Reading 19) an epidemic was the catastrophe most feared by the urban people of old America. The yellow fever epidemics that struck our seaboard cities in the 1790's forced medical discussion about their prevention and about public health measures in general. One result was the formation of early boards of public health, or at least the appointment of quarantine officials. But not until 1860 did a large majority of American towns have public health boards.

This is an eminent Philadelphian's memory of the epidemic of 1793, which was the worst disaster for an American city until then. The only sure precaution against contracting yellow fever was evacuation of the city. Samuel Breck (1771–1862), son of a wealthy Boston merchant, in 1792 had moved with his family to Philadelphia, then our national capital, where he was to lead a distinguished civic life. See his *Recollections* and the *Dictionary of American Biography*.

On Philadelphia in the age of Franklin see Carl and Jessica Bridenbaugh, *Rebels and Gentlemen* (New York, 1942), and J. F. Scharf and T. Westcott, *History of Philadelphia*, vol. I, chs. XIV–XX. On the epidemic see J. H. Powell, *Bring Out Your Dead* (Philadelphia, 1949), and R. H. Shryock, "The Yellow Fever Epidemics, 1793–1905," in Daniel Aaron (ed.), *America in Crisis* (New York, 1952), ch. III. On the long battle to improve public health see R. H. Shryock, *Medicine and Society in America: 1660–1860* (Ithaca, New York: Great Seal Books, 1960), ch. III.

⁘⁘

I HAD SCARCELY BECOME SETTLED IN PHILADELPHIA when in July, 1793, the yellow fever broke out, and, spreading rapidly in August, obliged all the citizens who could remove to seek safety

H. E. SCUDDER (ed.), *Recollections of Samuel Breck* (Philadelphia, 1877), 193–196.

in the country. My father took his family to Bristol on the Delaware, and in the last of August I followed him. Having engaged in commerce, and having a ship at the wharf loading for Liverpool, I was compelled to return to the city on the 8th of September, and spend the 9th there. My business took me down to the Swedes' church and up Front street to Walnut street wharf, where I had my countinghouse. Everything looked gloomy, and forty-five deaths were reported for the 9th. In the afternoon, when I was about returning to the country, I passed by the lodgings of the Vicomte de Noailles, who had fled from the Revolutionists of France. He was standing at the door, and calling to me, asked me what I was doing in town. "Fly," said he, "as soon as you can, for pestilence is all around us." And yet it was nothing then to what it became three or four weeks later, when from the first to the twelfth of October one thousand persons died. On the twelfth a smart frost came and checked its ravages.

The horrors of this memorable affliction were extensive and heart-rending. Nor were they softened by professional skill. The disorder was in a great measure a stranger to our climate, and was awkwardly treated. Its rapid march, being from ten victims a day in August to one hundred a day in October, terrified the physicians, and led them into contradictory modes of treatment. They, as well as the guardians of the city, were taken by surprise. No hospitals or hospital stores were in readiness to alleviate the sufferings of the poor. For a long time nothing could be done other than to furnish coffins for the dead and men to bury them. At length a large house in the neighborhood was appropriately fitted up for the reception of patients, and a few preeminent philanthropists volunteered to superintend it. At the head of them was Stephen Girard, who has since become the richest man in America.

In private families the parents, the children, the domestics lingered and died, frequently without assistance. The wealthy soon fled; the fearless or indifferent remained from choice, the poor from necessity. The inhabitants were reduced thus to one-half their number, yet the malignant action of the disease increased, so that those who were in health one day were buried the next. The burning fever occasioned paroxysms of rage which drove the patient naked from his bed to the street, and in some instances to the river, where he was drowned. Insanity was often the last stage of its horrors.

.   .   .   .

. . . . The attendants on the dead stood on the pavement in considerable numbers soliciting jobs, and until employed they were occupied in feeding their horses out of the coffins which they had provided in anticipation of the daily wants. These speculators were useful, and, albeit with little show of feeling, contributed greatly to lessen, by competition, the charges of interment. . . . The whole number of deaths in 1793 by yellow fever was more than four thousand. Again it took place in 1797, '98 and '99, when the loss was six thousand, making a total in these four years of ten thousand.

---

6 City of the New West: Lexington, Kentucky, in 1807

A wilderness fort in 1782, Lexington by the mid-1790's was the largest town in the new West, with close to 1600 residents. It became known as "the Philadelphia of Kentucky." Despite the severe blow to its economy in the panic and ensuing depression of 1819, with loss of prestige to Louisville, an Ohio River port so advantageously located in the new steamboat era, Lexington still retained its position as our western political and cultural center into the 1820's. Henry Clay made it famous in politics, and liberal Transylvania University, together with resident artists and literary figures, brought Lexington fame as "the Athens of the West."

Fortesque Cuming visited Lexington when it was reaching its prime. In 1810 the town held 4300 inhabitants. Little is known about Cuming, who appears to have been a widely traveled Englishman.

On early Lexington see Bernard Mayo, "Lexington:

Frontier Metropolis," in E. F. Goldman (ed), *Historiography and Urbanization* (Baltimore, 1941), ch. II, and N. H. Sonne, *Liberal Kentucky, 1780–1828* (New York, 1939).

THE COUNTRY HAD INSENSIBLY ASSUMED THE APPEARANCE OF AN APPROACH TO A CITY.—The roads very wide and fine, with grazing parks, meadows, and every spot in sight cultivated.

Soon after parting with the general, we were gratified with a view of Lexington, about half a mile distant, from an eminence on the road. On entering the town we were struck with the fine roomy scale on which every thing appeared to be planned. Spacious streets, and large houses chiefly of brick, which since the year 1795, have been rapidly taking the place of the original wooden ones, several of which however yet remain.

We turned up the main street, which is about eighty feet wide, compactly built, well paved, and having a footway, twelve feet wide on each side.—Passing several very handsome brick houses of two and three stories, numerous stores well filled with merchandize of every description, and the market place and court house, we dismounted at Wilson's inn, and entered the traveller's room, which had several strangers in it. Shortly after, the supper bell ringing, we obeyed the summons, and were ushered into a room about forty feet long, where, at the head of a table, laid out with neatness, plenty and variety, sat our well dressed hostess, who did the honours of it with much ease and propriety.

We retired early, and next morning, before breakfast, went to the market, which is held every Wednesday and Saturday. We were surprised at the number of horses belonging to the neighbouring farmers, which were fastened around on the outside, and on entering the market place we were equally astonished at the profusion and variety of most of the necessaries and many of the luxuries of life. There was not however such a display of fresh

FORTESQUE CUMING, *Sketches of a Tour to the Western Country . . . 1807 . . . 1809* (Pittsburgh, 1810), reprinted in Reuben Gold Thwaites, *Early Western Travels, 1748–1846*, IV (Cleveland, 1904), 181–189.

meat as is seen in Pittsburgh, which might be owing to the warmth of the climate at that season. Prices were nearly similar to those at Pittsburgh: beef four cents per pound, bacon eight, butter twelve and a half; lamb twenty-five cents a quarter, corn meal forty-two cents per bushel, and every thing else in proportion. Vegetables were in great abundance and very cheap, and were sold mostly by negro men and women; indeed that race were the most predominant both as to sellers and buyers.

Our beds had been very good, and our breakfast and dinner to-day, were correspondent to our supper last night—displaying a variety neatly and handsomely served up, with excellent attendance.

I employed the forenoon in running over and viewing the town. It contains three hundred and sixty-six dwelling houses, besides barns, stables and other out offices. The streets cross each other at right angles, and are from fifty to eighty feet wide. A rivulet which turns some mills below the town, runs through the middle of Water-street, but it is covered by an arch, and levelled over it the length of the street. It falls into the Elkhorn a few miles to the N.W.

There are societies of Presbyterians, Seceders, Episcopalians, Anabaptists and Roman Catholicks, each of which has a church, no way remarkable, except the Episcopalian, which is very neat and convenient. There is also a society of Methodists, which has not yet any regular house of worship. The court house now finishing, is a good, plain, brick building, of three stories, with a cupola, rising from the middle of the square roof, containing a bell and a town clock. The cupola is supported by four large brick columns in the centre of the house, rising from the foundation, through the hall of justice, and in my opinion adding nothing to its beauty or convenience. The whole building when finished, will cost about fifteen thousand dollars. The masonick hall, is a neat brick building, as is also the bank, where going for change for a Philadelphia bank note, I received in specie one per cent. advance, which they allow on the notes of the Atlantick cities for the convenience of remitting. There is a publick library and a university, called Transylvania, which is incorporated and is under the government of twenty-one trustees and the direction of a president, the Rev. James Blythe, who is also professor of natural philosophy, mathematicks, geography and English grammar. There are four professors besides: the Rev. Robert H. Bishop, professor of moral philosophy, belles lettres, logick and history; Mr. Ebenezer Sharpe, professor of the languages; Doctor James Fishback, professor of medicine, &c. and Henry Clay, Esq. professor of law. The funds of the university arise from the price of tuition, (which is lower than in any other seminary of learning in the United States) and from eight thousand acres of first rate land, granted to it by the state of Virginia; five thousand of which are in the neighbourhood of Lexington, and three thousand near Louisville at the falls of Ohio. The legislature of Kentucky have also granted to it six thousand acres of valuable land, south of Green river. Its yearly income from the lands, now amounts to about two thousand dollars, which will probably be soon much increased.

There are no fewer than three creditable boarding schools for female education, in which there are at present above a hundred pupils. An extract from Mrs. Beck's card, will convey some idea of the progress of polite education in this country.

"Boarders instructed in the following branches, at the rate of two hundred dollars per annum, viz. Reading, spelling, writing, arithmetick, grammar, epistolary correspondence, elocution and rhetorick; geography, with the use of maps, globes, and the armillary sphere; astronomy, with the advantage of an orrery; ancient and modern history; chronology, mythology, and natural history; natural and moral philosophy; musick, vocal and instrumental; drawing, painting, and embroidery of all kinds; artificial flowers, and any other fashionable fancy-work; plain sewing, marking, netting, &c."

The card designates a regular course of education, as it proceeds through the successional branches, all of which cannot be studied by any individual at the same time.

Mrs. Beck is an English lady, and is in high reputation as an instructress. She was now absent, having taken advantage of a vacation, to visit the Olympian Springs, about fifty miles from Lexington, much resorted, on account of their salubrious effects.

There is no regular academy for males, but there are several day schools.

The number of inhabitants in Lexington, in 1806, was 1655 free white inhabitants, and 1165 negro slaves, in all 2820. The whole number may now be safely estimated at 3000.

There are three nail manufacturies, which make about sixty tons of nails per annum; and there are ten blacksmith's shops, which find constant employment for a considerable number of hands.

There are two copper and tin manufacturies, one of which manufactures ware to the amount of ten thousand dollars yearly; the other is on a smaller scale.

There are four jewellers and silversmiths, whose business is very profitable.

Seven saddler's shops employ thirty hands, the proceeds of whose labour is annually from twenty-five to thirty thousand dollars.

There are four cabinet-maker's shops, where household furniture is manufactured in as handsome a style as in any part of America, and where the high finish which is given to the native walnut and cherry timber, precludes the regret that mahogany is not to be had but at an immense expense.

Three tan yards and five currying shops, manufacture about thirty thousand dollars worth of leather every year.

There is one excellent umbrella manufactury, one brush, one reed, four chair, and two tobacco manufacturies which make chewing tobacco, snuff and cigars. Three blue-dyers. Five hatters, who employ upwards of fifty hands, and manufacture about thirty thousand dollars worth of fur and wool hats annually. Ten tailors, who employ forty-seven journeymen and apprentices. Fifteen shoe and boot makers, who employ about sixty hands, and manufacture to the amount of about thirty thousand dollars yearly; and two stocking weavers.

Two brew-houses make as good beer as can be got in the United States. A carding machine for wool, is a great convenience to the manufacturers of that article. There is one manufacturer of baling cloth for cotton wool, who employs thirty-eight hands, and makes thirty-six thousand yards annually; and two cotton spinning machines, worked by horses, yield a handsome profit to the proprietors. An oil mill, worked by horses, makes fifteen hundred gallons of oil per year. Seven distilleries make near seven thousand gallons of spirits yearly. Four rope-walks employ about sixty hands, and make about three hundred tons of cordage annually, the tar for which is made on the banks of Sandy river, and is bought in Lexington at from eighteen to twenty-five cents per gallon. There are two apothecaries' shops, and five regular physicians. Twenty-two stores retail upwards of three hundred dollars worth of imported, foreign merchandize annually; and there is one book and stationary store on a very large scale, and two printing offices, where gazettes are printed weekly.

In the neighbourhood are six powder mills, that make about twenty thousand pounds of powder yearly.

There are seven brick yards which employ sixty hands, and make annually two million five hundred thousand bricks; and there are fifty brick-layers, and as many attendants, who have built between thirty and forty good brick houses each of the last three years. The Presbyterian society is now finishing a church which will cost eight thousand dollars. . . .

. . . . Last year there were in Lexington thirty-nine two wheel carriages, such as gigs and one horse chaises, valued at 5764 dollars, and twenty-one four wheel ones, coaches, chariots, &c. valued at 8900 dollars; since when four elegant ones have been added to the number. This may convey some idea of the taste for shew and expense which pervades this country. There are now here, fifteen hundred good and valuable horses, and seven hundred milk cows.

The police of Lexington seems to be well regulated: as one proof of which there is an established nightly watch.

The copper coinage of the United States is of no use in Kentucky—the smallest circulating coin being a silver sixteenth of a dollar.

There are four billiard tables in Lexington, and cards are a good deal played at taverns, where it is more customary to meet for that purpose than at private houses.

There is a coffee house here, where is a reading room for the benefit of subscribers and strangers, in which are forty-two files of different newspapers from various parts of the United States. It is supported by subscribers, who pay six dollars each annually, and of which there are now sixty. In the same house is a billiard table, and chess and back-gammon tables, and the guests may be accommodated with wine, porter, beer, spirituous liquors, cordials and confectionary. It is kept by a Mr. Terasse, formerly of the island of St. Bartholomew. He had been unfortunate in mercantile business in the West Indies, and coming to this country, and failing in the recovery of some property he had shipped to New York, he had no other resource left to gain a provision for his family, but the teaching of the French language and dancing, in Lexington. The trustees of Transylvania college (or university, as the Lexington people proudly call it) employed him in the former, but had it not been for the latter, he might have starved. And here it may not be impertinent to remark, that in most parts of the United States, teachers of dancing, meet with more encouragement than professors of any species of literary science.— Disgusted at length with the little encouragement he received, he bethought himself of his present business, in which he has become useful to the town and seems to be reaping a plentiful harvest from his ingenuity. He has opened a little publick garden behind his house, which he calls Vauxhall. It has a most luxuriant grape arbour, and two or three summer houses, formed also of grape vines, all of which are illuminated with variegated lamps, every Wednesday evening, when the musick of two or three decent performers sometimes excites parties to dance on a small boarded platform in the middle of the arbour. It is becoming a place of fashionable resort.

7   Cincinnati in 1835:
     Industry in the New West

Not until about 1830 was Lexington eclipsed as a cultural center by Cincinnati, "the Queen City of the West," or "Porkopolis." Incorporated in 1802, Cincinnati by 1810 had about 2400 inhabitants; by 1820, 9600; by 1830 nearly 25,000 and was the seventh ranking city in the country. Its most startling growth came in the 1840's when its population rose from 46,000 to 115,000.

Michael Chevalier (1806–1879) was a French economist and an influential advocate of industrialization and free trade. He was sent by his government in 1833 to study the development of the transportation network in the United States. His visit lasted two years, and his book originally appeared as letters from America in the *Journal des débats* (January 1, 1834–October 22, 1835). On Chevalier see A. L. Dunham, *The Anglo-French Treaty of Commerce* . . . (Ann Arbor, 1930), chs. II–IV, VII.

On Cincinnati in this period see Constance McL. Green, *American Cities in the Growth of the Nation* (London, 1957), pp. 41–56, and Clara L. de Chambrun, *Cincinnati: Story of the Queen City* (New York, 1939), chs. 9–12.

MEMPHIS, (TENN.), JAN. 1, 1835.

CINCINNATI HAS BEEN MADE FAMOUS BY MRS TROLLOPE, whose aristocratic feelings were offended by the pork-trade, which is here carried on on a great scale. From her accounts many persons have thought that every body in Cincinnati was a pork merchant, and the city a mere slaughter-house. The fact is that Cincinnati is a large and beautiful town, charmingly situated in one of those bends which the Ohio makes, as if unwilling to leave the spot. The hills which border the *Belle Rivière* (Beautiful River, the French name of the Ohio) through its whole course, seem here to have receded from the river bank, in order to form a lofty plain, to which they serve as walls, whenever the Ohio does not serve as a foss, and on which man might build a town above the reach of the terrible floods of the river. . . .

The architectural appearance of Cincinnati is very nearly the same with that of the new quarters of the English towns. The houses are generally of brick, most commonly three stories high,

MICHAEL CHEVALIER, *Society, Manners and Politics in the United States: Being a Series of Letters on North America,* translated by T. G. Bradford (Boston, 1839), 190–195, 200–204, 206. A recent edition is John William Ward's (New York: Anchor Books, 1961).

with the windows shining with cleanliness, calculated each for a single family, and regularly placed along well paved and spacious streets, sixty feet in width. Here and there the prevailing uniformity is interrupted by some more imposing edifice, and there are some houses of hewn stone in very good taste, real palaces in miniature, with neat porticoes, inhabited by the aristocratical portion of Mrs Trollope's hog-merchants, and several very pretty mansions surrounded with gardens and terraces. Then there are the common school-houses, where girls and boys together learn reading, writing, cyphering, and geography, under the simultaneous direction of a master and mistress.[1]

In another direction you see a small, plain church, without sculpture or paintings, without coloured glass or gothic arches, but snug, well carpeted, and well-warmed by stoves. In Cincinnati, as everywhere else in the United States, there is a great number of churches; each sect has its own, from Angelican Episcopalianism, which enlists under its banner the wealth of the country, to the Baptist and Methodist sects, the religion of the labourers and negroes. On another side, stands a huge hotel, which from its exterior you would take for a royal residence, but in which, as I can testify, you will not experience a princely hospitality; or a museum, which is merely a private speculation, as all American museums are, and which consists of some few crystals, some mammoth-bones, which are very abundant in the United States, an Egyptian mummy, some Indian weapons and dresses, and a half-dozen wax-figures, representing, for instance, Washington, General Jackson, and the Indian Chiefs, Black Hawk and Tecumseh, a figure of Napoleon afoot or on horseback, a French cuirass from Waterloo, a collection of portraits of distinguished Americans, comprising Lafayette and some of the leading men of the town, another of stuffed birds, snakes preserved in spirits,

[1] *According to the official report of the Trustees and visiters of the common schools, dated July 30, 1833, there were then in Cincinnati 6,000 children between the ages of 6 and 16 years, exclusive of 230 children of colour for whom there is a separate school. About 2,300 children attended the common schools and 1,700 private schools. The number of common schools is 18, under the care of 12 masters and 5 assistants, 6 mistresses and 7 assistant mistresses. The masters receive 400 dollars a year, and the assistants 250; the school mistresses 216, and the assistants 168. These salaries are thought to be too low.*

and particularly a large living snake, a boa constrictor, or an ana-
conda. One of these museums in Cincinnati is remarkable for its
collection of Indian antiquities, derived from the huge caves of
Kentucky, or from the numerous mounds on the banks of the
Ohio, of which there were several on the site of Cincinnati.[2]

As for the banks they are modestly lodged at Cincinnati, but a
plan of a handsome edifice, worthy of their high fortune, and
sufficient to accommodate them all, is at present under consideration. The founderies for casting steam-engines, the yards for
building steamboats, the noisy, unwholesome, or unpleasant
work-shops, are in the adjoining village of Fulton, in Covington
or Newport on the Kentucky bank of the river, or in the country. As to the enormous slaughter of hogs, about 150,000 annually, and the preparation of the lard, which follows, the town
is not in the least incommoded by it; the whole process takes
place on the banks of a little stream called Deer Creek, which has
received the nickname of the Bloody Run, from the colour of its
waters during the season of the massacre, or near the basins of the
great canal, which extends from Cincinnati towards the Maumee
of Lake Erie. Cincinnati has, however, no squares planted with
trees in the English taste, no parks nor walks, no fountains, although it would be very easy to have them. It is necessary to wait
for the ornamental, until the taste for it prevails among the inhabitants; at present the useful occupies all thoughts. Besides, all
improvements require an increase of taxes, and in the United
States it is not easy to persuade the people to submit to this. . . .
Cincinnati also stands in need of some public provision for lighting the streets, which this repugnance to taxes has hitherto prevented.

Cincinnati has had water-works, for supplying the inhabitants
with water, for about 20 years; for an annual rate, which amounts
to about 8 or 12 dollars for a family, each has a quantity amply
sufficient for all its wants. A steam-engine on the banks of the

[2] *This museum has one show which I never saw anywhere else; it is a
representation of the Infernal Regions, to which the young Cincinnati
girls resort in quest of that excitement which a comfortable and peaceful, but cold and monotonous manner of life denies them. This strange
spectacle seems to afford a delicious agitation to their nerves, and is the
principal source of revenue to the museum.*

river raises the water to a reservoir on one of the hills near the city, 300 feet high, whence it is conducted in iron pipes in every direction. The height of the reservoir is such that the water rises to the top of every house, and fire-plugs are placed at intervals along the streets to supply the engines in case of fire. Several of the new towns in the United States have water-works, and Philadelphia, among the older cities, has an admirable system of works, which, owing to a series of unsuccessful experiments, have cost a large sum. At this moment, a plan for supplying Boston with water is under discussion, which will cost several millions, because the water must be brought from a distance. New York is also engaged in a similar work, the expense of which will be about five millions. The Cincinnati water-works have not cost much above 150,000 dollars, although they have been several times completely reconstructed. It is generally thought in the United States, that the water-works ought to be owned by the towns, but those in Cincinnati belong to a company, and the water-rate is, therefore, higher than in Philadelphia and Pittsburg. The city has three times been in negotiation for the purchase of the works, and has always declined buying on advantageous terms; the first time the establishment was offered for 35,000 dollars, and the second time for 80,000; the third time, 125,000 dollars were demanded, and 300,-000 or 400,000 will finally be paid for it. In this case, as in regard to lighting the streets, the principal cause of the refusal of the city to buy was the unwillingness to lay new taxes.

.   .   .   .

NATCHEZ, (MISS.) JAN. 4, 1835.

CINCINNATI contains about 40,000 inhabitants, inclusive of the adjoining villages; although founded 40 years ago, its rapid growth dates only about 30 years back. It seems to be the rendezvous of all nations; the Germans and Irish are very numerous, and there are some Alsacians; I have often heard the harsh accents of the Rhenish French in the streets. But the bulk of the population, which gives its tone to all the rest, is of New England origin. What makes the progress of Cincinnati more surprising is, that the city is the daughter of its own works. Other towns, which have sprung up in the United States in the same rapid manner, have been built on shares, so to speak. Lowell, for example, is an enterprise of Boston merchants, who, after having raised the necessary funds, have collected workmen and told them, "Build us a town." Cincinnati has been gradually extended and embellished, almost wholly without foreign aid, by its inhabitants, who have for the most part arrived on the spot poor. The founders of Cincinnati brought with them nothing but sharp-sighted, wakeful, untiring industry, the only patrimony which they inherited from their New England fathers, and the other inhabitants have scrupulously followed their example and adopted their habits. They seem to have chosen Franklin for their patron-saint, and to have adopted Poor Richard's maxims as a fifth gospel.

. . . .

. . . . In spite of the superior advantages of Louisville as an *entrepôt*, in spite of the manufacturing resources of Pittsburg, Cincinnati is able to maintain a population twice that of Louisville and half as large again as that of Pittsburg in a state of competence, which equals, if it does not surpass, the average condition of that of each of the others. The inhabitants of Cincinnati have fixed this prosperity among them, by one of those instinctive views with which the sons of New England are inspired by their eminently practical and calculating genius. A half-word, they say, is enough for the wise, but cleverer than the wisest, the Yankees understand each other without speaking, and by a tacit consent direct their common efforts toward the same point. To work Boston fashion means, in the United States, to do anything with perfect precision and without words. The object which the Cincinnatians have had in view, almost from the origin of their city, has been nothing less than to make it the capital, or great interior mart of the West. The indirect means which they have employed, have been to secure the manufacture of certain articles, which, though of little value separately considered, form an important aggregate when taken together, and getting the start of their neighbours, with that spirit of diligence that characterises the Yankees, they have accordingly distributed the manufacture of these articles among themselves. This plan has succeeded.

Thus with the exception of the pork trade, one is surprised not to see any branch of industry carried on on the great scale of the manufacturing towns of England and France. The Cincinnatians make a variety of household furniture and utensils, agricultural and mechanical implements and machines, wooden clocks, and a thousand objects of daily use and consumption, soap, candles, paper, leather, &c., for which there is an indefinite demand throughout the flourishing and rapidly growing States of the West, and also in the new States of the Southwest, which are wholly devoted to agriculture, and in which, on account of the existence of slavery, manufactures cannot be carried on. Most of these articles are of ordinary quality; the furniture, for instance, is rarely such as would be approved by Parisian taste, but it is cheap and neat, just what is wanted in a new country, where, with the exception of a part of the South, there is a general ease and but little wealth, and where plenty and comfort are more generally known than the little luxuries of a more refined society. The prosperity of Cincinnati, therefore, rests upon the sure basis of the prosperity of the West, upon the supply of articles of the first necessity to the bulk of the community; a much more solid foundation than the caprice of fashion, upon which, nevertheless, the branches of industry most in favour with us, depend. The intellectual also receives a share of attention; in the first place, there is a large type-foundery in Cincinnati, which supplies the demand of the whole West, and of that army of newspapers that is printed in it. According to the usual English or American mode of proceeding, the place of human labour is supplied as much as possible by machinery, and I have seen several little contrivances here, that are not probably to be found in the establishments of the Royal Press or of the Didots. Then the printing-presses are numerous, and they issue nothing but publications in general demand, such as school-books, and religious books, and newspapers. By means of this variety of manufactures, which, taken separately appear of little consequence, Cincinatti has taken a stand, from which it will be very difficult to remove her, for, in this matter, priority of occupation is no trifling advantage. The country trader, who keeps an assortment of everything vendible, is sure to find almost everything he wants in Cincinnati, and he, therefore, goes thither in preference to any other place in order to lay in his stock of goods. Cincinnati is thus in fact the great central mart of the West; a great quantity and variety of produce and manufactured articles find a vent here, notwithstanding the natural superiority of several other sites, either in regard to the extent of water-communication or mineral resources.

.   .   .   .

. . . . Hemmed in by the laborious habits of the country, by political notions, and by religion, a man must either resign himself to the same mode of life with the mass, or seek a soil less unfriendly to his tastes in the great cities of New York, Philadelphia, or New Orleans, or even in Europe. There is, therefore, no such thing in Cincinnati as a class of men of leisure, living without any regular profession on their patrimony, or on the wealth acquired by their own enterprise in early life, although there are many persons of opulence, having one hundred thousand dollars and upwards. I met a young man there, the future heir of a large fortune, who, after having been educated at West Point and received a commission, had retired from the service in order to live at home. Wearied out with his solitary leisure, burdened with the weight of his own person, he could find no other relief than to open a fancy-goods shop.

<hr>

8   Early Chicago in 1833 and 1848

Cincinnati held its economic pre-eminence among western towns until the 1850's when Chicago emerged as the leading rail, real estate, and packing center, and St. Louis as the chief river port, of the Middle West. Chicago's rise was phenomenally rapid. With a population of 250 in 1833, it rose to over 4000 in 1837. By 1844 there were 8000 residents, and over 20,000 by 1848. In 1860 the city held over 109,000 people. Between 1854 and 1860 the population nearly quintupled. In the east, Boston, New York, and Philadelphia also experienced a rapid rate of growth between 1850 and 1870, but the gain was greater in the cities of the Old Northwest.

John Dean Caton (1812–1895), author of the following reminiscence written in 1869, was typical of the young men from the East who came to Chicago to seek their fortunes. If they stayed, most of them made a place for themselves. Caton, the town's first practicing lawyer, became Chief Justice of the Illinois Supreme Court and later made his fortune from the Illinois and Mississippi Telegraph Company. On Caton see the *Dictionary of American Biography*.

John Lewis Peyton (1824–1896), writer of the second account, was a Virginian who lived in Illinois for three years in the 1850's. The wildcat banking practices and the corner lot speculations in Chicago's outskirts described by him had been even more frenzied in Chicago before the Panic of 1837, which lessened the speculative fever. But by the mid 1840's Chicago was again booming with promise of completed transportation routes and her place as the transfer point for western farm produce headed for eastern markets. On Peyton, who during the Confederacy was state agent for North Carolina, see the *Dictionary of American Biography*.

On Chicago in this era, see Bessie L. Pierce, *A History of Chicago*, I, *The Beginning of a City, 1673–1848* (New York, 1937), and II, *From Town to City, 1848–1871* (New York, 1940).

THE TOWN WAS FULL OF STRANGERS AND MORE FLOCKING IN DAILY. All was activity and enterprise, and preparations for building everywhere. I arrived in Chicago at what may be termed the very commencement of its improvements. Already a few frames had been raised and every few days witnessed another and only a few weeks elapsed till almost each day witnessed the rise

HARRY E. PRATT (ed.), "John Dean Caton's Reminiscences of Chicago in 1833 and 1834," *Journal of the Illinois State Historical Society*, XXVIII (April, 1935), 10–12, 22–23, 25. Reprinted with the permission of the Illinois State Historical Society.

of a new building as the increase of the supply of lumber and of mechanics enabled the newcomers to build houses for themselves and places for their business. . . .

. . . Nearly all the buildings put up that year were, what was aptly described as Balloon frames, that is two by six joists for sills, studs two by four toed onto the sills by nails, a strip of inch board for plate and, if one story strips of inch boards for joists or if two story, two inch joists to support the upper floor spiked to the studs and supported also by strips of inch boards under them nailed to the studs. The rafters were one or two inches according to the size of the building. No braces were introduced. For this the siding and lathing or casing was alone depended upon and yet they rarely blew down, and I have known but few lives lost in that way. It required but little mechanical skill to build one. It was not uncommon to see one rise in a single day, and constituting the next day the snug home of a young and enterprising couple, the next with a blanket hanging up for a door with perhaps one or two flaxen-haired bright-eyed urchins lifting one corner and peeping out on the busy world around them. *Such was the first stage of Chicago growth.*

.   .   .   .

In . . . the new Mansion House . . . was provided for the first time in Chicago a room of sufficient size to accommodate a pretty large dancing party and in order to utilize it, it was resolved to have a grand ball. There were gentlemen enough, no doubt, but they alone would make a dry ball. Ladies in Chicago were very scarce and in order to make up the deficiency as far as possible every servant girl in town was invited. The streets happened to be very muddy, which was always the case in wet weather. I never saw worse roads than Chicago afforded when the unimproved prairie was used. After a few hot days of spring I have seen a dried crust over the semi-fluid of which the streets were composed to a great depth over which one could walk but which would vibrate and tremble for yards around. I once noticed four yoke of oxen with an empty wagon stalled at the corner of Wells and Lake streets. . . .

Then Chicago had *no carriages* as the term is ordinarily understood. The ordinary lumber wagon, was better adapted to the purpose of transporting passengers and so it was when the weather was bad and the roads deep and mirey for some years later. Even as late as 1837 the most convenient and the most common vehicle in which the ladies made their calls was a one-horse cart in the bottom of which was a thick course of prairie hay, over which was a buffalo robe on which the ladies seated themselves with another robe over their laps. In this way they went in a jolly mood on their round of calls or to attend a party or a wedding. The driver was seated on a front corner of the box as we now see him with a load of gravel instead of a bevy of ladies. Nothing could be more convenient than this arrangement for when the cart was backed up to the front door the ladies could get in or alight with the greatest convenience and laugh at the sea of mud around them. . . .

At the time of the ball, however, carts were unknown in Chicago, and the heavy lumber wagon monopolized the passenger transportation. In this way were the ladies gathered up and brought to the Mansion House, mistresses and maids seated side by side, all in their gayest rigs.

.   .   .   .

It was early in that spring of 1834 that I found myself standing at the crossing of Dearborn and Lake streets looking west; and for the first time I could see where the street was by the line of buildings on either side of it. This was the first time I ever noticed a street in Chicago made perceptible by the buildings on both sides of it. Then for the first time could I fully realize that our little settlement was assuming the appearance of a town. . . .

::::::::::::::::

THE CITY IS SITUATED ON BOTH SIDES OF THE CHICAGO RIVER, a sluggish, slimy stream, too lazy to clean itself, and on both sides of its north and south branches, upon a level piece of ground, half dry and half wet, resembling a salt marsh, and contained a population of 20,000. There was no pavement, no macadamized streets, no drainage, and the three thousand houses in which the

JOHN L. PEYTON, *Over the Alleghenies and Across the Prairies*, 2nd ed. (London, 1870), 325–29, 333–36.

people lived, were almost entirely small timber buildings, painted white, and this white much defaced by mud. I now recall but a single exception to this rule, in a red brick, two story residence in the north division. . . . To render the streets and side walks passable, they were covered with deal boards from house to house, the boards resting upon cross sills of heavy timber. This kind of track is called "the plank road." Under these planks the water was standing on the surface over three-fourths of the city, and as the sewers from the houses were emptied under them, a frightful odour was emitted in summer, causing fevers and other diseases, foreign to the climate. This was notably the case during the summer of 1854, when the cholera visited the place, destroying the population at the rate of one hundred and fifty a day. It not unfrequently happened that from the settling or rolling of a sleeper, that a loose plank would give way under the weight of a passing cab, when the foul water would spurt into the air high as the windows.[1]

On the outskirts of the town where this kind of road terminated, the highways were impassable, except in winter when frozen, or in summer when dry and pulverized into the finest and most penetrating of dust. At all other seasons they were little less than quagmires. As may be imagined, the communication with the interior was principally carried on in canoes and batteaux. Of architectural display there was none. The houses were built hurriedly to accommodate a considerable trade centering here, and were devoid of both comforts and conveniences. Every one in the place seemed in a hurry, and a kind of restless activity prevailed which I had seen no where else in the West, except in Cincinnati.

[1] *To correct this state of affairs, the authorities have since, at an enormous cost, covered the entire city, four feet deep with sand, thus driving out the water and making a dry spot of what was once a swamp. They have also constructed fine stone drains, leading into the country south of the city, and thence communicating with the waters of the Illinois river, by which they are borne south to the Mississippi. At this moment, I believe, they are cutting a canal to convey through the city the waters of the lake—the lake being higher than the bed of the Illinois river—and thus, while making a canal connecting Lake Michigan and the Mississippi, they will provide the means of thoroughly draining the city, and keeping it clean by this rapid current of pure water. Chicago has thus been turned into a healthy spot.*

A central point in the western route of emigrants, it was even at this inclement season animated by passing parties. . . .

Chicago was already becoming a place of considerable importance for manufactures. Steam mills were busy in every part of the city preparing lumber for buildings which were contracted to be erected by the thousand the next season. Large establishments were engaged in manufacturing agricultural implements of every description for the farmers who flocked to the country every spring. A single establishment, that of McCormick, employed several hundred hands, and during each season completed from fifteen hundred to two thousand grain-reapers and grass-mowers. Blacksmith, wagon and coachmaker's shops were busy preparing for a spring demand, which, with all their energy, they could not supply. Brickmakers had discovered on the lake shore, near the city and a short distance in the interior, excellent beds of clay, and were manufacturing, even at this time, millions of brick by a patent process, which the frost did not hinder, or delay. Hundreds of workmen were also engaged in quarrying stone and marble on the banks of the projected canal; and the Illinois Central Railway employed large bodies of men in driving piles, and constructing a track and depôt on the beach. Real estate agents were mapping out the surrounding territory for ten and fifteen miles in the interior, giving fancy names to the future avenues, streets, squares and parks. A brisk traffic existed in the sale of corner lots, and men with nothing but their wits, had been known to succeed in a single season in making a fortune—sometimes, certainly, it was only on paper.

This process was somewhat in this wise—A. sells a lot to B. for 10,000 dollars, B. sells to C. for 20,000 dollars, no money passing, C. writes to his friend D. in New York of the rapid rise in the price. The property had gone in a very short time from 10,000 dollars to 20,000 dollars and would double within ninety days, such was the *rush* of capitalists to the West. . . .

.   .   .   .

Wishing to change a few American (gold) eagles, for I had provided myself with this kind of solid currency for my Western tour, my friend Shirley accompanied me to a timbershed, or shanty, bespattered with mud and defaced by the sun and storm,

where the great banking establishment of those days was conducted by George Smith and Co. When there, placing my eagles
upon the counter, Mr. Willard, the manager . . . returned me
notes of the denomination of one, two, three and four dollars,
which read as follows:

"The Bank of Atlanta, Georgia, promises to pay the bearer on
demand, one dollar, when five is presented at their banking-house
at Atlanta.

"George Smith, President.

"Willard, Cashier."

I objected most decidedly to receiving this currency, because Atlanta was by the usual route of travel nearly two thousand miles
distant; because when the notes were presented, the bank of
Atlanta might pay them in the currency of another 'wild cat'
bank, probably conducted by Tom Mackenzie in Texas or New
Mexico, and because they would only pay them in particular
amounts of five dollars, a sum, I said ironically, which a judicious
man was not likely to accumulate in his hands of this kind of
currency. Stating these objections, both Messrs. Willard and
Shirley smiled at my ignorance and inexperience, my "old fogy-
ism," and explained that these notes were as current in Chicago
and the State of Illinois as gold; and much more plentiful, thought
I to myself. Nevertheless, on their assurances I accepted them,
with a mental reservation, however, that I would divest myself
of the trash before my departure. . . .

. . . Returning to the hotel, Mr. Rossiter informed me that
my bank notes (and my pocket was stuffed with them) were
called "wild cat money," and such institutions as that at Atlanta
"Wild Cat Banks;" but he said the circulating medium of the
United States was so far below the actual wants of the people,
that they were compelled to resort to such systems of credit to
get on rapidly and improve the country, and as long as farmers
would take the money (as they now did) there would be no
difficulty.

"Why, sir," said Mr. Rossiter, looking around his establishment
with pride, "this hotel was built with that kind of stuff, and what
is true of 'The American,' is very nearly true of every other house
in Chicago. I will take 'wild cats' for your bill, my butcher takes

them of me, and the farmer from him, and so we go, making it
pleasant all round. I only take care," continued Mr. Rossiter, "to
invest what I may have at the end of a given time in corner lots.
Then I'll be prepared, I guess, for the deluge, or crash, when it
comes, and sooner or later it must come, as sure as the light of
day. . . . On this kind of worthless currency, based on Mr.
Smith's supposed wealth and our wants, we are creating a great
city, building up all kind of industrial establishments, and covering the lake with vessels—so that suffer who may when the inevitable hour of reckoning arrives, the country will be the
gainer. . . .

9   The Levee at St. Louis, 1848

No one who traveled by river steamboat soon forgot it
or the excitement of the great port towns along the Ohio
and the Mississippi. Here is one of the best descriptions
we have of the levee at St. Louis, written ten years before
Mark Twain sailed the river but true to his account. St.
Louis at this time was the crossroads for far western commerce and migration, soon to be the chief emporium for
those going overland to the California gold fields. By
1850 St. Louis would have a population of 77,000, an increase of 60,000 since 1840. In 1860 St. Louis, with 160,-
773 residents, was the seventh ranking city in the nation,
just behind Cincinnati and ahead of Chicago.

John S. Robb joined the gold seekers in 1849: he was
one of the secretaries of the California constitutional convention, and he died in San Francisco in 1856.

On St. Louis, see C. McL. Green, *American Cities*, pp.
56–66; W. W. Belcher, *The Economic Rivalry between
St. Louis and Chicago, 1850–1880* (New York, 1947);
and I. H. Lionberger, *The Annals of St. Louis . . .* (St.
Louis, 1930).

THE ST. LOUIS LEVEE IS A PAVED CAUSEWAY OF GRADUAL DESCENT TO LOW WATER MARK, bounded on the west by a row of stores, and east by the river. The paved portion extends in shape like a bow, for about the distance of one mile, commencing in the neighborhood of the Centre Market or Town Hall, and terminating at "Battle Row." Within these limits the principal shipping trade of St. Louis is transacted. Below the Town Hall is the flat boat landing and wood market, and above Battle Row are the *docks*, where our steamers are built, repaired, or where they "lay up" in dull seasons. During eight months in the year, an average of forty steamers may be seen loading and unloading in front of the paved portion of this causeway.

The row of stores bounding it upon the west may be termed the city's *face*, and, rightly studied, it is an index to the living municipal world beyond it. It has its fine features and its blemishes, but through the general expression is beaming forth unmistakable evidences of a substantial trade. Its stately store houses stand side by side with primitive cabins, and the kind of dealers who congregate there run through the whole catalogue, from the merchant, who deals in cargoes, to the youthful apple trader, who carries his stock about upon his arm. . . . The puffing steamers which bound it on the east, may not always bring profit to the merchant, but they certainly bring general trade to his neighbors, and, therefore, they are the ever welcome couriers of western commerce.

Our Levee may be likened to a *patch* of many colored stripes, in which are a promiscuous assemblage of human threads, ranging from the finest silk to the coarsest tow. Here strides a merchant of unblemished reputation, whose word is his bond, and who scorns the petty arts of deception by which less scrupulous traders take advantage of their neighbors. He steps as solidly as if every tread was an indorsement of the sufficiency of his capital. Cautiously watching the current of trade, he is always ready to take

"SOLITAIRE" [JOHN S. ROBB], "St. Louis in Patches," in "Glimpses of the Past," *Missouri Historical Quarterly*, VI (January–March, 1939), 18–20, 25–27. First printed in St. Louis *Weekly Revelle*, October 22–29, 1848. Reprinted with permission of the Missouri Historical Society.

advantage of that tide which flows to fortune. Here is his clerk, full of commercial importance, aspiring to be a jobber, and here the jobber wishing to be considered a representative of unbounded capital. There struts one who claims to be a representative of *high* society, and here another who claims fellowship with none. Here pushes along, with an independent, sailor kind of a swing, the steam boat officer—a true representative of the citizen of the world—and there goes the country merchant, holding tightly to his saddle-bags, and gazing at every thing. The trader at home and the stranger from abroad; the Jew and the Gentile; black and white; vehicles of all kinds, from the costly chariot, with its spanking bays, down to the humble ox team, all help to make up the moving portion of this city panorama. Occasionally this busy scene is heightened in interest by a pugilistic encounter, and a sudden emigration from "Battle Row," to the southern boundary of the Levee, where lies the inebriate's harbor, described in our last as the *calaboose*.

To see our Levee in its glory it should be viewed in the busy season, when it hums with the whirl of trade—when its whole length is covered with the various products of not only our own fruitful country, but the commercial riches of other lands. The spectator may then see hemp and tobacco from the Missouri, lead from the Upper Mississippi, grain from the Illinois, lumber from the St. Croix and Wisconsin, iron from Pittsburgh, sugar and molasses from New Orleans, furs from the Rocky Mountains, fish from the Northern Lakes, manufactured goods from Massachusetts, furniture from Cincinnati, fruits from Cuba and the West Indies, coffee from South America, hardware and porcelain from England, cloths and liquors from France, and tea from China, accompanying which rolls in upon our shore, a continuous tide of emigrants, seeking homes on the rich land of our valley. None of the great commercial marts of the Old World, either of ancient or modern days, ever exhibited more unmistakable signs of greatness in their progress than is foreshadowed for St. Louis. A quarter of a century has made her an inland Tyre, with the various products and people from all quarters of the civilized world flowing into her lap. In walking the length of our Levee, besides the peculiarities of expression which distinguish men from different States in our own confederacy, a keen ear may recognize every language of Europe. The Babel is a compound of German, French, Spanish, Italian, English cockneyism, Scotch drawl, or Irish brogue. Human *flats*, as well as flat boats, float along our city front, and we would advise them while they are perusing its face to examine carefully all its features, for the stranger is sometimes, in that neighborhood, as a stranger, taken in. *"Sharp"* is the word upon the levee, not only for those who trade, but those, also, who travel.

.   .   .   .

A row of Mississippi steamers along our levee front, form the border *patch* of our municipal quilt; and if you should select any *great* name, from the catalogue of earthly creatures or things, it is more than probable you would name one of the vast fleet which plough our inland seas. Their officers are proverbial throughout the world for courtesy; a liberality which sometimes runs into extravagance, a generosity and warmth of friendship which never tires, where their confidence is once gained; an excess of courage which too often disdains peril; and a spirit of accommodation which makes them frequently delay a boat a whole day for the purpose of taking along *all* the passengers who may wish to go in the same direction which they are about journeying.

Arriving, or departing, is the most interesting time to see a western steamer—she is then "alive," and all hands on board are "kicking." Her entry into port resembles a nautical contest. It is a struggle between the shore men to get on board, and the passengers to get on shore. A crowd gathers upon each boat lying near where she is about to land, and the moment the new arrival touches a craft moored at the levee, a very correct exhibition of American character is at once displayed—every body "goes with a *rush!*" Amid the roar of steam, the jingling of bells, the shout of the mate to "stand by that bow-line!" the crowd pours on the guard of the incoming craft; as if they had received the order to *"boarders away!"* Stranger passengers stand still, amazed, as the steam rolls up the stairway and into the cabin. Merchants, reporters, peddlers, steamboat and hotel runners, draymen, porters, hackmen, white and black, fashionable and ragged, dash in glorious confusion into their midst. Then commence a Babel of sounds:

"Planters' House, sir?" "Virginia Hotel, gentlemen?" "Baggage for the Monroe! Baggage wagon ready!" Each runner is proffering a card to the stranger thus saluted. "Going up the Missouri, gentlemen? our boat is going this evening!" "Our first class boat, with *su-pe-rior* accommodations, leaves in the morning for Illinois river—any body going *up?*"

.   .   .   .

The scene at starting is somewhat different. There is first the *preliminary smoke*. Freight is tumbling in; slow-goers are selecting comfortable berths, and hasty travellers are watching the appearances. The Captain has great *hopes* of getting off "this evening." Those who have taken passage and moved their trunks on board, step timidly along the levee, but keep the boat in sight, and watch her smoke, ready to run if she shows the least sign of starting. Night comes, the smoke ceases rolling from the flues, and it is finally concluded to start *early* in the morning. Morning comes, and with it comes more passengers and more freight. Up goes the steam; *chug!* goes the 'scape pipe; jingle goes the bell, and passengers now look lively, for matters *begin* to wear a sure enough moving appearance. So they continue to look *all day!* Another day comes, and now the parties that the Captain was waiting for come on board—freight is bouncing in after them—all is hurry and confusion. The bell is sounding an alarm, and the 'scape pipe is screaming like a panther.

━━━

10 San Francisco of the 49'ers

Bayard Taylor (1825–1875) was one of our best-known travel writers and journalists in the nineteenth century. Fame came to him also as a scholar and a translator of Goethe's *Faust*. Taylor's commission from the *New York Tribune* to visit the California gold fields resulted in these views of San Francisco in its boisterous early days. They helped to fix the image of a romantic city by the Golden

Gate in the minds of Americans then and since. Taylor remained in California during the winter of 1849–1850 to witness the rapid rise of San Francisco within only four months. On Taylor see the *Dictionary of American Biography* and citations therein.

On San Francisco see John Philip Young, *San Francisco, A History of the Pacific Coast Metropolis*, vol. I (San Francisco and Chicago, 1912), chs. XVIII–XXI, XXII–XXXIII.

A‌T LAST WE ARE THROUGH THE GOLDEN GATE—fit name for such a magnificent portal to the commerce of the Pacific! Yerba Buena Island is in front; southward and westward opens the renowned harbor, crowded with the shipping of the world, mast behind mast and vessel behind vessel, the flags of all nations fluttering in the breeze! Around the curving shore of the Bay and upon the sides of three hills which rise steeply from the water, the middle one receding so as to form a bold amphitheatre, the town is planted and seems scarcely yet to have taken root, for tents, canvas, plank, mud and adobe houses are mingled together with the least apparent attempt at order and durability. But I am not yet on shore. The gun of the Panama has just announced our arrival to the people on land. We glide on with the tide, past the U.S. ship Ohio and opposite the main landing, outside of the forest of masts. A dozen boats are creeping out to us over the water; the signal is given—the anchor drops—our voyage is over.

. . . .

. . . The Ohio's boat put us ashore at the northern point of the anchorage, at the foot of a steep bank, from which a high pier had been built into the bay. A large vessel lay at the end, discharging her cargo. We scrambled up through piles of luggage, and among the crowd collected to witness our arrival, picked out two Mexicans to carry our trunks to a hotel. The barren side of the hill before us was covered with tents and canvas houses, and

BAYARD TAYLOR, *Eldorado, or, Adventures in the Path of Empire* . . . , 3rd ed. (New York, 1850); I, 52–61; II, 55–63.

nearly in front a large two-story building displayed the sign: "Fremont Family Hotel."

As yet, we were only in the suburbs of the town. Crossing the shoulder of the hill, the view extended around the curve of the bay, and hundreds of tents and houses appeared, scattered all over the heights, and along the shore for more than a mile. A furious wind was blowing down through a gap in the hills, filling the streets with clouds of dust. On every side stood buildings of all kinds, begun or half-finished, and the greater part of them mere canvas sheds, open in front, and covered with all kinds of signs, in all languages. Great quantities of goods were piled up in the open air, for want of a place to store them. The streets were full of people, hurrying to and fro, and of as diverse and bizarre a character as the houses: Yankees of every possible variety, native Californians in *sarapes* and sombreros, Chilians, Sonorians, Kanakas from Hawaii, Chinese with long tails, Malays armed with their everlasting creeses, and others in whose embrowned and bearded visages it was impossible to recognize any especial nationality. We came at last into the plaza, now dignified by the name of Portsmouth Square. It lies on the slant side of the hill, and from a high pole in front of a long one-story adobe building used as the Custom House, the American flag was flying. On the lower side stood the Parker House—an ordinary frame house of about sixty feet front—and towards its entrance we directed our course.

Our luggage was deposited on one of the rear porticos, and we discharged the porters, after paying them two dollars each—a sum so immense in comparison to the service rendered that there was no longer any doubt of our having actually landed in California. There were no lodgings to be had at the Parker House— not even a place to unroll our blankets; but one of the proprietors accompanied us across the plaza to the City Hotel, where we obtained a room with two beds at $25 per week, meals being in addition $20 per week. I asked the landlord whether he could send a porter for our trunks. "There is none belonging to the house," said he; "every man is his own porter here." . . .

Many of the passengers began speculation at the moment of landing. The most ingenious and successful operation was made by a gentleman of New York, who took out fifteen hundred copies of The Tribune and other papers, which he disposed of in two hours, at one dollar a-piece! Hearing of this I bethought me of about a dozen papers which I had used to fill up crevices in packing my valise. There was a newspaper merchant at the corner of the City Hotel, and to him I proposed the sale of them, asking him to name a price. "I shall want to make a good profit on the retail price," said he, "and can't give more than ten dollars for the lot." I was satisfied with the wholesale price, which was a gain of just four thousand per cent! . . .

It may be interesting to give here a few instances of the enormous and unnatural value put upon property at the time of my arrival. The Parker House rented for $110,000 yearly, at least $60,000 of which was paid by gamblers, who held nearly all the second story. Adjoining it on the right was a canvas-tent fifteen by twenty-five feet, called "Eldorado," and occupied likewise by gamblers, which brought $40,000. On the opposite corner of the plaza, a building called the "Miner's Bank," used by Wright & Co., brokers, about half the size of a fire-engine house in New York, was held at a rent of $75,000. A mercantile house paid $40,000 rent for a one-story building of twenty feet front; the United States Hotel, $36,000; the Post-Office, $7,000, and so on. . . .

The prices paid for labor were in proportion to everything else. The carman of Mellus, Howard & Co. had a salary of $6,000 a year, and many others made from $15 to $20 daily. Servants were paid from $100 to $200 a month, but the wages of the rougher kinds of labor had fallen to about $8. Yet, notwithstanding the number of gold-seekers who were returning enfeebled and disheartened from the mines, it was difficult to obtain as many workmen as the forced growth of the city demanded. . . .

. . . .

. . . One who has been some time in the country will lay down . . . [in a shop] money, without wasting words. The only exception I found to this rule was that of a sharp-faced Down-Easter just opening his stock, who was much distressed when his clerk charged me seventy-five cents for a coil of rope, instead of one dollar. This disregard for all the petty arts of money-making was really a refreshing feature of society. Another equally agree-

able trait was the punctuality with which debts were paid, and
the general confidence which men were obliged to place, perforce, in each other's honesty. Perhaps this latter fact was owing,
in part, to the impossibility of protecting wealth, and consequent
dependence on an honorable regard for the rights of others. . . .

. . . We sallied out for a night-view of San Francisco. . . .
Business was over about the usual hour, and then the harvest-time
of the gamblers commenced. Every "hell" in the place, and I did
not pretend to number them, was crowded, and immense sums
were staked at the monte and faro tables. A boy of fifteen, in one
place, won about $500, which he coolly pocketed and carried off.
One of the gang we brought in the Panama won $1,500 in the
course of the evening, and another lost $2,400. A fortunate miner
made himself conspicuous by betting large piles of ounces on a
single throw. His last stake of 100 oz. was lost, and I saw him the
following morning dashing through the streets, trying to break
his own neck or that of the magnificent *garañon* he bestrode. . . .

.   .   .   .

Of all the marvellous phases of the history of the Present, the
growth of San Francisco is the one which will most tax the belief
of the Future. Its parallel was never known, and shall never be
beheld again. I speak only of what I saw with my own eyes.
When I landed there, a little more than four months before, I
found a scattering town of tents and canvas houses, with a show
of frame buildings on one or two streets, and a population of
about six thousand. Now, on my last visit, I saw around me an
actual metropolis, displaying street after street of well-built edifices, filled with an active and enterprising people and exhibiting
every mark of permanent commercial prosperity. Then, the town
was limited to the curve of the Bay fronting the anchorage and
bottoms of the hills. Now, it stretched to the topmost heights, followed the shore around point after point, and sending back a
long arm through a gap in the hills, took hold of the Golden
Gate and was building its warehouses on the open strait and almost fronting the blue horizon of the Pacific. Then, the gold-
seeking sojourner lodged in muslin rooms and canvas garrets,
with a philosophic lack of furniture, and ate his simple though
substantial fare from pine boards. Now, lofty hotels, gaudy with

verandas and balconies, were met with in all quarters, furnished with home luxury, and aristocratic restaurants presented daily their long bills of fare, rich with the choicest technicalities of the Parisian cuisine. Then, vessels were coming in day after day, to lie deserted and useless at their anchorage. Now scarce a day passed, but some cluster of sails, bound *outward* through the Golden Gate, took their way to all the corners of the Pacific. . . .

.   .   .   .

There had been a vast improvement in the means of living since my previous visit to San Francisco. Several large hotels had been opened, which were equal in almost every respect to houses of the second class in the Atlantic cities. The Ward House, the Graham House, imported bodily from Baltimore, and the St. Francis Hotel, completely threw into the shade all former establishments. The rooms were furnished with comfort and even luxury, and the tables lacked few of the essentials of good living, according to a 'home' taste. The sleeping apartments of the St. Francis were the best in California. The cost of board and lodging was $150 per month—which was considered unusually cheap. A room at the Ward House cost $250 monthly, without board. The principal restaurants charged $35 a week for board, and there were lodging houses where a berth or "bunk"—one out of fifty in the same room—might be had for $6 a week. The model of these establishments—which were far from being "model lodging-houses"— was that of a ship. A number of staterooms, containing six berths each, ran around the sides of a large room, or cabin, where the lodgers resorted to read, write, smoke and drink at their leisure. The state-rooms were consequently filled with foul and unwholesome air, and the noises in the cabin prevented the passengers from sleeping, except between midnight and four o'clock.

The great want of San Francisco was society. Think of a city of thirty thousand inhabitants, peopled by men alone! The like of this was never seen before. Every man was his own housekeeper, doing, in many instances, his own sweeping, cooking, washing and mending. . . .

Towards the close of my stay, the city was as dismal a place as could well be imagined. The glimpse of bright, warm, serene weather passed away, leaving in its stead a raw, cheerless, southeast storm. The wind now and then blew a heavy gale, and the cold, steady fall of rain, was varied by claps of thunder and sudden blasts of hail. The mud in the streets became little short of fathomless, and it was with difficulty that the mules could drag their empty wagons through. . . . I saw occasionally a company of Chinese workmen, carrying bricks and mortar, slung by ropes to long bamboo poles. The plank side-walks, in the lower part of the city, ran along the brink of pools and quicksands, which the Street Inspector and his men vainly endeavored to fill by hauling cart-loads of chapparal and throwing sand on the top; in a day or two the gulf was as deep as ever. The side-walks, which were made at the cost of $5 per foot, bridged over the worst spots, but I was frequently obliged to go the whole length of a block in order to get on the other side. One could not walk any distance, without getting at least ankle-deep, and although the thermometer rarely sank below 50°, it was impossible to stand still for even a short time without a death-like chill taking hold of the feet. As a consequence of this, coughs and bronchial affections were innumerable. The universal custom of wearing the pantaloons inside the boots threatened to restore the knee-breeches of our grandfathers' times. Even women were obliged to shorten their skirts, and wear high-topped boots. The population seemed to be composed entirely of dismounted hussars. . . .

The severe weather occasioned a great deal of sickness, especially among those who led an exposed life. The city overflowed with people, and notwithstanding buildings were continually growing up like mushrooms, over night, hundreds who arrived were obliged to lodge in tents, with which the summits of the hills were covered. Fever-and-ague and dysentery were the prevailing complaints, the great prevalence of which was owing undoubtedly to exposure and an irregular habit of life. An association was formed to relieve those in actual want, many of the wealthiest and most influential citizens taking an honorable part in the matter. Many instances of lamentable destitution were by this means brought to light. Nearly all the hospitals of the place were soon filled, and numbers went to the Sandwich Islands to recruit. The City Hospital, a large, well ventilated and regulated establishment, contained about fifty patients. The attending physician described to me several cases of nearly hopeless lunacy which had come under his care, some of them produced by disappointment and ill-luck, and others by sudden increase of fortune. Poor human nature!

.   .   .   .

The effect of a growing prosperity and some little taste of luxury was readily seen in the appearance of the business community of San Francisco. The slouched felt hats gave way to narrow-brimmed black beavers; flannel shirts were laid aside, and white linen, though indifferently washed, appeared instead; dress and frock coats, of the fashion of the previous year in the Atlantic side, came forth from trunks and sea-chests; in short, a San Francisco merchant was almost as smooth and spruce in his outward appearance as a merchant anywhere else. The hussar boot, however, was obliged to be worn, and a variation of the Mexican sombrero—a very convenient and becoming head-piece—came into fashion among the younger class.

.   .   .   .

Part Three

The Cities
Mature

The urban life of commerce, banking, and venture capital that made Boston flourish in the 1820's also tended to strengthen class lines, separating the established families of trade and shipping from the Yankees, often from the hills of New England, who were making their way through manufacturing and retail selling. The rise of new men of wealth to power was often what produced Jacksonian political leaders in Boston, as in many another American town. Boston was securing its place as the great provincial city of New England, but to all its inhabitants it was the "Hub of the Universe." The devotion of its residents to education and letters, coupled with its liberal Unitarian leadership, produced a cultural climate in which Reform became a byword.

This brief description by Anne Royall (1769–1854) emphasizes the prison and the library, of which Bostonians were proud, and the speech pattern of Yankees which, for Mrs. Royall, identified a "lower class." At the time of her visit Boston had about 45,000 inhabitants.

Anne Royall was a Marylander and a penniless widow at the age of 54; she traveled widely to earn a living from the ten travel books she published between 1826 and 1831. On Royall see the *Dictionary of American Biography*.

On Boston at this time, see S. E. Morison, *The Maritime History of Massachusetts, 1783–1860* (Boston: Sentry Books, 1961), chs. XII–XVIII; W. M. Whitehill, *Boston: A Topographical History*, chs. III–IV; O. B.

Frothingham, *Boston Unitarianism, 1820–1850* (New York, 1890); and Oscar Handlin, *Boston's Immigrants* (Cambridge, 1959), chs. 1–5.

B OSTON CONTAINS 1 NEW STATE-HOUSE, 1 old do., a court-house, a hall for police, Fanueil hall, a prison, an alms-house, a house of correction, a hospital, a dispensary, a theatre, a circus, a custom-house, a city library, a law library, an athenæum, a museum, 2 market-houses, 6 bridges, 3 wharves and the mall, an observatory, and 7 banks. It has also 32 houses for public worship, viz. 12 Congregationalists and Unitarians, 4 Episcopalians, 4 Baptists, 4 Universalists, 3 Methodists, 1 Roman Catholic, 1 Friends, 1 New-Jerusalem, 1 Seamen's chapel, and 1 African. The wharves of Boston are among the first public buildings in the city, and a subject of admiration to all who visit them: they extend to a great distance in the water, to wit, central and long wharf, 1,240 feet. The India wharf is also of considerable length. These wharves are lofty brick houses, with a street on each side, for the landing of vessels, the water being too shallow for vessels to come near the shore, as they do at New-York. The buildings on those wharves surpass any idea that can be formed of symmetry and proportion: so uniform in height, that no line can be drawn with more exactness; particularly central wharf, the whole of the buildings being four stories high, built of the best burnt brick, and occupied for stores. I mean the wharves are all four stories high, and of brick, but the central wharf being more recently built, is more showy. Nothing can look more grand than these wharves stretching out into the bay to such an amazing length. The state-house requires little more to be said. It is called the *new* state-house, to distinguish it from the old one. It stands upon a lofty eminence, called Mount Vernon, at the head of the mall.[1]

ANNE ROYALL, *Sketches of History, Life and Manners in the United States* (New Haven, 1826), 310–311, 318, 320–321, 324–325.

[1] *Pronounced Mal by the citizens.*

It is built of brick, and very high in proportion to its relative size. It has a splendid dome and cupola of astonishing height, with stairs leading many a weary round, out upon the top. It fronts the mall, with a colonnade of singular beauty. The legislature of the state holds its sessions in the state-house; the treasurer of the state, the adjutant general, and secretary of state have their offices there. The governor and council also sit in the state-house. The interior is not very splendidly decorated, but quite enough so. The legislative halls are on the second story, and are very simple indeed; the members sitting upon semi-circular seats, without desks; the speaker's chair is distinguished by no frippery or pomp. . . .

STATE PRISON. The state prison of Massachusetts is organized upon the same plan as those of New-York and Philadelphia, with this difference, however, the convicts of the former are more lively and active, perform their work with more cheerfulness, and receive the full amount of their labor. The prison is in Charlestown, and like those mentioned, has a large yard for the prisoners to perform their labor. The out-door laborers are chiefly stone-cutters, and never did men exceed them in application to business. The prison-yard is in one continual roar of hammers and chissels. Not a man lifted his head to look at me, as I walked through the sheds, while the dust or sand, raised by the instruments, almost blinded me. The mechanics work in shops, which make a part of the prison wall, some hundred feet in length. In these shops mechanics of every description are at work, even at jewelry, printing, and engraving: many of these convicts clear their expenses, and have money to take with them when they are discharged. . . .

The whole of the prison is neatly plastered and whitewashed, even to the floors: from two to four sleep in one cell, upon straw beds, with pillows and blankets, and stools to sit on. They eat three times a day, mush with molasses or milk, for breakfast; supper the same; pork or fish, with beans or peas, and bread, for dinner; all who labor hard, drink beer. None are put in for life. It is under the government of a warden, deputy warden, commissary, clerk, keeper, three turnkeys, eleven watchmen, and attended by a chaplain and physician. The number of prisoners in when I called, was about 300—280 is about the average. They cleared $17,139.46 last year, (1824,) after paying all expenses.

This is the best prison, and the best kept, of any in the U. States, at least, that I have seen. The wardens and keepers are gentlemen of education, and discharge their trust with great humanity.

ATHÆNEUM. But the pride of Boston is the Athenæum. Here the citizens "drink deep of the Pierian Spring." It contains a library of 19,000 volumes, of the best authors, both ancient and modern. Here I saw for the first time Confucius, Terence, Dante, and Leland's translation of Demosthenes. Being honored with the privilege of the Athenæum, I spent some pleasant hours in its apartments; the books are classed in different rooms, and you have only to name those you wish to read, when you are shewn into that part of the building which contains them. No one is permitted, not even the proprietors, to take a book so much as from one room to another; those, and those only, who are proprietors, can go into the Athenæum without special leave from one of their number. The privilege is certainly one of the greatest treats; the building being one of the largest in the city, pleasantly shaded with trees, the rooms spacious, and as silent as night; no one is allowed to speak above their breath lest they might interrupt the readers. Each room is accommodated with chairs, tables, pen and ink, for taking extracts if you wish so to do. Besides the library, the Athenæum contains a choice collection of statuary and painting. . . . Besides this library, there are several in the city. The law library has been mentioned; the city library contains 6060 volumes. The books in all the libraries are well selected; want what author you will, it is to be found in Boston.

MARKETS. The market of Boston yields to none, and in many things it excels, particularly in its fish; the butter is sweet and abundant, much more so than in New-York; but there is no market that I have seen which equals Boston for its excellence in fish. The meat and vegetables also are fine and plentiful, with early fruit of delicious flavor; but they have no market-house worth the name. The butchers assemble under Fanueil Hall, and another place adjoining; but the venders of vegetables line themselves in rows at random, or sell out of carts the best way they can; the fishmongers have a kind of a shed, with a long bench, near to which they have large tubs of water with the finest salmon, fresh from the ocean, and every kind of fish that can be mentioned. The fish market is exemplary for neatness. . . .

MANNERS AND APPEARANCE. Whatever may be the cause, and how-ever strange it may appear, yet it is nevertheless true, that in pro-portion as one part of society advance in science and civilization, the other part sink into vapid ignorance; like turbid water, the pure particles rise to the top, while the dregs settle to the bottom. Whether the cause of this difference is to be sought for in the physical or moral structure of the human mind, I leave to those whom it may more deeply concern to investigate. This truth is perhaps in no community more clearly manifested than in Boston. The people differ as widely as tho' they lived on opposite sides of the globe. How happens this? The means of education are the same to all; there are not less than an hundred schools in Boston and its vicinity, free to all, many of them without money and without price; Cambridge is in sight! Never were the means so ample as in Boston; the whole state is one seminary of education; no excuse for ignorance; the poor are taught gratis.

One part of the community have realized these advantages while the other has not. In no city, perhaps, in America, are to be found a greater body of what may be called gentlemen than in Boston: whatever can be conceived of wealth, whatever can be conceived of talent, or intellect embellished by education or im-proved by business, is eminently displayed in the gentlemen of Boston. Here the human mind appears to be perfectly unfolded; most of them, indeed all of them, are men of liberal education, whether professional or not, and by associating constantly to-gether, and reciprocating those delicious waters which flow from the fountain of knowledge, their manners, of course, accords with the excellence of those attainments. They are affable, mild, and liberal, in every sense of the word. They are mostly Unitarians and Universalists in religion, the most humane and benevolent sects I have met with; the former, however, predominate. The ladies, like the gentlemen, are not exceeded by any on the con-tinent; in accomplished manners, they possess all the yielding soft-ness of the southern ladies, with warmer hearts, and minds im-proved by travelling, most of them having made the tour of Europe. Their countenance is diffused with a magic charm of irresistible sweetness, to which they join the utmost grace of ges-ture and harmony of voice. As to beauty, the ladies of Boston are celebrated throughout the world. But that which deserves our

greatest applause, is their unbounded benevolence and charity towards the distressed; "Which things the angels desired to look
into." All the females, of every class, have a flexible softness in
their manners peculiar to them. What may be called the lower
class, for their opportunity, are ignorant, proud, and abrupt in
their manners, particularly the men; nor do they mix at all with
the higher class, or have any intercourse with them, more than
with the inhabitants of a distant country. They do not know them
in the streets, they are as absolutely separated as though an impassable gulph lay between them. These last, I cannot call them
clowns, for a clown though awkward is bashful; but these are
presuming, pert, and in some cases rude, nor have they a spark
of that yielding charity which distinguishes their more refined
neighbors. Their manners and their dialect perfectly correspond,
though they can read and write, and many, in fact, all, I am told,
go to the grammar schools; a chambermaid will read as correct
as the most finished scholar, and yet their dialect is wretchedly
defective. Here are a few of their phrases; *had'nt ought*, ought
not, *I be*, I am, *do what you'r mine'to*, use your pleasure, *on to it*,
on it, with a number of such. But *guess*, and *what'say*, are their
favorites, and make a part of every sentence. It is amusing enough
to hear about a dozen of their *what'says* and *guesses* assembled
together. What'say is a substitute for sir or madam, (which
amongst them you seldom hear,) and answers to the *how*, of
New-York; it is a habit they have contracted from asking a question to be repeated again, although they have heard it distinctly.
They have the *hickups* here too. All the learning in the world will
never break them of those vulgar habits. . . .

12 Davy Crockett at the Lowell Mills, 1834

The famed cotton manufacturing community established
by Patrick Tracy Jackson (1780–1847) at a site where
water power was plentiful on the Merrimac River was

visited by many from here and abroad. It was considered a model community in America's industrial revolution, and it became known as the "Manchester of America." In one sense this forerunner of modern manufacturing cities was an industrial reform that paralleled the humanitarian reforms of New Englanders in education, prisons, or care of the insane. On Jackson, see the *Dictionary of American Biography;* and on the city of Lowell in this era, see C. F. Ware, *The Early New England Cotton Manufacture* (Boston, 1931), chs. 4–5.

Davy Crockett (1786–1836), frontiersman and Whig congressman, made his "tour of the north" in 1834. Due to his opposition to Andy Jackson and his fame as a hunter, he was wined and dined by New England Whigs. It is doubtful that his autobiographical writings, including this one, were entirely his own. On his life see the *Dictionary of American Biography.*

NEXT MORNING I ROSE EARLY, and started for Lowell in a fine carriage, with three gentlemen who had agreed to accompany me. I had heard so much of this place that I longed to see it; not because I had heard of the "mile of gals;" no, I left that for the gallantry of the president, who is admitted, on that score, to be abler than myself: but I wanted to see the power of machinery, wielded by the keenest calculations of human skill; I wanted to see how it was that these northerners could buy our cotton, and carry it home, manufacture it, bring it back, and sell it for half nothing; and, in the mean time, be well to live, and make money besides.

We stopped at the large stone house at the head of the falls of the Merrimac river, and having taken a little refreshment, went down among the factories. The dinner bells were ringing, and the folks pouring out of the houses like bees out of a gum. I looked at them as they passed, all well dressed, lively, and genteel

DAVID CROCKETT [?], *An Account of Colonel Crockett's Tour to the North and Down East* . . . (Philadelphia, 1835), 91–94.

in their appearance; indeed, the girls looked as if they were coming from a quilting frolic. We took a turn round, and after dining on a fine salmon, again returned, and entered the factories.

The out-door appearance was fully sustained by the whole of the persons employed in the different rooms. I went in among the young girls, and talked with many of them. Not one expressed herself as tired of her employment, or oppressed with work: all talked well, and looked healthy. Some of them were very handsome; and I could not help observing that they kept the prettiest inside, and put the homely one on the outside rows.

I could not help reflecting on the difference of condition between these females, thus employed, and those of other populous countries, where the female character is degraded to abject slavery. Here were thousands, useful to others, and enjoying all the blessings of freedom, with the prospect before them of future comfort and respectability: and however we, who only hear of them, may call their houses workshops and prisons, I assure my neighbours there is every enjoyment of life realized by these persons, and there can be but few who are not happy. It cannot be otherwise: respectability depends upon being neighbour-like: here everybody works, and therefore no one is degraded by it; on the contrary, those who don't work are not estimated.

There are more than five thousand females employed in Lowell; and when you come to see the amount of labour performed by them, in superintending the different machinery, you will be astonished.

Twelve years ago, the place where Lowell now rises in all its pride was a sheep-pasture. It took its name from Francis C. Lowell, the projector of its manufactories, and was incorporated in 1826—then a mere village. The fall, obtained by a canal from the Merrimac river, is thirty-two feet, affording two levels for mills, of thirteen and seventeen feet; and the whole water of the river can be used.

There are about fourteen thousand inhabitants. It contains nine meeting-houses; appropriates seven thousand five hundred dollars for free schools; provides instruction for twelve hundred scholars, daily; and about three thousand annually partake of its benefits. It communicates with Boston by the Middlesex canal (the first ever made in the United States); and in a short time the rail-road

to Boston will be completed, affording every facility of intercourse to the seaboard.

This place has grown by, and must depend on, its manufactures. Its location renders it important, not only to the owners,
but to the nation. Its consumption not only employs the thousands of its own population, but many thousands far away from
them. It is calculated not only to give individual happiness and
prosperity, but to add to our national wealth and independence;
and instead of depending on foreign countries, to have our own
material worked up in our own country.

Some of the girls attended three looms; and they make from
one dollar seventy-five cents to three dollars per week, after paying their board. These looms weave fifty-five yards per day; so
that one person makes one hundred and sixty-five yards per day.
Every thing moves on like clockwork, in all the variety of em-
ployments; and the whole manufacture appears to be of the very
best.

The owner of one of the mills, Mr. Lawrence, presented me
with a suit of broadcloth, made out of wool bought from Mark
Cockral, of Mississippi, who sold them about four thousand
pounds; and it was as good cloth as the best I ever bought for
best imported.

The calico made here is beautiful, and of every variety of
figure and colour. To attempt to give a description of the manner
in which it is stamped and coloured is far beyond my abilities.
One thing I must state, that after the web is wove, and before
they go further, it is actually passed over *a red-hot cylinder*, to
scorch off the furze. The number of different operations is truly
astonishing; and if one of my countrywomen had the whole of
the persons in her train that helped to make her gown, she would
be like a captain on a field-muster: and yet, when you come to
look at the cost, it would take a trunk full of them to find these
same people in living for one day.

I never witnessed such a combination of industry, and perhaps
never will again. I saw the whole process, from the time they put
in the raw material, until it came out completely finished. In fact,
it almost came up to the old story of a fellow walking into a
patent machine with a bundle of wool under his arm, and coming
out at the other end with a new coat on.

Nothing can be more agreeable than the attention that is paid by every one connected with these establishments. Nothing appears to be kept secret; every process is shown, and with great cheerfulness. I regret that more of our southern and western men do not go there, as it would help much to do away with their prejudices against these manufactories.

13   New York City Comes
        of Age in the 1830's

With the completion of the Erie Canal in 1825, New York City came into its own as the first city of the nation. Its population rose from 123,706 in 1820 to 202,589 in 1830. In the 1830's the city received almost 100,000 new residents, chiefly immigrants, and by 1850 its population stood at 515,394. New York, including Brooklyn, held one million people by 1860.

Successful measures to guard a city against fire were always sought and acclaimed by city people. In the first account here Mrs. Royall (see Reading 11) briefly describes New York's well-organized fire department.

The second account of New York in the Jacksonian period is one of the best views of the city left us by a contemporary. Its author, Asa Green (1789–1837)—a Yankee from the Berkshires—was a physician and newspaper man. Among his other books was a satire on the medical profession and an account of his travels in the South.

On New York City in this period see R. G. Albion, *The Rise of New York Port, 1815–1860* (New York, 1939); Robert Ernst, *Immigrant Life in New York City, 1825–1863* (New York, 1949); Bayrd Still, *Mirror for Gotham* (New York, 1956), ch. 5.

THE FIRE DEPARTMENT. The Fire Company is at once, the most respectable and useful society in the city; but I can only afford a brief remark on this establishment. The Fire Department is "a Body Corporate and Politic," consisting of Fire Companies in every Ward, under the control of one *chief* Engineer.

ENGINEERS AND FIRE WARDENS. The common council carry a wand, with a gilded flame at the top. The engineers wear a leathern cap, painted white, with a gilded front, and a fire engine blazoned thereon, and carry a speaking trumpet, painted black, with the words "engine, No. 1," (or as the case may be,) in white, painted on their caps. The fire wardens wear a hat, the brim black, and the crown white, with the city arms blazoned on the front, and carry speaking trumpets, painted white, with the word "warden," in black: the firemen also have badges. When a building takes fire in the night, the watchmen cry "Fire," the bells are set to ringing; the companies attend as above described, with all possible dispatch, with their engines, which are pulled by the firemen running at full speed; the constables and marshals of the city attend with their staves of office, and obey the corporation under the penalty of a heavy fine. Every man, even the mayor of the city are under the control of the fire corporation, during a fire. They use no buckets, or at least rarely, the rivers being so near, and their hose [1] extending from one engine to another, and finally to the river, it is conveyed through them to the fire. The engineers, chief engineers, and fire wardens only direct; they are constantly running to and fro, directing the firemen. The firemen when they are fixed each in his station, stand still and play the engine; their superiors speaking to them through the trumpets, calling to each engine, to "play away No. 2, No. 3," or whatever it may be; for the noise and crackling of the fire, and that of the multitude which gather, would effectually drown their voice. None but the fire companies join in extinguishing fires; the citizens which gather in crowds, are kept at a distance by the city officers. The engines are the most superb piece of mechanism in the city, most of them being richly gilded, and the fire companies consist

ANNE ROYALL, *Sketches of History, Life and Manners in the United States* (New Haven, 1826), 257–259.

[1] *A leathern pipe, from four to five inches in circumference, of great length.*

wholly of reputable men. The membership is deemed one of
honour, but it is one dearly bought; the smoke from the fires, as
near as they are obliged to approach, would strangle any one
else. Very little damage has accrued from fire, since the department has been organized upon its present plan.

B ROAD AS BROADWAY IS, . . . it is now quite too narrow for the
immense travel, business, and locomotion of various kinds, of
which it is the constant scene. This is particularly the case with
that part below Canal-street; and more particularly so south of
the Park. Here the attempt at crossing is almost as much as your
life is worth. . . . We daily see persons waiting at the crossing
places, for some minutes, before they can find an opening, and a
chance to get over, between the omnibuses, coaches, and other
vehicles, that are constantly dashing up and down the street; and,
after waiting thus long, deem themselves exceedingly fortunate
if they get over with sound bones and a whole skin. . . .

Most of the houses in New York are built of brick; and are in
height from two to six stories. A few of the old wooden buildings
remain; and a few of the more new and elegant structures are of
stone. At least they appear to be stone; though few of them, we
believe, have the entire fabric, or the solid walls of that durable
material. For instance, the Astor House, which seems to the eye
a structure of pure granite, is merely covered with slabs of that
material, while the principal thickness of the entire outer wall,
and all the partition walls, are of brick. . . .

Each of these buildings appears in itself, of a uniform and excellent material, and betrays not, by any outward appearance, the
diversity of its composition. The same cannot be said of all those
buildings in which granite or marble forms a part of the material.
They present a front of very beautiful stone, while the gable end
is exposed in all the nakedness of bare bricks. Such are several of
the houses in Broadway; and such is that pretty row of new buildings composing Lafayette Place. . . .

ASA GREENE, *A Glance at New York* (New York, 1837), 4–8,
12–13, 17–18, 30, 33, 42–43, 46–49, 52–55, 165–168, 180–183,
187–188, 193, 222–225, 227–229, 252–256, 258–264.

Granite pillars in front of the stores are of recent introduction. Five or six years ago there were scarcely a dozen of such fronts in all New York. Now every new store is built with granite columns, as high as the first story; and some of them higher. But the new stores are not the only recipients of these improvements. The brick walls are knocked away from the fronts of many of the old ones, and granite pillars inserted. . . .

All the modern structures of New-York are built sufficiently slight; and, like the child's cob-house, are but too ready, elevated as they are, to totter and fall. . . .

The inhabitants of New York . . . derive their origin from every part of the world. They exhibit a sort of human patchwork, in which the materials are brought together from all quarters; and, as might be expected, the whole piece is most strangely and curiously diversified. . . .

As yet the groundwork of this variously patched piece may be seen—though in fainter and fainter colors—in the descendants of the ancient Dutch population. In a few years more this will fade away entirely. The influx of emigrants from New England and Europe will overspread and characterize the whole. In the active business of the place the Yankees are taking, and will take, the lead. Where headwork is to be done the Yankees will do it. The manual operatives will be, as they are becoming more and more, the natives of the Emerald Isle. . . .

House-rent and the price of fuel have equally increased: so that it is next to impossible for a man, on a moderate income, to support a wife and children. If he rent a house, it takes all his income to pay his landlord, and he has nothing left wherewith to purchase food, clothing, and fuel. Or, if he provide himself with these latter articles, he has nothing left wherewith to pay his rent. So that in either event he is pretty sure to suffer destitution.

To show the difference in the prices of sundry articles now, and at a period not beyond the memory of some persons still living—say a little more than seventy years ago—we will place side by side the cost of the articles at that period and the present (p. 84). For the former we are indebted to Watson's "Olden Time in New York."

.   .   .   .

All, or nearly all these hotels are situated in the southerly part
of the city, and most of them in the three lower wards. There
they are convenient to the steamboat landings, and also to the
business operations of the city. Nearly half of the whole number
are situated in Broadway; and these, with two or three exceptions,
no further north than the Park. . . .

PRICES IN 1773			DITTO IN 1837		
	s	*d*		*s*	*d*
Best Oysters per hundred,	1		Do.	20	
Beef per pound,		3 a 4	Do.	1 a 1	6
Fowls each,		9	Do.	2 a 3	
A cock Turkey,	4		Do.	16	
A hen Turkey,	2		Do.	12	
A Goose,	2		Do.	12	
A Duck,	1		Do.	4	
Butter per pound,		9	Do.	2	6
Oak wood per load,	2		Do.	20	

The price of lodging per week, at the Custom House Hotel, is
$2,50. At Tammany Hall and at Lovejoy's it varies from $2,50 to
$3,50, according as your room is situated, up one or more pair of
stairs—the price being lower, the nearer you approach heaven;
and higher, the closer you cling to earth. In the eating department of these houses, the price of a meal consisting of one dish,
varies from 12½ to 31¼ cents.

.   .   .   .

There are, in all, about 150 churches, or religious societies, in
New York. If we suppose their congregations, on an average, to
amount to 1000 each—and this we think is not rating them too
high—there are assembled weekly in this city 150,000 worshippers
—or one half the entire population. The balance, then, in favor
of church-going, and against the theatres, is just equal to 29 in
every 30 persons. So much does the taste in this great metropolis,
run on the side of religion, and so much more popular are ser-
mons than plays. . . .

[Sermons] are better attended than plays—they are less expensive. It will cost a man some hundreds of dollars per annum
for a nightly ticket at the theatre; while it will scarcely cost him

so many cents for admission at a church twice every Sunday. Nay, for that matter, it need not cost him any thing if he chooses to go free. The doors of all the churches are open to all who wish to enter, provided they demean themselves in a sober and orderly manner. . . .

Of all the numerous sects into which this religious community is divided, the Presbyterians are the most numerous, having no less than 39 churches. Next to these are the Episcopalians, who have 29. The Baptists have 20; the Methodists of all sorts, Wesleyan and Independent, 20; Dutch Reformed, 14; Roman Catholic, 6; Universalist, 4; Orthodox, or Trinitarian, Quakers, 1; Hicksite, or Unitarian Quakers, 3; Congregationalists, 2; Unitarians, 2; Lutherans, 2; Moravians, 1; Swedenborgians, 1; Christian, 1; German Reformed, 1; Mariner's Church, 1: total 147 Christian churches. Add to these 3 Jewish Synagogues, and you have the whole number of 150.

These have meetings for public worship from one to three times every Sunday: except the Jews, whose Sabbath is on the seventh day of the week. Of course, as the Israelites are too small a number to do business successfully, without Christian aid, they have also a second day of rest, on the first day of the week.

Besides these religious societies, there is a congregation of Atheists who meet regularly on Sunday, at Tammany Hall.

These different sects for the most part, walk together—or rather walk apart—in great harmony. They agree perfectly well, to differ, with few exceptions. Among these exceptions, for instance, the Atheist, sneers at the Christian; while the Christian, on the contrary, descends from his dignity to lash the Atheist.

But the most bitter animosity prevails between certain of the different sects of Christians; or rather perhaps, it should be said, between the leaders of these different sects. These are, in general the Roman Catholics on the one side, and the Protestants on the other. But the more particular and bitter division is between certain of the pastors of the Dutch Reformed and of the Roman Catholic Churches. . . .

.   .   .   .

The members of the three learned professions in New York amount, in all, to about 1400. We have already stated the number of churches to be 150. . . .

Taking the 150 clergymen from the whole number engaged in the learned professions, and there remain, to be divided amongst the doctors and lawyers, 1250: of whom 650 are lawyers, and the remaining 600, doctors. If, therefore, we divide the population among them in equitable proportions, each lawyer will have about 461½ persons to his share, and each doctor 500. If body and estate, in this great metropolis, be not well taken care of, it will evidently not be for lack of numbers in the professions of law and physic. . . .

In considering the great number of lawyers and doctors, in proportion to the number of inhabitants, it will naturally be asked how they all—i.e. the lawyers and doctors—live. Some will answer, that they do not *live*, but merely *stay*. We will not make so nice distinction; but suppose the stayers to be also livers.

If we suppose each man, woman, and child to pay, on an average, $1.50 per annum for medical attendance, then each physician in New York—allowing "the spoils" were divided equally—would receive $750. This would decently maintain a single man; but leave nothing for wife and children. The division of profits, however, is very far from being equal. . . .

.   .   .   .

The mayor, aldermen, and assistants of New York, are chosen annually, on the 2d Tuesday of April; or to speak more properly, they begin to be chosen on that day; for they do not fairly succeed in getting in, until two days afterwards. So great an affair is an election in the "empire state." . . .

Such crowding!—such jostling!—such pushing!—such swearing!—you would suppose the whole thing were to be done in a single day, and that the freemen were pushing so to get in their votes, because they were pushed for time. No such thing. We have just said they have three days allowed them. But the truth is, the more they swear the less they do. . . .

To get in 60 votes an hour, is a very thriving business in New York. Some wards, indeed, have exceeded it, where the presiding officers have been dexterous, and where there was very little challenging and less swearing. These are apt to take up a great deal of time; especially in those very contested elections, where votes, that are even known to be legal, are disputed. . . .

Some honest citizens of New York have tried hard to obtain a law for the registry of voters: to obviate the necessity of challenging, to do away with the profane practice of swearing, and at the same time secure the purity of elections. But such a law would prove ruinous to the trade in politics; and therefore cannot reasonably be expected to pass. . . .

.   .   .   .

There is not perhaps in the Union a city more destitute of the blessing of good water than New-York.

The present supply, such as it is, comes from three sources, to wit: the town pumps, the Manhattan Company, and Knapp's spring. To this we should add a fourth source, namely, the clouds; from which the chief supply for washing is obtained.

The town pumps are conveniently situated at the corners of the streets, every where throughout the city; so that no person who is athirst, need perish for want of water, if he will take the trouble of walking the length of a square. . . . Besides the virtue derived from the neighboring sinks, the pump-water is also impregnated with certain saline properties, which render it peculiarly efficacious in certain complaints.

Little less so is that—if we may judge from its peculiar hue and taste—which comes from the Collect; and is called Manhattan water. This is ready pumped up to the people's hands, by the Manhattan Banking Company, which was chartered many years ago, for the purpose of supplying the city with "pure and wholesome water." Not that the people get it gratis, as they do the town pump beverage. But they can have it brought to their houses in pipes, on application to the Manhattan Company, and paying the regular price. . . .

The third source, namely Knapp's Spring, furnishes the only tolerable water in the city. This is conveyed about the streets in hogsheads, and sold, we believe, at a penny a gallon. Small as this price seems, their supply of spring water, we are informed, costs some of the larger hotels more than $300 each, per annum. The hotels, boarding houses, and respectable private families make use of this water for tea, coffee, and ordinary drink. The poor all resort to the street pumps.

. . . The great difficulty in supplying the city properly—that is, plentifully and with a good article—is the very great distance from which it must be brought. Various projects have from time to time been started, examined, discussed, debated, and finally thrown aside as impracticable; until very recently, when it was resolved, after a scientific survey of the river and the ground, and duly calculating the expense, to bring hither the waters of the Croton. For this purpose an act has been obtained of the legislature; and if money can be raised, the water will probably be forthcoming, sometime within the life-lease of the present generation. . . .

What is the entire number of dram-shops in New York, we know not. But they may be found at almost every corner throughout the city, and at almost every door of the buildings bordering on the North and East rivers. Besides those places devoted to the mere sale and swilling of liquors; almost every grocery is likewise a dram-shop. Not only tea, coffee, sugar, molasses, butter and cheese are sold at these establishments; but likewise ardent spirits of all sorts, by the gallon and the glass. And the trade in these latter articles is thought to be the most lucrative of the two. . . .

Wine in New York is better; and, if we except that compound called Port, is the best liquor in the city. . . .

.   .   .   .

The New York Society Library . . . is now among the most valuable in the character, as well as number of its books, to be found in the United States. It contains more than 25,000 volumes. The price of a share is now $25, and the annual tax $4.

The next, in number of volumes, is the clerk's library, a collection belonging to the merchants' clerks, united together under the name of the Mercantile Library Association. This library was founded in the year 1821, by the union of a few clerks who thought they could devote their leisure hours more profitably, if not more agreeably, to books than to the theatres, ball rooms, and other fashionable amusements. They began by uniting their own little collections with such books as they could get together by way of donation. Thus a few hundred volumes were collected, which have since been increasing in number, chiefly by means of the subscriptions of members and by an annual tax, until they now amount to more than 13,500: enabling the Mercantile Library to rank as the tenth, in point of numbers in the United States.

The increase in 1836, was 1845 volumes; and the number of members added during the same year was 867. The whole number of members is now about 3,500. The initiation fee is $1; and the annual tax $2, payable by quarterly instalments of 50 cents each. To the library is added a reading room, furnished with all the most valuable periodical literature of the day.

Merchants are allowed all the privileges of the library and the reading room, by paying an annual subscription of $5. And so far they are considered members but they are not allowed the privilege of voting.

The sole management of the concern belongs to the clerks; who, not far from the first of January, elect their officers for each year, and hear the report of those entrusted with the rule for the year preceding.

. . . .

Next to the Mercantile Library in number of volumes, and not inferior to it in point of usefulness, is the Apprentices Library. It was founded in the year 1820, and has now upwards of 12,000 volumes. This library is the property of the General Society of Mechanics and Tradesmen, a benevolent association formed in 1784, thirty-six years before the establishment of the library. The initiation fee, for members of this society, is $10; and $12 more, paid in four annual instalments of $3 each—or $20, paid in the beginning—constitutes a man a life member.

The books of this library are loaned to mechanics' apprentices —for whose use alone it is intended—free of all expense; their masters engaging to become responsible for the safe return of the books. . . .

. . . .

There are several other public libraries in this city, the largest of which is that belonging to the New York Historical Society, founded in 1809, and containing upwards of 10,000 volumes. That of the American Institute, established in 1828, contains about 3,000 volumes; and that of the Law Institute, founded in the same year, upwards of 2,000. The Mechanics' Institute, founded in 1831, has a library of about 1,200 volumes. . . .

The use of hackney coaches is comparatively, of recent date. . . . The number of hackney coaches in New York, at the present time, is upwards of 200: a number twice as great, in proportion to the population, as that of London. These coaches are taxed $5 each for their yearly license, besides a dollar for the coachman. The prices for carrying passengers, as fixed by law, are: for any distance, not exceeding a mile, $37\frac{1}{2}$ cents; and for each additional passenger 25 cents. For any distance over one mile, and not exceeding two the fare is 50 cents; and for each additional passenger 25 cents. For children between two and fourteen years of age, the price is 50 per cent less. For a carriage to Harlem, and back, with the privilege of remaining three hours, the price is $4; to King's Bridge, remaining all day, $5. The price per day for a hack, driven in any direction, is $5. In each of these last cases, the fare is the same, whether there be a single passenger, or whether the coach be full. For attending a funeral within the lamp and watch district, the price is $2; to Potter's Field, $3. . . .

The penalty for a hackney coachman demanding more than the legal rates, is the forfeiture of his whole fare, and a fine of $10. The fine is the same for refusing—when he is not otherwise engaged—to carry a paassenger any where on the island of New York—the legal fee being tendered. . . .

Rainy days are the harvest times for the hackmen. They eye the clouds with as much anxiety as so many ducks; and rejoice, like them, in a long and copious shower. Nothing is so dull—nothing so discouraging to them—as a melancholy time of fair weather. No class of persons in this city—not even those who are paid for it in the pulpit—it is believed, pray so often and so devoutly for rain as the hackney coachmen.

.   .   .   .

From hacks we must ascend to omnibuses. We say ascend, because, although fewer steps are required to get into them, they are nevertheless, for the most part, superior in magnitude and in the number of steeds, to the hackney coaches. This kind of vehicle first got the name of *omnibus* in London, and that not much more than a dozen years since. It is a Latin word, signifying *to all* or *with all:* and was doubtless given to one of these lumbering coaches, because they are open to all, carry all, and are crowded withal.

.   .   .   .

. . . It was not until about the year '30, or '31, that four horses began to be attached to the [New York] city stages.

.   .   .   .

The four-horse stages pay a licence of $20; the two-horse, $10. The fare generally throughout the city is 12½ cents. To York-ville it is 18¾ cents; to Harlem and to Manhattanville, 25 cents. A deduction of one third is made from these prices, where a dozen, or even half a dozen tickets are purchased at once. The number of persons, who take the benefit of the omnibuses, is believed to average not less than 25,000 per day, Sundays ex-cepted, when the horses are allowed to rest.

As these carriages run on certain fixed routes, there is never any occasion for dispute about the price. . . .

The dining hour being from twelve to three, it is between those two periods that the stages—the homeward bound ones—are most apt to be crowded. Indeed, during the whole space of those three important hours, it is exceedingly difficult to get a seat. You may sometimes stand at the corner of a street, beckon-ing to all the stages that pass for half an hour, and not one of them has a seat to give you. The best way, on such occasions, is to march leisurely, but steadily on; and you will probably arrive at your journey's end much sooner than you can get a stage to carry you there, and save your shilling into the bargain. . . .

.   .   .   .

The conclusion, naturally to be drawn from the foregoing pages, is, that New York is a very great city; a very populous city; a very expensive city; a very scarce-of-hotels city; a re-markably religious city; a sadly overrun-with-law-and-physic city; a surprisingly newspaperial city; a rather queerly governed city; an uncommon badly watered city; a very considerable of a rum city; a very full-of-fires city; a pretty tolerably well-hoaxed city; and, moreover, a city moderately abounding in foul streets, rogues, dandies, mobs, and several other things, concerning which it is not necessary to come to any specific conclusion.

Old and New Natchez
of the 1830's

In the 1830's Natchez retained some of its rough frontier
aspects, still seen by arrivals on the levee at Natchez-
under-the-Hill. But on the bluff 200 feet above the Mississippi River Natchez was showing all the signs of a
newer, prosperous ante-bellum planter town. Indeed,
Natchez was becoming typical of many a river town
and provincial capital in the Old South.

J. H. Ingraham (1809–1860) was a New Englander
who went to teach at Jefferson College in Mississippi. He
grew to love the South. A high income came to him from
his voluminous output of novels, published in various
newspapers. In 1852 he became a priest of the Protestant
Episcopal church. On Ingraham see the *Dictionary of
American Biography*.

On Natchez see Harnett T. Kane, *Natchez on the Mississippi* (New York, 1947); C. S. Sydnor, *A Gentleman
of the Old Natchez Region: Benjamin L. C. Wailes*
(Durham, 1938), ch. V; and N. N. Oliver, *Natchez:
Symbol of the old South* (New York, 1940).

WE ARE NOW WITHIN TWENTY MILES OF NATCHEZ. The river
is here very circuitous, making the distance much greater
than by land. The shores continue to exhibit the peculiarly
gloomy and inhospitable features which, with the occasional exception of a high bluff, plantation or village, they present nearly
to the mouth of the Ohio. The loud and startling report of a

JOSEPH HOLT INGRAHAM, *The South-West by a Yankee*, (New
York, 1835), Vol. II, 15–24, 28–29, 33–41, 48–51, 160.

cannon in the bows of the boat, making her stagger and tremble through every beam, is the signal that our port is in sight—a pile of gray and white cliffs with here and there a church steeple, a roof elevated above its summit, and a light-house hanging on the verge! At the foot of the bluffs are long straggling lines of wooden buildings, principally stores and store-houses; the Levée is fringed with flat boats and steamers, and above all, tower majestically the masts of two or three ships. The whole prospect from the deck presents an interesting scene of commercial life and bustle. But this is not Natchez! The city proper is built upon the summit level, the tops of whose buildings and trees can be seen from the boat, rising higher than the cliff. The ascent from the lower town, or as it is commonly designated, "under the hill," is by an excavated road, of moderate elevation. The whole appearance of the place from the deck is highly romantic. On our left, opposite Natchez, is Vidalia, in Louisiana, a pleasant village of a few houses, built on one street parallel with the river. Here, in a pleasant grove above the town, is the "field of honour," where gentlemen from Mississippi occasionally exchange leaden cards—all in the way of friendship.

.   .   .   .

We landed last evening at the Levée, amid the excitement, noise, and confusion which always attend the arrival or departure of a steamer in any place. But here the tumult was varied and increased by the incessant jabbering, hauling, pulling, kicking and thumping, of some score or two of ebony-cheeked men and urchins, who were tumbling over each other's heads to get the first trunk. . . .

.   .   .   .

. . . On looking round me for a moment, on landing, I was far from agreeably impressed with the general appearance of the buildings. This part of the town is not properly Natchez—and strangers passing up and down the river, who have had the opportunity of seeing only this place, have, without dreaming of the beautiful city over their heads, gone on their way, with impressions very inaccurate and unfavourable. These impressions, derived only, but justly, from this repulsive spot, have had a tendency to depreciate the city, and fasten upon it a bad name, which it is very far from meriting. Like the celebrated "Five Points," in New-York, "Natchez under the Hill," as it has been aptly named, has extended its fame throughout the United States, in wretched rhyme and viler story. For many years it has been the nucleus of vice upon the Mississippi. But, for two or three years past, the establishment of respectable mercantile houses, and an excellent hotel, combined with an efficient police, and a spirit of moral reform among the citizens, has, in a great measure, redeemed the place—changed its repulsive character and cancelled its disgraceful name. Though now on the high way of reform, there is still enough of the cloven-hoof visible, to enable the stranger to recognise that its former reputation was well earned.

The principal street, which terminates at the ascent of the hill, runs parallel with the river, and is lined on either side with a row of old wooden houses; which are alternately gambling-houses, brothels, and bar-rooms: a fair assemblage! As we passed through the street—which we gained with difficulty from the boat, picking our way to it as we could, through a filthy alley—the low, broken, half-sunken side-walks, were blocked up with fashionably-dressed young men, smoking or lounging, tawdrily arrayed, highly rouged females, sailors, Kentucky boatmen, negroes, negresses, mulattoes, pigs, dogs, and dirty children. The sounds of profanity and Bacchanalian revels, well harmonizing with the scene, assailed our ears as we passed hastily along, through an atmosphere of tobacco smoke and other equally fragrant odours. After a short walk we emerged into a purer air, and in front of a very neat and well-conducted hotel. From near this place, extending along the Levée to the north, commences the mercantile part of the "landing," lined with stores and extensive warehouses, in which is transacted a very heavy business. The whole of this lower town is built upon a reclaimed flat, from one to two hundred yards broad, and half a mile in length; bounded upon one side by the river, and on the other by the cliff or bluff, upon which Natchez stands, and which rises abruptly from the *Batture*, to the height of one hundred and sixty feet. . . . With but a little excavation, a fine road has been constructed along this way, with an inclination sufficiently gentle to enable the heaviest teams to ascend with comparative ease. . . .

On arriving at the summit of the hill, I delayed a moment, for the double purpose of taking breath and surveying the scene spread out around me. Beneath lay the roofs of warehouses, stores, and dwellings, scattered over a flat, sandy surface, which was bordered, on the water side, by hundreds of up-country flat-boats, laden with the produce of the rich farming states bordering the Ohio and "Upper Mississippi." Lower down, steamers were taking in and discharging freight; while the mingled sounds of the busy multitude rose like the hum of a hive upon the ear. . . . Natchez, mantled with rich green foliage like a garment, with its handsome structures and fine avenues, here a dome and there a tower, lies immediately before me. It is the very contrast to its straggling namesake below. The city proper consists of six streets, at right angles with the river, intersected by seven others of the same length, parallel with the stream. The front, or first parallel street, is laid out about one hundred yards back from the verge of the bluff, leaving a noble green esplanade along the front of the city, which not only adds to its beauty, but is highly useful as a promenade and parade ground. Shade trees are planted along the border, near the verge of the precipice, beneath which are placed benches, for the comfort of the lounger. From this place the eye commands one of the most extensive prospects to be found on the Mississippi. . . .

.   .   .   .

. . . The buildings on the front street face the river, and, with the exception of one or two private houses, with galleries and shrubbery, reminding one of the neat and beautiful residences on the "coast," [1] possess no peculiar interest. The town is entered from the parade by rude bridges at the termination of each street, spanning a dry, dilapidated brick aqueduct of large dimensions, which has been constructed along the whole front of the city, but is now, from some unknown cause, suffered to fall

---

[1] *The banks of the Mississippi are termed* "the coast," *as far up the river as Baton Rouge. It is usual to say one lives on the* coast, *if he lives on the river shore.*

to ruin. It was probably intended as a reservoir and conductor
of the water which, after heavy rains, rushes violently down the
several streets of the city. . . .

.   .   .   .

Main-street is the "Broadway" of Natchez. It extends from the
river to the eastern extremity of the city, about half a mile in
length, dividing the town into nearly equal portions, north and
south. This street is to Natchez what Chartres-street is to New-
Orleans, though on a much smaller scale. Here are all the banks
and most of the dry goods and fancy stores. Here, consequently,
is the centre of business, and, to the ladies, that of attraction; although the stores are not turned inside out every morning, to
adorn their fronts and create zigzags on the side-walks, to the
great edification of the shopmen, who are the operators, and the
little comfort of gouty or hurrying pedestrians. In passing up
this street, which is compactly built with handsome brick blocks,
generally but two stories in height, the stranger is struck with
the extraordinary number of private carriages, clustered before
the doors of the most fashionable stores, or millineries, rolling
through the street, or crossing and recrossing it from those by
which it is intersected, nearly every moment, from eleven till
two on each fair day. But few of these equipages are of the city:
they are from the plantations in the neighbourhood, which spread
out from the town over richly cultivated "hill and dale,"—a pleasant and fertile landscape—far into the interior. . . .

. . . The moving galaxy of grace and beauty that floats down
Chesnut-street, cannot at any time present more fashionable and
elegantly-dressed promenaders than now enliven the street, or
than that fair bevy of young ladies clustered round yonder carriage door, all chattering together, with their sweet pleasant
voices, to a pale, beautiful, and interesting girl within, apparently
an invalid. So far as I can judge, as much of "the ton," in dress
and society, prevails here as in Philadelphia, where many residents of the city and country spend a portion of every summer—
certainly more than at New-Orleans, which is by far the most
unfashionable city in the United States. The gentlemen of
Natchez are less particular in their dress, though much more
punctilious than they were five or six years since, when there

was not to be found what would be termed a "fashionable man," (according to the acceptation of the term in New-York) among the residents of this city. And where is the southern gentleman that ever dressed *fashionably?* They dress well and richly, but seldom fashionably. Their garments hang upon them loosely, as though made for larger men; and they wear them with a sort of free and easy air, enviable but inimitable by the stiffer and more formal northerner. . . .

. . . .

A circumstance that very soon arrests the attention of the stranger, is the number of gentlemen with riding-whips in their hands to be met with in all parts of the city, particularly on days when any public meeting is held. Every third or fourth person is thus, to a northerner, singularly armed. At the north few ride except in gigs. But here all are horsemen; and it is unusual to see a gentleman in a gig or carriage. If his wife rides out, he attends her *à cheval*. Instead of gigs, therefore, which would fill the streets of a northern town, saddle-horses, usually with high pummelled Spanish saddles, and numerous private carriages, in which are the ladies of the family, drawn by long-tailed horses, throng the streets and line the outside of the pavé. At least a third of the persons who fill the streets are planters and their families from the country, which every day pours forth its hundreds from many miles around the city, that like a magnet attracts all within its influence.

. . . .

Natchez, like most of the minor cities of this country, cannot boast of any public buildings remarkable for harmonious conformity to the rules or orders of architecture. They are, nevertheless, well deserving of notice, highly ornamental to the city, and reflect honour upon the public spirit of its citizens. The Agricultural bank is unquestionably the finest structure in the city. It has been erected very recently on the south side of Main-street, presenting a noble colonnaded front, of the modernized Grecian style; being built somewhat after the model of the United States bank at Philadelphia; though brick and stucco are here substituted for marble, and heavy pillars for the graceful

column. . . . A short distance above this fine building is the
Masonic Hall. . . . The first story of the building is used as an
academy—the only one in this state. It is a well-conducted institution, and its pupils are thoroughly instructed by competent
officers, who are graduates of northern colleges, as are most of
the public and private instructors of this state. The number of
students is generally large. Those who are destined for professional life, after completing their preparatory course here, usually
enter some one of the colleges at the north. Yale, Princeton, and
Harvard annually receive several from this state; either from this
academy or from under the hands of the private tutors, who are
dispersed throughout the state, and from whom a great majority
of the planters' sons receive their preparatory education. . . .
There is a female seminary also in the city, which, though of a
very respectable character, is not so celebrated and flourishing as
many others in the state.

. . . The citizens of Natchez are not a play-going community;
consequently they take little pride in the possession of a fine
theatre. Its interior, however, is well arranged, convenient, and
handsomely painted and decorated. Its boards are supplied, for
two or three months during every season, by performers from
New-Orleans or New-York. . . . Of the other public buildings
of Natchez, the Presbyterian church is the finest and most imposing. It stands on a commanding site, overlooking the public
square, a pleasant green flat, in the center of which is the court-
house. . . .

The court-house is a fine, large, square building, opposite to
the church, surmounted by a cupola. It is surrounded by a beautiful, though not spacious, green. On the streets which bound the
four sides of it are situated the lawyers' and public offices, which
are generally plain, neat, wooden buildings. . . .

.   .   .   .

The society of Natchez, now, is not surpassed by any in America. Originally, and therein differing from most western cities,
composed of intelligent and well-educated young men, assembled
from every Atlantic state, but principally from New England and
Virginia, it has advanced in a degree proportionate to its native
powers. English and Irish gentlemen of family and fortune have

here sought and found a home—while the *gentilhomme* of sunny France, and the dark-browed don of "old Castile," dwell upon the green hills that recede gently undulating from the city; or find, in their vallies, a stranger's unmarbled and unhonoured grave.

The citizens of Natchez are, however, so inseparably connected with the neighbouring planters, that these last are necessarily included in the general term "society of Natchez." The two bodies united may successfully challenge any other community to produce a more intelligent, wealthy, and, I may say, *aristocratic* whole. But I do not much like the term applied to Americans; though no other word will express so clearly that refinement and elegance to which I allude, and which everywhere indicate the opulence and high breeding of their possessors. This is not so manifest, however, in the external appearance of their dwellings, as it is in their mode or style of living. To this their houses, especially the residences of those who have *made* their wealth, and who yet occupy the same cabins, but little improved, which they originally erected, present a sad contrast. Many of the wealthiest planters are lodged wretchedly; a splendid sideboard not unfrequently concealing a white-washed beam—a gorgeous Brussels carpet laid over a rough-planked floor—while uncouth rafters, in ludicrous contrast to the splendour they look down upon, stretch in coarse relief across the ceiling.—These discrepancies, however, always characteristic of a new country, are rapidly disappearing; and another generation will be lodged, if not like princes, at least, like independent American gentlemen. . . .

. . . Natchez is one hundred and fifty-five miles from New-Orleans by land, and two hundred and ninety-two by water. It contains a population of about three thousand, the majority of whom are coloured. The influx of strangers—young merchants from the north, who have within the last four years, bought out nearly all the old standing merchants—numerous mechanics, and foreign emigrants— is rapidly increasing the number, and in five years, if the rail-road already surveyed from this city to the capital, a distance of one hundred and nine miles, is brought into operation, it will probably contain twice the present number of souls. . . . Cotton is now shipped directly to the northern states

and Europe, from this port, instead of being conveyed by steamboats to New-Orleans and there reshipped. There are two oil
mills in this city worked by steam. The oil is manufactured from
cotton-seed, which heretofore was used as manure. This oil is said
to be superior to sperm oil, and the finest paint oil. Similar manufactories are established in New-Orleans, and I think, also, in
Mobile. . . .

15 High Society in Charleston, 1850's

Charleston was the social capital of southern planters and
traders. The elite of the South gravitated there for the
winter season of racing and fancy dress balls. Charleston
was not so much a city as a kind of urban club, founded
upon a cotton empire. By 1830, the town held about 15,500
Negro slaves and about 12,700 white residents. South
Carolina's turn to headstrong political agrarianism around
1830 was due in part to Charleston's loss of prestige as
a commercial port to Savannah and its inability to link
up with the West by interstate railroad. The capital of
the Confederacy would be located elsewhere, but for
many southerners Charleston was the sentimental capital
of the South, a noble city that spoke for an entire region
in denouncing the urban life of the North.

J. M. Mackie (1813–1894) of Massachusetts was a
teacher and biographer. This account is based upon his
trip to the South just before the Civil War.

On old Charleston see C. McL. Green, *American
Cities*, pp. 18–26; H. H. Ravenel [Mrs. St. Julien Rave-
nel], *Charleston, the Place and the People* (New York,
1922), chs. XVIII–XXI; D. D. Wallace, *The History
of South Carolina*, vol. III (New York, 1934), ch.
LXXXIV.

I HAD BEGUN TO HEAR THE FEBRUARY RACES IN CHARLESTON TALKED OF AS FAR NORTH AS WASHINGTON, and had been told much of the fine horses, much of the beautiful women, who, in *grande toilette*, grace these festive occasions. . . .

As to the ladies, they were not to be cheated out of their holiday by the rain. They were there in full feather; in ermine and point lace; in light brocades and cashmeres of India. They were there in the latest *nouveautés;* gay with flowers and graceful with fringes, as well as in perfect little loves of parasols, and fans fluttering with coquetry. One or two dowagers sported their diamonds and jewels more appropriate for the ballroom. Nearly all, as it seemed to me, were rather over-dressed for the occasion; though, as it is the fashion of the Charlestonians to put on new bonnets for the February races, as the Philadelphians do at Easter, perhaps the temptation to make too much of the toilet at this time might well be irresistible. . . .

The lords of this part of creation, likewise, were tall and fine-looking; though it struck me that their easy morning costumes, if adapted to the occasion, were not quite in harmony with the elaborate toilets of the sex. Certain it is, that the tip-top beaux were generally dressed in overcoats, sacks, raglans, sticks, and umbrellas. I could but think, also, that many of them carried a trifle too much weight in the watch chain, and, in some instances, selected their waistcoats of a crimson slightly too emphatic for the black of their pantaloons. But, on the whole, the crowd of clubmen were well attired; and I did not see among them a single specimen of the black-satin-vest gentry.

For the rest, considering that ladies came to the race in full dress, I was a little surprised at seeing that the floor of the saloon wherein they were assembled was, in places, wet with tobacco juice, and sprinkled with nutshells. Lads, whose bringing up in the best families of the town should have taught them better, threw the shells on the floor as unceremoniously as if they had been in a beer garden, or a cockpit. Even a lady arrayed in ermine, and deep frills of Chantilly lace, who was holding a

JOHN MILTON MACKIE, *From Cape Cod to Dixie* (New York, 1864), 93–100, 108–109.

court, at the moment, consisting of four gentlemen, all in waxed
mustaches, suffered two out of the four to stand in her presence
munching peanuts.

.   .   .   .

. . . My first impressions of Charleston were extremely agreeable. It was a pleasant thing to find an American city containing
so many memorials of the times colonial, and not wearing the
appearance of having been all built yesterday. The atmosphere,
charged with an unusual dampness in consequence of the low
position of the town on coast and river banks, helps materially to
deepen the marks of years; soon discoloring the paint upon the
houses and facilitating the progress of the green moss, which here
is ever creeping over the northern side of roofs and walls. The
whole town looks picturesquely dingy, and the greater number
of buildings have assumed something of the appearance of European antiquity. The heavy brick walls and the high gateways are
such as one sees in London or Paris. Many front doors and piazzas
had been wrought after the graceful models brought from England in the old colonial period. The verandas, story above story,
and generally looking toward the south, or the sea, form another
pleasant feature in the prevailing style of building. Nor less attractive are the gardens and courtyards invariably attached to
the best houses, where, in winter, the hedges are green with
pitosporum and the dwarf orange; and where blow the first
fragrant violets and daffodils of spring. . . .

.   .   .   .

In winter, many of the wealthy South Carolinian planters come
to Charleston to enjoy the gay season of February; and a few
spend several months here for the sake of the greater advantages
in educating their children. But all come to town with less parade
than did the grand seigneurs of the generation preceding. For a
quarter of a century, the number of coaches and four has been
gradually diminishing. Fewer outriders herald the planter's advance. The family carriage has grown a little rickety, and the
worse for wear; though the horses are still well blooded. . . .
Comparatively few are the masters who nowadays pass through
the country with a retinue of from fifteen to twenty servants;

who, at a wedding, or other festive occasion, open wide their doors to all comers, entertaining troops of friends, twoscore and more, with for every one a couch, as well as for every one a month's welcome. . . .

The February balls in Charleston are scarcely less known to fame than the races. The most select and fashionable are those of the Saint Cecilia, and they have been given here from times running back past the memory of all the dancers now living. Only the gentry and the more favored strangers are admitted. They go at ten o'clock, and stay until three. The attendance, however, is principally confined to the younger portion of the fashionable community, who, before setting off for the dance, see the mammas and papas comfortably to bed. . . .

. . . .

Returning to town, we passed along the Battery, the principal promenade of the Charlestonians, and a truly beautiful one. Two rivers, the Cooper and the Ashley, flow past it into the bay, which here spreads out to view a pleasant expanse of waters. Almost entirely landlocked, the Palmetto Islands bound it on the south; to the eastward project into the water the two salient points of Forts Sumter and Moultrie; while in the west, when I first saw it, lay diffused over all the beautiful tints of the sunset. . . . A little later in the year, all the fashion of Charleston will be met, at the hour of twilight, promenading on this smoothly laid sea wall. Nightly the cool breeze from the water fans them, and refreshes their languid spirits, when May-day introduces the season of hot weather. And hence has grown up the proverb, that the Charlestonians live but during two months of the year—in February, for the sake of the races, and in May, for that of the promenade upon the Battery.

Part Four

⸻⸻⸻⸻⸻⸻⸻⸻⸻⸻⸻⸻

The Impact of Civil War

⸻⸻⸻⸻⸻⸻⸻⸻⸻⸻⸻⸻

16 Washington on the Eve of Civil War

Washington, our national capital since 1800, did not reach maturity until the era of the Civil War. The town that in 1850 held 40,000 people grew by 1860 to a population of 75,000. The War brought to Washington not only Union soldiers by the thousands, many of them wounded at the front and hospitalized in the city, but also as many clerks and seekers after government contracts or offices. With wartime disease and death also came wartime prosperity. Washington began to catch up with northern cities in her urban facilities: the city hall, begun in 1820, was completed in 1860; an adequate water supply was brought in by aqueduct; a salaried fire department was established; and the school system was greatly expanded. By the summer of 1863 Washington held nearly 200,000 people.

George William Bagby (1828–1883) wrote and lectured on Old Virginia themes. Trained in medicine, he abandoned it to edit the Lynchburg, Virginia, *Express* in the 1850's. He next was a newspaperman in Washington, and when this piece was published he was editor of the *Southern Literary Messenger* in Richmond. On Bagby see the *Dictionary of American Biography*.

For Washington in this period see Constance McLaughlin Green, *Washington: Village and Capital, 1800–1878* (Princeton, 1962).

Washington is the paradise of paradoxes,—a city of magnificent distances, but of still more magnificent discrepancies.
Anything may be affirmed of it, everything denied. What it seems
to be it is not; and although it is getting to be what it never was,
it must always remain what it now is. It might be called a city,
if it were not alternately populous and uninhabited; and it would
be a wide-spread village, if it were not a collection of hospitals
for decayed or callow politicians. It is the hybernating-place of
fashion, of intelligence, of vice,—a resort without the attractions
of waters either mineral or salt, where there is no bathing and no
springs, but drinking in abundance and gambling in any quantity.
Defenceless, as regards walls, redoubts, moats, or other fortifications, it is nevertheless the Sevastopol of the Republic, against
which the allied army of Contractors and Claim-Agents incessantly lay siege. It is a great, little, splendid, mean, extravagant,
poverty-stricken barrack for soldiers of fortune and votaries of
folly. . . .

.   .   .   .

Traversing a rocky prairie infested with hacks, you arrive late
in the afternoon at a curbed boundary, too fatigued in body and
too suffocated with dust to resent the insult to your common-
sense implied in the announcement that you have merely crossed
what is called an Avenue. Recovered from your fatigue, you
ascend the steps of a marble palace, and enter but to find it garrisoned by shabby regiments armed with quills and steel pens.
The cells they inhabit are gloomy as dungeons, but furnished
like parlors. Their business is to keep everybody's accounts but
their own. They are of all ages, but of a uniformly dejected aspect. Do not underrate their value. Mr. Bulwer has said, that, in
the hands of men entirely great, the pen is mightier than the
sword. Suffer yourself to be astonished at their numbers, but permit yourself to withdraw from their vicinity without questioning
too closely their present utility or future destination. No personal affront to the public or the nineteenth century is intended

[G. W. BAGBY] "Washington City," *Atlantic Monthly*, VII
(January, 1861), 1–8.

by the superfluity of their numbers or the inadequacy of their capacities. Their rapid increase is attributable not to any incestuous breeding in-and-in among themselves, but to a violent seduction of the President and the Heads of Department by importunate Congressmen; and you may rest assured that this criminal multiplication fills nobody with half so much righteous indignation and virtuous sorrow as the clerks themselves.

Emerging from the palace of quill-drivers, a new surprise awaits you. The palace is surmounted by what appear to be gigantic masts and booms, economically, but strongly rigged, and without any sails. In the distance, you see other palaces rigged in the same manner. The effect of this spectacle is painful in the extreme. . . . It is not without pain that you are forced at last to the commonplace belief that these remarkable mountings of the Public Buildings are neither masts nor booms, but simply derricks, —mechanical contrivances for the lifting of very heavy weights. It is some consolation, however, to be told that the weakness of these derricks has never been proved by the endeavor to elevate by means of them the moral character of the inhabitants of Washington. Content yourself, after a reasonable delay for natural wonderment, to leave the strange scene. This shipping-like aspect of the incomplete Departments is only a nice architectural tribute to the fact that the population of Washington is a floating population. This you will not be long in finding out. The oldest inhabitants are here to-day and gone to-morrow, as punctually, if not as poetically, as the Arabs of Mr. Longfellow. A few remain,—parasitic growths, clinging tenaciously to the old haunts. Like tartar on the teeth, they are proof against the hardest rubs of the tooth-brush of Fortune.

As with the people, so with the houses. Though they retain their positions, seldom abandoning the ground on which they were originally built, they change almost hourly their appearance and their uses,—insomuch that the very solids of the city seem fluid, and even the stables are mutable,—the horse-house of last week being an office for the sale of patents, or periodicals, or lottery-tickets, this week, with every probability of becoming an oyster-cellar, a billiard-saloon, a cigar-store, a barber's shop, a bar-room, or a faro-bank, next week. And here is another astonishment. You will observe that the palatial museums for the tem-

porary preservation of fossil or fungous penmen join walls, virtually, with habitations whose architecture would reflect no credit
on the most curious hamlet in tide-water Virginia. To your
amazement, you learn that all these houses, thousands in number,
are boarding-houses. Of course, where everybody is a stranger,
nobody keeps house. It would be pardonable to suppose, that, out
of so many boarding-houses, some would be in reality what they
are in name. Nothing can be farther from the fact. These houses
contain apartments more or less cheerless and badly furnished,
according to the price (always exorbitant, however small it may
be) demanded for them, and are devoted exclusively to the storage of empty bottles and demijohns, to large boxes of vegetable-
and flower-seeds, to great piles of books, speeches, and documents
not yet directed to people who will never read them, and to an
abominable odor of boiling cabbages. . . .

.   .   .   .

. . . The entire male population is constantly eating in the
oyster-cellars. Indeed, if ocular evidence may be relied on, the
best energies of the metropolis are given to the incessant consumption of "half a dozen raw," or "four fried and a glass of
ale." The bar-rooms and eating-houses are always full or in the
act of becoming full. By a fatality so unerring that it has ceased
to be wonderful, it happens that you can never enter a Washington restaurant and find it partially empty, without being instantly
followed by a dozen or two of bipeds as hungry and thirsty as
yourself, who crowd up to the bar and destroy half the comfort
you derive from your lunch or your toddy.

.   .   .   .

Seeing the multitude of boarding-houses, oyster-cellars, and
ivory-banks [faro houses], you may suppose there are no hotels
in Washington. You are mistaken. There are plenty of hotels,
many of them got up on the scale of magnificent distances that
prevails everywhere, and somewhat on the maritime plan of the
Departments. Outwardly, they look like colossal docks, erected
for the benefit of hacks, large fleets of which you will always
find moored under their lee, safe from the monsoon that prevails
on the open sea of the Avenue. Inwardly, they are labyrinths. . . .

The differential calculus by which all Washington is computed obtains at the hotels as elsewhere, with this peculiarity,—that the differences are infinitely great, instead of infinitely small. While the fronts are very fine, showy, and youthful as the Lecompton Constitution, the rears are coarse, common, and old as the Missouri Compromise. The furniture in the rooms that look upon Pennsylvania Avenue is as fresh as the dogma of Squatter Sovereignty; that in all other rooms dates back to the Ordinance of '87. Some of the apartments exhibit a glaring splendor; the rest show beds, bureaus, and washstands which hard and long usage has polished to a sort of newness. Specimens of ancient pottery found on these washstands are now in the British Museum, and are reckoned among the finest of Layard's collections at Nineveh.

The dining-rooms are admirable examples of magnificent distance. The room is long, the tables are long, the kitchen is a long way off, and the waiters a long time going and coming. The meals are long,—so long that there is literally no end to them; they are eternal. . . .

The people of Washington are as various, mixed, dissimilar, and contrasted as the edifices they inhabit. Within the like area, which is by no means a small one, the same number of dignitaries can be found nowhere else on the face of the globe,—nor so many characters of doubtful reputation. If the beggars of Dublin, the cripples of Constantinople, and the lepers of Damascus should assemble in Baden-Baden during a Congress of Kings, then Baden-Baden would resemble Washington. Presidents, Senators, Honorables, Judges, Generals, Commodores, Governors, and the Exs of all these, congregate here as thick as pick-pockets at a horse-race or women at a wedding in church. Add Ambassadors, Plenipotentiaries, Lords, Counts, Barons, Chevaliers, the great and small fry of the Legations, Captains, Lieutenants, Claim-Agents, Negroes, Perpetual-Motion-Men, Fire-Eaters, Irishmen, Plug-Uglies, Hoosiers, Gamblers, Californians, Mexicans, Japanese, Indians, and Organ-Grinders, together with females to match all varieties of males, and you have a vague notion of the people of Washington. . . .

In spite of numberless receptions, levees, balls, hops, parties, dinners, and other reunions, there is, properly speaking, no soci-

ety in Washington. Circles are said to exist, but, like that in the
vortex of the whirlpool, they are incessantly changing. . . .

The Circle of the Mudsill includes Negroes, Clerks, Irish Laborers, Patent and other Agents, Hackmen, Faro-Dealers, Wash-
erwomen, and Newspaper-Correspondents. In the Hotel Circle,
the Newest Strangers, Harpists, Members of Congress, Concer-
tina-Men, Provincial Judges, Card-Writers, College-Students, Un-
protected Females, "Star" and "States" Boys, Stool-Pigeons, Con-
tractors, Sellers of Toothpicks, and Beau Hickman, are found.
The Circle of the White House embraces the President, the Cab-
inet, the Chiefs of Bureaus, the Embassies, Corcoran and Riggs,
formerly Mr. Forney, and until recently George Sanders and
Isaiah Rynders. The little innermost circle is intended to represent a select body of residents, intense exclusives, who keep aloof
from the other circles and hold them all in equal contempt. This
circle is known only by report; in all probability it is a myth. It
is worthy of remark that the circles of the White House and the
Hotels rise higher and sink lower than that of the Mudsill. . . .

Everybody is "busted." No matter what may be the state of a
man's funds when he gets to Washington, no matter how long
he stays or how soon he leaves, to this "busted" complexion must
he come at last. He is in Rome; he must take the consequences.
Shall he insult the whole city with his solvency? Certainly
not. . . .

Where morals are loose, piety is seldom in excess. But there
are a half-dozen of churches in Washington, besides preaching
every Sunday in the House of Representatives. The relative size
and cost of the churches, as compared with the Public Buildings,
indicates the true object of worship in Washington. Strange to
say, the theatre is smaller than the churches. Clerical and dramatic entertainments cannot compete with the superior attractions of the daily rows in Congress and the nightly orgies at the
faro-banks. Heaven is regarded as another Chihuahua or Sonora,
occupied at present by unfriendly Camanches, but destined to be
annexed some day. In the mean time, a very important election is
to come off in Connecticut or Pennsylvania. That must be attended to immediately. Such is piety in Washington. . . .

In conclusion, it must be admitted that Washington is the Ely-
sium of oddities, the Limbo of absurdities, an imbroglio of ludi-

crous anomalies. Planned on a scale of surpassing grandeur, its architectural execution is almost contemptible. Blessed with the name of the purest of men, it has the reputation of Sodom. The seat of the law-making power, it is the centre of violence and disorder which disturb the peace and harmony of the whole Republic,—the chosen resort for duelling, clandestine marriages, and the most stupendous thefts. It is a city without commerce and without manufactures; or rather, its commerce is illicit, and its manufacturers are newspaper-correspondents, who weave tissues of fiction out of the warp of rumor and the web of prevarication. The site of the United States Treasury, it is the home of everything but affluence. Its public buildings are splendid, its private dwellings generally squalid. The houses are low, the rents high; the streets are broad, the crossings narrow; the hacks are black, the horses white; the squares are triangles, except that of the Capitol, which is oval; and the water is so soft that it is hard to drink it, even with the admixture of alcohol. It has a Monument that will never be finished, a Capitol that is to have a dome, a Scientific Institute which does nothing but report the rise and fall of the thermometer, and two pieces of Equestrian Statuary which it would be a waste of time to criticize. It boasts a streamlet dignified with the name of the river Tiber, and this streamlet is of the size and much the appearance of a vein in a dirty man's arm. It has a canal, but the canal is a mud-puddle during one half the day and an empty ditch during the other. In spite of the labors of the Smithsonian Institute, it has no particular weather. It has the climates of all parts of the habitable globe. It rains, hails, snows, blows, freezes, and melts in Washington, all in the space of twenty-four hours. After a fortnight of steady rain, the sun shines out, and in half an hour the streets are filled with clouds of dust. Property in Washington is exceedingly sensitive, the people alarmingly callous. The men are fine-looking, the women homely. The latter have plain faces, but magnificent busts and graceful figures. The former have an imposing presence and an empty pocket, a great name and a small conscience. Notwithstanding all these impediments and disadvantages, Washington is progressing rapidly. It is fast becoming a large city, but it must always remain a deserted village in the summer. Its destiny is that of the Union. It will be the greatest

capital the world ever saw, or it will be "a parched place in the
wilderness, a salt land and not inhabited," and "every one that
passeth thereby shall be astonished and wag his head."

17 New York City's Growth
1862-1865

The city that had come of age in the 1830's grew into a
great metropolis during the 1860's. More important for
determining the relationship between New York City
and the Civil War than the draft riots of July, 1863,
which are frequently cited by historians as the outstanding wartime incidents in this city, is the immense up-
turn in the city's material prosperity. The war brought
wealth to many New Yorkers and after its close New
York City became the commercial, financial, and merchandising capital of the nation. One index of this rise
is that the value of real and personal property in New
York County nearly doubled in the 1860's. The arrival
on the social scene of a new "shoddy" rich, displacing
the older established families in pretentious living, was
paralleled by a turn in New York's theatrical and residential life. New theatres opened, many showing the
forerunners of modern musical comedies. By the early
1870's the first modern apartment houses with elevators
were being erected. A new pattern of commuter life was
being drawn in the 1860's: although the city did not
reach above Forty-second Street, Brooklyn was becoming a bedroom for New York. And to the city annually
came thousands of immigrants, anticipating the even
greater number of newcomers in the last quarter of the
nineteenth century.

The first selection, a brief reminder that New York
City was losing its old town character, was written by
George William Curtis (1824–1892), author, orator, and

traveler. A New Englander and one time disciple of Ralph Waldo Emerson, Curtis for several years conducted *Harper's* "Easy Chair." On Curtis see the *Dictionary of American Biography*.

The longer selection describing New York's growth in this period was written by Fitzhugh Ludlow (1836–1870), a native of New York City and dramatic, art, and music critic for the New York *Evening Post* and *Home Journal*. On Ludlow see the *Dictionary of American Biography*.

On New York City in this period see Bayrd Still, *Mirror for Gotham*, ch. 7; Robert Ernst, *Immigrant Life in New York City: 1825–1863*, ch. XV; and J. G. Wilson (ed.), *The Memorial History of the City of New York*, vol. III, ch. XIV.

Those who remember the Broadway of twenty years ago can hardly walk the street now without incessant wonder and surprise. For although the transformation is gradually wrought, it is always going on before the eye. Twenty years ago it was a street of three-story red brick houses. Now it is a highway of stone, and iron, and marble buildings. The few older ones that remain and are individually remembered as among the best of their kind and time, are now not even quaint, but simply old-fashioned and unhandsome.

And yet, among all the costly and colossal buildings that have of late been erected how few show any real taste or grace; how little but stone, and iron, and space has been bought for the money! The fine architectural effects of some streets in Genoa, in Naples, in Rome, in Paris, in Berlin, in Venice, and other great foreign cities, are unknown in New York. There are some exceptions. Some of the new stores in Broadway are almost as imposing as some of the palaces in Italian cities. But how very few the exceptions are! And how the best are disfigured by the ugliest signs!

[George William Curtis] "Editor's Easy Chair," *Harper's New Monthly Magazine*, CXLI (February, 1862), 409.

The changes, too, in the business character of Broadway are
not less striking; and the change is not a gain to the brilliancy
and gayety of the city. The chief promenading thoroughfare of
a metropolis should sparkle with the small retail shops, in which
the details finish the street with pretty arabesque. . . .

But in Broadway the cellar and wareroom are invading the
boudoir. Great wholesale stores stand where the pretty shops
stood, and if you go below Canal Street of an evening there is
something ghastly in the gloom of the closed warehouses. Twenty
years ago you sauntered from Canal Street to Chamber, stopping
at Contoit's Garden to eat an ice-cream. City civilization then
paused at Bleecker or Fourth streets. The New York Hotel stands
now, down town, where then a quiet farm-house stood aloof in
leafy seclusion. Beyond Ninth Street the city raveled out into the
fields. Union Park was an inclosure. Madison Square was out
upon the island. Where now the choicest fashion dwells cows
and donkeys browsed. Dear me, how changed every thing is!

Of course in all these changes the city has lost much of its old
town character, and becomes every year more and more a metropolis. The crowd in Broadway, when Broadway is fullest,
seems to have come from out of town. It has a strange, wondering
air. And the population of the city itself is so incessantly reinforced by those who come from the country that the city has
always a little air of novelty to its own citizens. The customs of
smaller towns, the street distinction of certain people, are gradually going. It is not many years since every noted man was
known to all Broadway. It is not long since, on Sunday mornings,
the clergymen, with wide-flying black-silk gowns, floated and
ambled along the street to church. These things have disappeared
almost unconsciously. They belonged to the age of three-story
red brick houses, and they have gone together.

.   .   .   .

THE PROPERTY ON THE NORTHWEST CORNER OF BROADWAY AND
CHAMBER STREET, now occupied in part by one of Delmonico's restaurants, was purchased by a New York citizen, but lately

FITZHUGH LUDLOW, "The American Metropolis," *Atlantic
Monthly*, XV (January, 1865), 73–83, 85–86.

deceased, for the sum of $1,000: its present value is $125,000. A single Broadway lot, surveyed out of an estate which cost the late John Jay $500 per acre, was recently sold at auction for $80,000, and the purchaser has refused a rent of $16,000 per annum, or twenty per cent on his purchase-money, for the store which he has erected on the property. In 1826, the estimated total value of real estate in the city of New York was $64,804,050. In 1863, it had reached a total of $402,196,652, thus increasing more than sixfold within the lifetime of an ordinary business-generation. In 1826, the personal estate of New York City, so far as could be arrived at for official purposes, amounted to $42,434,981. In 1863, the estimate of this class of property-values was $192,000,161. It had thus more than quadrupled in a generation.

.   .   .   .

During the year 1862, 75,000 immigrants landed at the port of New York; in 1863, 150,000 more; and thus far in 1864 (we write in November) 200,000 have debarked here. Of these 425,000 immigrants, 40 per cent have stayed in the city. Of the 170,000 thus staying, 90 per cent, or 153,000, are British subjects; and of these, it is not understating to say that five eighths are dependent for their livelihood on physical labor of the most elementary kind. By comparing these estimates with the tax-list, it will appear that we have pushed our own inherent vitality to an extent of forty millions increase in our taxable property, and contributed to the support of the most gigantic war in human annals, during the period that we received into our grand civic digestion a city of British subjects as large as Bristol, and incorporated them into our own body politic with more comfort both to mass and particles than either had enjoyed at home.

.   .   .   .

Let us invite the map to help us in our investigation of New York's claim to the metropolitan rank. There are three chief requisites for the chief city of every nation. It must be the city in easiest communication with other countries,—on the sea-coast, if there be a good harbor there, or on some stream debouching into the best harbor that there is. It must be the city in easiest communication with the interior, either by navigable streams, or valleys and mountain-passes, and thus the most convenient rendezvous for the largest number of national interests,—the place where Capital and Brains, Import and Export, Buyer and Seller, Doers and Things to be Done, shall most naturally make their appointments to meet for exchange. Last, (and least, too,—for even cautious England will people jungles for money's sake,) the metropolis must enjoy at least a moderate sanitary reputation; otherwise men who love Fortune well enough to die for her will not be reinforced by another large class who care to die on no account whatever.

New York answers all these requisites better than any metropolis in the world. She has a harbor capable of accommodating all the fleets of Christendom, both commercial and belligerent. . . .

.   .   .   .

. . . Philadelphia and Baltimore are forever precluded from competing with New York, both by their greater distance from open water and the comparative inferiority of the interior tracts with which they have ready communication. . . .

Considered with regard to the tributary interior, New York occupies a position no less central than with respect to the coast. It is impossible to study a map of our country without momently increasing surprise at the multiplicity of natural avenues which converge in New York from the richest producing districts of the world. The entire result of the country's labor seems to seek New York by inevitable channels. Products run down to the managing, disbursing, and balancing hand of New York as naturally as the thoughts of a man run down to the hand which must embody them. . . .

.   .   .   .

Finally, New York has been prevented only by disgraceful civic mismanagement from becoming long ago the healthiest city in the world. In spite of jobbed contracts for street-cleaning, and various corrupt tamperings with the city water-front, by which the currents are obstructed, and injury is done the sewage as well as the channels of the harbor, New York is now undoubtedly a healthier city than any other approaching it in size. Its natural sanitary advantages must be evident. The crying need of a great city is good drainage. To effect this for New York, the civil engineer has no struggle with his material. He need only avail himself dexterously of the original contour of his ground. . . . In the matter of climate, New York experiences such comparative freedom from sudden changes as belongs to her position in the midst of large masses of water. She enjoys nearly entire immunity from fogs and damp or chilly winds. Her weather is decided, and her population are liable to no one local and predominant class of disease. So far as her hygienic condition depends upon quantity and quality of food, her communications with the interior give her an exceptional guaranty. Despite the poverty which her lower classes share in kind, though to a much less degree, with those of other commercial capitals, there is no metropolis in the world where the general average of comfort and luxury stands higher through all the social grades. . . .

.   .   .   .

The natural advantages which allured New York's first population have been steadily developed and reinforced by artificial ones. For the ships of the world she has built about her waterfront more than three hundred piers and bulkheads. Allowing berth-room for four ships in each bulkhead, and for one at the end of each pier, (decidedly an under-estimate, considering the extent of some of these structures,)—the island water-front already offers accommodation for the simultaneous landing of eight hundred first-class foreign cargoes. The docks of Brooklyn, Jersey City, and Hoboken may accommodate at least as many more. . . .

Besides the various berths or anchorages and the warehouses of New York, commerce is still further waited on in our metropolis by one of the most perfect systems of pilot-boat, steam-tug, and lighter service which have ever been devised for a harbor. No vessel can bring so poor a foreign cargo to New York as not to justify the expense of a pilot to keep its insurance valid, a tug to carry it to its moorings, and a lighter to discharge it, if the harbor be crowded or time press. Indeed, the first two items are matters of course; and not one of them costs enough to be called a luxury.

The American river-steamboat—the palatial American *steamboat*, as distinguished from the dingy, clumsy English *steamer* —is another of the means by which Art has supplemented New

York's gifts of Nature. This magnificent triumph of sculpturesque beauty, wedded to the highest grade of mechanical skill, must be from two hundred and fifty to four hundred feet long,—must accommodate from five hundred to two thousand passengers,—must run its mile in three minutes,—must be as *rococo* in its upholsterings as a bedchamber of Versailles,—must gratify every sense, consult every taste, and meet every convenience. Such a boat as this runs daily to every principal city on the Sound or the Hudson, to Albany, to Boston, to Philadelphia. A more venturous class of coasting steamers in peaceful times are constantly leaving for Baltimore, Wilmington, Charleston, Savannah, Key West, Mobile, New Orleans, and Galveston. The immense commerce of the Erie Canal, with all its sources and tributaries, is practically transacted by New York City. Nearly everything intended for export, plus New York's purchases for her own consumption, is forwarded from the Erie Canal terminus in a series of *tows*, each of these being a rope-bound fleet, averaging perhaps fifty canal-boats and barges, propelled by a powerful steamer intercalated near the centre. . . .

Turning to New York's land communication with the interior, we find the following railroads radiating from the metropolitan centre.

1. A Railroad to Philadelphia.
2. A Railroad to the Pennsylvania Coal Region.
3. A Railroad to Piermont on the Hudson.
4. A Railroad to Bloomfield in New Jersey.
5. A Railroad to Morristown in New Jersey.
6. A Railroad to Hackensack in New Jersey.
7. A Railroad to Buffalo.
8. A Railroad to Albany, running along the Hudson.
9. Another Railroad to Albany, by an interior route.
10. A Railroad to New Haven.
11. A Railroad to the chief eastern port of Long Island.
12. The Delaware and Raritan Road to Philadelphia, connecting with New York by daily transports from pier.
13. The Camden and Amboy Railroad, connecting similarly.
14. The Railroad to Elizabeth, New Jersey.

Let us turn to consider how New York has provided for the people as well as the goods that enter her precincts by all the ways we have rehearsed. She draws them up Broadway in twenty thousand horse-vehicles per day, on an average, and from that magnificent avenue, crowded for nearly five miles with elegant commercial structures, over two hundred miles more of paved street, in all directions. She lights them at night with eight hundred miles of gas-pipe; she washes them and slakes their thirst from two hundred and ninety-one miles of Croton main; she has constructed for their drainage one hundred and seventy-six miles of sewer. She victimizes them with nearly two thousand licensed hackmen; she licenses twenty-two hundred car- and omnibus-drivers to carry them over twenty-nine different stage-routes and ten horse-railroads, in six hundred and seventy-one omnibuses and nearly as many cars, connecting intimately with every part of the city, and averaging ten up-and-down trips per day. She connects them with the adjoining cities of the main-land and with Staten and Long Island by twenty ferries, running, on the average, one boat each way every ten minutes during the twenty-four hours. She offers for her guests' luxurious accommodation at least a score of hotels, where good living is made as much the subject of high art as in the Hôtel du Louvre, besides minor houses of rest and entertainment, to the number of more than five thousand. She attends to their religion in about four hundred places of public worship. She gives them breathing-room in a dozen civic parks, the largest of which both Nature and Art destine to be the noblest popular pleasure-ground of the civilized world, as it is the amplest of all save the Bois de Boulogne. Central Park covers an area of 843 acres, and, though only in the fifth year of its existence, already contains twelve miles of beautifully planned and scientifically constructed carriage-roads, seven miles of similar bridle-path, four sub-ways for the passage of trade-vehicles across the Park, with an aggregate length of two miles, and twenty-one miles of walk. As an item of city property, Central Park is at present valued at six million dollars; but this, of course, is quite a nominal and unstable valuation. The worth of the Park to New York property in general is altogether beyond calculation.

.   .   .   .

We have no room for the details—which would embarrass us, if we should attempt a statement—of the cost of clothing the New York people. We will merely remark, in passing, that one of the largest retail stores in the New York dry-goods trade sells at its counters ten million dollars' worth of fabrics per annum, and that another concern in the wholesale branch of the same trade does a yearly business of between thirty and forty millions. As for tailors' shops, New York is their fairy-land,—many eminent examples among them resembling, in cost, size, and elegance, rather a European palace than a republican place of traffic. . . .

On the 31st day of December, 1863, there were 101 joint-stock companies for the underwriting of fire-risks, with an aggregate capital of $23,632,860; net assets to the amount of $29,269,423; net cash receipts from premiums amounting to $10,181,031; and an average percentage of assets to risks in force equalling 2.995. Besides these 101 joint-stock concerns, there existed at the same date twenty-one mutual fire-insurance companies, with an aggregate balance in their favor of $674,042. The rapidity with which mutual companies have yielded to the compacter and more efficient form of the joint-stock concern will be comprehended when it is known that just twice the number now in being have gone out of existence during the last decade. There are twelve marine insurance companies in the metropolis, with assets amounting to $24,947,559. The life-insurance companies number thirteen, with an aggregate capital of $1,885,000. We may safely set down the property invested in New York insurance companies of all sorts at $51,139,461. Add this sum to the aggregate banking capital above stated, and we have a total of $120,359,224. This vast sum merely represents New York's interest in the management of other people's money. The bank is employed as an engine for operating debt and credit. Its capital is the necessary fuel for running the machine; and that fuel ought certainly not to cost more than a fair interest on the products of the engine. The insurance companies guard the business-man's fortune from surprise, as the banks relieve him from drudgery; they put property and livelihood beyond the reach of accident: in other words, they manage the estates of the community so as to secure them from deterioration, and charge a commission for their stewardship. . . .

.   .   .   .

I do not know how much I may assist any reader's further comprehension of the energies of the metropolis by stating that it issues fifteen daily newspapers, one hundred and thirty-three weekly or semi-weekly journals, and seventy-four monthly, semi-monthly, or weekly magazines,—that it has ten good and three admirable public libraries,—a dozen large hospitals, exclusive of the military,—thirty benevolent societies, (and we are in that respect far behind London, where every man below an attorney belongs to some "union" or other, that he may have his neighbors' guaranty against the ever-impending British poor-house,)— twenty-one savings-banks,—one theatre where French is spoken, a German theatre, an Italian opera-house, and eleven theatres where they speak English. In a general magazine-article, it is im-possible to review the hundreds of studios where our own Art is painting itself into the century with a vigor which has no rival abroad. . . .

.   .   .   .

18   The Burning of Richmond, 1865

The destruction of war has been visited upon very few American cities. But long remembered by their inhabit-ants has been the wartime burning of cities—Washington City by the British during the War of 1812, the Southern cities of Atlanta, Columbia, Charleston, and Richmond at the close of the Civil War. Only the peacetime fires in New York City in 1835, in Chicago in 1871 (the most disastrous), in Boston in 1872, or in San Francisco fol-lowing the earthquake of 1906 brought as much or more devastation and human misery as these wartime fires. This vivid description of the burning and evacuation of Rich-mond is included not because it marks the end of the city as capital of the Confederacy but because it depicts an urban catastrophe of the first order: a beleaguered city in flames with its residents in disorder and flight. Richmond, however, was to be rebuilt. By 1870 it held 51,000 inhabitants, an increase of 13,000 over its population of 1860. By 1880 it had a population of 63,600.

Sallie A. Brock Putnam came from a family long prominent in Virginia affairs. She began her literary career in 1866 under the pseudonym of Virginia Madison and became a contributor to various journals and newspapers with her travel sketches, editorials, and reviews. In 1882 she married a Boston clergyman, Richard F. Putnam.

On Richmond during the war see A. H. Bill, *The Beleaguered City: Richmond, 1861–1865* (New York, 1946).

THE MORNING OF THE 2d OF APRIL, 1865, dawned brightly over the capital of the Southern Confederacy. . . . No sound disturbed the stillness of the Sabbath morn, save the subdued murmur of the river, and the cheerful music of the church bells. . . . At St. Paul's church the usual congregation was in attendance. President Davis occupied his pew. . . . A messenger was observed to make his way up the aisle, and to place in the hands of the President a sealed package. Mr. Davis arose, and was noticed to walk rather unsteadily out of the church. An uneasy whisper ran through the congregation, and intuitively they seemed possessed of the dreadful secret of the sealed dispatch— the unhappy condition of General Lee's army and the necessity for evacuating Richmond. The dispatch stated that this was inevitable unless his lines could be reformed before eight o'clock that evening. . . . Late in the afternoon the signs of evacuation became obvious to even the most incredulous. Wagons were driven furiously through the streets, to the different departments, where they received as freight, the archives of the government, and carried them to the Danville Depot, to be there conveyed away by railroad.

Thousands of the citizens determined to evacuate the city with the government. Vehicles commanded any price in any currency possessed by the individual desiring to escape from the

SALLIE A. BROCK PUTNAM, *Richmond During the War: Four Years of Personal Observation* (New York, 1867), 362–369.

doomed capital. The streets were filled with excited crowds hurrying to the different avenues for transportation, intermingled with porters carrying huge loads, and wagons piled up with incongruous heaps of baggage, of all sorts and descriptions. The banks were all open, and depositors were busily and anxiously collecting their specie deposits, and directors were as busily engaged in getting off their bullion. Millions of dollars of paper money, both State and Confederate, were carried to the Capitol Square and buried.

Night came on, but with it no sleep for human eyes in Richmond. Confusion worse confounded reigned, and grim terror spread in wild contagion. The City Council met, and ordered the destruction of all spirituous liquors, fearing lest, in the excitement, there would be temptation to drink, and thus render our situation still more terrible. In the gutters ran a stream of whiskey, and its fumes filled and impregnated the air. After nightfall Richmond was ruled by the mob. In the principal business section of the city they surged in one black mass from store to store, breaking them open, robbing them, and in some instances (it is said) applying the torch to them.

In the alarm and terror, the guards of the State Penitentiary fled from their posts, and numbers of the lawless and desperate villains incarcerated there, for crimes of every grade and hue, after setting fire to the workshops, made good the opportunity for escape. . . .

But a still more terrible element was destined to appear and add to the horrors of the scene. From some authority—it seems uncertain what—an order had been issued to fire the four principal tobacco warehouses. They were so situated as to jeopardize the entire commercial portion of Richmond. At a late hour of the night, Mayor Mayo had dispatched, by a committee of citizens, a remonstrance against this reckless military order. But in the mad excitement of the moment the protest was unheeded. The torch was applied, and the helpless citizens were left to witness the destruction of their property. The rams in the James River were blown up. The "Richmond," the "Virginia" No. 2 and the "Beaufort" were all scattered in fiery fragments to the four winds of heaven. The noise of these explosions, which occurred as the first grey streaks of dawn broke over Richmond, was like that of a hundred cannon at one time. The very foundations of the city were shaken; windows were shattered more than two miles from where these gunboats were exploded, and the frightened inhabitants imagined that the place was being furiously bombarded. The "Patrick Henry," a receiving-ship, was scuttled, and all the shipping at the wharves was fired except the flag-of-truce steamer "Allison."

As the sun rose on Richmond, such a spectacle was presented as can never be forgotten by those who witnessed it. To speed destruction, some malicious and foolish individuals had cut the hose in the city. The fire was progressing with fearful rapidity. The roaring, the hissing, and the crackling of the flames were heard above the shouting and confusion of the immense crowd of plunderers who were moving amid the dense smoke like demons, pushing, rioting and swaying with their burdens to make a passage to the open air. From the lower portion of the city, near the river, dense black clouds of smoke arose as a pall of crape to hide the ravages of the devouring flames, which lifted their red tongues and leaped from building to building as if possessed of demoniac instinct, and intent upon wholesale destruction. All the railroad bridges, and Mayo's Bridge, that crossed the James River and connected with Manchester, on the opposite side, were in flames.

The most remarkable scenes, however, were said to have occurred at the commissary depot. Hundreds of Government wagons were loaded with bacon, flour and whiskey, and driven off in hot haste to join the retreating army. In a dense throng around the depot stood hundreds of men, women and children, black and white, provided with anything in which they could carry away provisions, awaiting the opening of the doors to rush in and help themselves. A cascade of whiskey streamed from the windows. About sunrise the doors were thrown open to the populace, and with a rush that seemed almost sufficient to bear off the building itself, they soon swept away all that remained of the Confederate commissariat of Richmond.

By this time the flames had been applied to or had reached the arsenal, in which several hundred car loads of loaded shell were left. At every moment the most terrific explosions were sending forth their awful reverberations, and gave us the idea of a general bombardment. All the horrors of the final conflagration, when the earth shall be wrapped in flames and melt with fervent heat, were, it seemed to us, prefigured in our capital.

At an early hour in the morning, the Mayor of the city, to whom it had been resigned by the military commander, proceeded to the lines of the enemy and surrendered it to General Godfrey Weitzel, who had been left by General Ord, when he withdrew one-half of his division to the lines investing Petersburg, to receive the surrender of Richmond.

As early as eight o'clock in the morning, while the mob held possession of Main street, and were busily helping themselves to the contents of the dry goods stores and other shops in that portion of the city, and while a few of our cavalry were still to be seen here and there in the upper portions, a cry was raised: "The Yankees! The Yankees are coming!" Major A. H. Stevens, of the Fourth Massachusetts Cavalry, and Major E. E. Graves, of his staff, with forty cavalry, rode steadily into the city, proceeded directly to the Capitol, and planted once more the "Stars and Stripes"—the ensign of our subjugation—on that ancient edifice. As its folds were given to the breeze, while still we heard the roaring, hissing, crackling flames, the explosions of the shells and the shouting of the multitude, the strains of an old, familiar tune floated upon the air—a tune that, in days gone by, was wont to awaken a thrill of patriotism. But now only the most bitter and crushing recollections awoke within us, as upon our quickened hearing fell the strains of "The Star Spangled Banner." For us it was a requiem for buried hopes.

.   .   .   .

By one o'clock in the day, the confusion reached its height. As soon as the Federal troops reached the city they were set to work by the officers to arrest the progress of the fire. By this time a wind had risen from the south, and seemed likely to carry the surging flames all over the northwestern portion of the city. The most strenuous efforts were made to prevent this, and the grateful thanks of the people of Richmond are due to General Weitzel and other officers for their energetic measures to save the city from entire destruction.

The Capitol Square now presented a novel appearance. On the

south, east, and west of its lower half, it was bounded by burning
buildings. The flames bursting from the windows, and rising from
the roofs, were proclaiming in one wild roar their work of destruction. Myriads of sparks, borne upward by the current of
hot air, were brightening and breaking in the dense smoke above.
On the sward of the Square, fresh with the emerald green of
early spring, thousands of wretched creatures, who had been
driven from their dwellings by the devouring flames, were con-
gregated. Fathers and mothers, and weeping, frightened children
sought this open space for a breath of fresh air. But here, even,
it was almost as hot as a furnace. Intermingled with these miserable beings were the Federal troops in their garish uniform,
representing almost every nation on the continent of Europe, and
thousands of the *Corps d'Afrique*. All along on the north side of
the Square were tethered the horses of the Federal cavalry, while,
dotted about, were seen the white tents of the sutlers, in which
there were temptingly displayed canned fruits and meats,
crackers, cheese, etc.

-    .   .   .   .

The sun had set upon this terrible day before the awful reverberations of exploding shells at the arsenal ceased to be heard over
Richmond. The evening came on. A deathlike quiet pervaded the
late heaving and tumultuous city, broken only by the murmuring
waters of the river. . . .

-    .   .   .   .

19   Atlanta After the War

In Richmond, Atlanta, and Nashville the New South began its urban rebuilding as soon as the Civil War ended.
Prosperity returned to these cities more rapidly than to
their sister cities of the South. Particularly was this true
of Atlanta. Whitelaw Reid on a trip to the South after
the War wrote: "The burnt district of Richmond was

hardly more thoroughly destroyed than the central part of Atlanta; yet, with all the advantages of proximity to the North, abundant capital, and an influx of business and money from above the Potomac, Richmond was not half so far rebuilt as Atlanta."

Incorporated as Atlanta in 1847 at the junction of railroad lines, the city had a population of about 6000 in 1854 and only about 11,500 on the eve of the Civil War. During the war, martial law ruled the city while it was becoming a center for manufacturing and the storage of supplies. Some 80,000 wounded soldiers were quartered in the city during the war. After General Sherman ordered the city destroyed upon its surrender, September 2, 1863, the city was evacuated and fired on November 15. As a result, all but 400 of Atlanta's 4500 houses and commercial buildings were razed. By January, 1865, many citizens were returning to the city to begin the rebuilding. By 1866 the population was estimated at 20,228, and in 1868 Atlanta became the state capital. By 1900 its population reached 89,900; and in 1920, despite a great fire in 1917, the city held nearly 201,000 people. Ever since the days of Reconstruction, when Yankee money and energy were sent to the city, Atlanta has stood first among our southeastern cities as a railroad and commercial center.

This account of Atlanta after the war was written by Sidney Andrews (1835–1880), a journalist from New England who toured the Carolinas and Georgia in the fall of 1865 as special correspondent for the *Chicago Tribune* and the *Boston Advertiser*. On Andrews see the *Dictionary of American Biography*.

On Atlanta after the war see E. M. Coulter, *The South During Reconstruction, 1865–1877* (Baton Rouge, 1947), ch. XII.

ATLANTA IS BUILT ON SOMETHING LESS THAN A HUNDRED HILLS; and, excepting Boston, is the most irregularly laid out city I ever saw. In fact, the greater portion of it seems never to have been laid out at all till Sherman's army came in here. That did the work pretty thoroughly,—so thoroughly, indeed, as to prove remarkably destructive ability in his men.

Coming here has dispelled two illusions under which I rested: first, that Atlanta was a small place; and second, that it was wholly destroyed. It was a city of about fourteen thousand inhabitants two years ago, and it was not more than half burned last fall. The entire business portion, excepting the Masonic Hall building and one block of six stores and a hotel, was laid in ruins, and not a few of the larger residences in all parts of the city were also burned. But the City Hall and the Medical College, and all the churches, and many of the handsomer and more stylish private dwellings, and nearly all the houses of the middling and poorer classes, were spared; and on the first of last June there was ample shelter here for at least six or eight thousand persons. Of course, however, when the entire business portion of the place had disappeared, the city had been practically put out of the way for the time being, even if nothing be said of the fact that it was depopulated by military orders.

The marks of the conflict are everywhere strikingly apparent. The ruin is not so massive and impressive as that of Columbia and Charleston; but as far as it extends it is more complete and of less value. The city always had a mushroom character, and the fire-king must have laughed in glee when it was given over into his keeping. There is yet abundant evidence of his energy,—not so much in crumbling walls and solitary chimneys, as in thousands of masses of brick and mortar, thousands of pieces of charred timber, thousands of half-burned boards, thousands of scraps of tin roofing, thousands of car and engine bolts and bars, thousands of ruined articles of hardware, thousands upon thousands of tons of *débris* of all sorts and shapes. Moreover, there are plenty of cannon-balls and long shot lying about the streets, with

SIDNEY ANDREWS, *The South Since the War: As Shown by Fourteen Weeks of Travel and Observation in Georgia and the Carolinas* (Boston, 1866), 338–342.

not a few shell-struck houses in some sections; and from the court-house square can be seen a dozen or more forts, and many a hillside from which the timber was cut so that the enemy might not come upon the city unawares.

From all this ruin and devastation a new city is springing up with marvellous rapidity. The narrow and irregular and numerous streets are alive from morning till night with drays and carts and hand-barrows and wagons,—with hauling teams and shouting men,—with loads of lumber and loads of brick and loads of sand,—with piles of furniture and hundreds of packed boxes,—with mortar-makers and hod-carriers,—with carpenters and masons,—with rubbish removers and house-builders,—with a never-ending throng of pushing and crowding and scrambling and eager and excited and enterprising men, all bent on building and trading and swift fortune-making.

Chicago in her busiest days could scarcely show such a sight as clamors for observation here. Every horse and mule and wagon is in active use. The four railroads centring here groan with the freight and passenger traffic, and yet are unable to meet the demand of the nervous and palpitating city. Men rush about the streets with little regard for comfort or pleasure, and yet find the days all too short and too few for the work in hand. The sound of the saw and plane and hammer rings out from daylight till dark, and yet master-builders are worried with offered contracts which they cannot take. Rents are so high that they would seem fabulous on Lake Street, and yet there is the most urgent cry for store-room and office-room. Four thousand mechanics are at work, and yet five thousand more could get immediate employment if brick and lumber were to be had at any price. There are already over two hundred stores, so called, and yet every day brings some trader who is restless and fretful till he secures a place in which to display another stock of goods.

Where all this eagerness and excitement will end no one seems to care to inquire. The one sole idea first in every man's mind is to make money. That this apparent prosperity is real no outsider can believe. That business is planted on sure foundations no merchant pretends. That there will come a pause and then a crash, a few prudent men prophesy.

Meantime Atlanta is doing more than Macon and Augusta combined. The railroad from here to Chattanooga clears over one hundred thousand dollars per month, and could add fifty thousand more to that enormous sum if it had plenty of engines and rolling stock. The trade of the city is already thirty per cent greater than it was before the war, and it is limited only by the accommodations afforded, and has even now spread its wings far out on streets heretofore sacred to the privacy of home.

Wonderful as is the new growth of the city, its original existence is still more wonderful. It is two hundred and fifty miles from the sea-coast, in the midst of a country but moderately productive, not in the vicinity of any navigable river, and without facilities of any kind for manufacturing purposes; yet it was founded less than twenty years ago, is now the fourth place in population in the State, and bids fair to be the second in less than five years.

It can never be a handsome city, but its surrounding hills and slopes offer beautiful sites for elegant residences. Many of the buildings now going up are of frail and fire-tempting character, but in several instances owners are putting in solid one or two-story brick blocks,—intending at some future time to add two or three stories more. Few of the present merchants were here before the war,—few of them are yet to be considered as permanent residents of the city. The streets never were either neat or tasty; now, what with the piles of building material and the greater piles of *débris* and rubbish, and the vast amount of teaming and hauling over them, they are simply horrible. The former residents are coming home, and in the private portions, as well as the business section, there is great activity of repair and refurnishing. The place has no decent hotel,—no one has yet found time to build a large house. Of small and wretched fifth-rate hotels there are half a dozen; but better than any of these are several of the very numerous so-called private boarding-houses, which send their porters and runners to every train, receive all classes of transient guests, charge the usual four dollars per day, and are hotels in everything but name. The city handsomely supports two of the largest daily newspapers in the State, has five or six churches, a medical college, two or three select schools, and is talking about an academy.

.   .   .   .

Part Five

Life in Urban America

20   Pittsburgh in the 1880's

Since the 1830's Pittsburgh has been renowned here and abroad as an industrial center laden with soot and grime —the "Birmingham of America." By the end of the Civil War Pittsburgh was manufacturing half of the steel and one-third of the glass produced in this country. The influx before the war of freed Negroes from Maryland and Virginia and of thousands of German immigrants, who went to work in Pittsburgh's rolling mills, mines, and foundries, anticipated the arrival in the 1880's of new workers and residents from Italy, Poland, Russia, and central Europe. By 1890 Pittsburgh held a quarter million people. Recovering slowly from the business crisis of 1873–1879 under the leadership of industrialists such as Henry Clay Frick, Charles M. Schwab, and Andrew Carnegie, and seeing support for its laboring people grow through organization of the American Federation of Labor in 1886 and the United Mine Workers in 1890, Pittsburgh became the barometer of industrial production for urban America.

Willard Glazier's description is included here because it represents the typical impression made by the city at the Golden Triangle upon its visitors, from the 1830's into the twentieth century. Glazier (1841–1905) was a New Yorker who participated in over sixty engagements in the Civil War. After the war, as author and lecturer, he toured the United States and Canada, making one famous trip by horseback from New York to San Francisco in 1876.

On Pittsburgh see L. D. Baldwin, *Pittsburgh: The
Story of a City* (Pittsburgh, 1937).

░░░

BY ALL MEANS MAKE YOUR FIRST APPROACH TO PITTSBURG IN THE
NIGHT TIME, and you will behold a spectacle which has not
a parallel on this continent. Darkness gives the city and its surroundings a picturesqueness which they wholly lack by daylight.
It lies low down in a hollow of encompassing hills, gleaming with
a thousand points of light, which are reflected from the rivers,
whose waters glimmer, it may be, in the faint moonlight, and
catch and reflect the shadows as well. Around the city's edge, and
on the sides of the hills which encircle it like a gloomy amphitheatre, their outlines rising dark against the sky, through numberless apertures, fiery lights stream forth, looking angrily and
fiercely up toward the heavens, while over all these settles a
heavy pall of smoke. It is as though one had reached the outer
edge of the infernal regions, and saw before him the great furnace of Pandemonium with all the lids lifted. . . .

Failing a night approach, the traveler should reach the Iron
City on a dismal day in autumn, when the air is heavy with moisture, and the very atmosphere looks dark. All romance has disappeared. . . . There is only a very busy city shrouded in gloom.
The buildings, whatever their original material and color, are
smoked to a uniform, dirty drab; the smoke sinks, and mingling
with the moisture in the air, becomes of a consistency which may
almost be felt as well as seen. Under a drab sky a drab twilight
hangs over the town, and the gas-lights, which are left burning
at mid-day, shine out of the murkiness with a dull, reddish glare.
Then is Pittsburg herself. Such days as these are her especial
boast, and in their frequency and dismalness, in all the world she
has no rival, save London.

In truth, Pittsburg is a smoky, dismal city, at her best. At her
worst, nothing darker, dingier or more dispiriting can be imagined. The city is in the heart of the soft coal region; and the
smoke from her dwellings, stores, factories, foundries and steam-

WILLARD GLAZIER, *Peculiarities of American Cities* (Philadelphia, 1885), 332–335, 337–339.

boats, uniting, settles in a cloud over the narrow valley in which she is built, until the very sun looks coppery through the sooty haze. According to a circular of the Pittsburg Board of Trade, about twenty per cent., or one-fifth, of all the coal used in the factories and dwellings of the city escapes into the air in the form of smoke, being the finer and lighter particles of carbon of the coal, which, set free by fire, escapes unconsumed with the gases. The consequences of several thousand bushels of coal in the air at one and the same time may be imagined. But her inhabitants do not seem to mind it; and the doctors hold that this smoke, from the carbon, sulphur and iodine contained in it, is highly favorable to lung and cutaneous diseases, and is the sure death of malaria and its attendant fevers. And certainly, whatever the cause may be, Pittsburg is one of the healthiest cities in the United States. Her inhabitants are all too busy to reflect upon the inconvenience or uncomeliness of this smoke. Work is the object of life with them. It occupies them from morning until night, from the cradle to the grave, only on Sundays, when, for the most part, the furnaces are idle, and the forges are silent. For Pittsburg, settled by Irish-Scotch Presbyterians, is a great Sunday-keeping [city]. Save on this day her business men do not stop for rest or recreation, nor do they "retire" from business. They die with the harness on, and die, perhaps, all the sooner for having worn it so continuously and so long.

.   .   .   .

. . . The crowning glory of Pittsburg is her monster iron and glass works. One-half the glass produced in all the United States comes from Pittsburg. This important business was first established here in 1787, by Albert Gallatin, and it has increased since then to giant proportions. Probably, not less than one hundred millions of bottles and vials are annually produced here, besides large quantities of window glass. The best wine bottles in America are made here, though they are inferior to those of French manufacture. A great number of flint-glass works turn out the best flint glass produced in the country.

In addition to these glass works—which, though they employ thousands of workmen, represent but a fraction of the city's industries—there are rolling mills, foundries, potteries, oil refineries, and factories of machinery. All these works are rendered possible by the coal which abounds in measureless quantities in the immediate neighborhood of the city. All the hills which rise from the river back of Pittsburg have a thick stratum of bituminous coal running through them, which can be mined without shafts, or any of the usual accessories of mining. All that is to be done is to shovel the coal out of the hill-side, convey it in cars or by means of an inclined plane to the factory or foundry door, and dump it, ready for use. . . .

. . . . Probably not less than ten thousand men are employed in these coal mines in and near Pittsburg, adding a population not far from fifty thousand to that region. Pittsburg herself consumes one-third of the coal produced, and a large proportion of the rest is shipped down the Ohio and Mississippi rivers, some of it as far as New Orleans.

The monster iron works of Pittsburg consume large quantities of this coal, and it is the abundance and convenience of the latter material which have made the former possible. No other city begins to compare with Pittsburg in the number and variety of her factories. Down by the banks of the swift-flowing Allegheny most of the great foundries are to be discovered. . . .

.   .   .   .

21   St. Louis During Fair Week, 1880's

Towns have become cities due to their geographical position, their commerce, or their industries. Another compelling reason for their growth has been their existence as social centers, as places for the exchange of news or gossip, for meeting people, or for feeling the cultural pulse of a day or age. St. Louis as a regional cultural center, a focal point of popular education, is here described by Willard Glazier (see Reading 20). In his listing of the city's cultural attractions he might have included the St. Louis Symphony Orchestra, which was founded in

1880 and is the second oldest in the country. The atmosphere of St. Louis he describes during its Fair Week was the same in many Middle Western states at the time of state fairs, and it was even more charged with excitement in St. Louis in 1904 when the famous Centennial Exposition was held there and all America knew the song, "Meet Me in St. Louie, Louie, Meet Me at the Fair." By 1880 St. Louis had lost out to Chicago in the rivalry for urban leadership in the Middle West. St. Louis in 1880 ranked sixth among American cities with a population of 350,500, while Chicago stood fourth with 503,200 people.

On St. Louis in this period see W. W. Belcher, *The Economic Rivalry Between St. Louis and Chicago, 1850–1880* (New York, 1947), chs. IX–XI.

⁞⁞

FAIR WEEK, WHICH IS USUALLY THE FIRST WEEK IN OCTOBER, is the great holiday and gala season of St. Louis. . . . Every train of cars on the many lines which centre at St. Louis, and every steamboat which came up or down the river, brought its living freight of men and women, who were out for a week's holiday, and, it may have been, paying their annual visit to the greatest city west of the Mississippi. The country roads leading to town were black with vehicles of all descriptions, and laden with men and merchandise. The laborers and mules upon the levee were busier than ever, receiving and transporting the articles to be exhibited and sold. Every hotel was crowded, and the surplus overflowed into boarding and lodging houses, so that their keepers undoubtedly reaped a golden harvest for that one week, at least. The streets were thronged with an immense and motley multitude: business men, on the alert to extend their trade and add to their gains; working women, who found an opportunity for a brief holiday; ladies of fashion who viewed the scene resting at their ease in their carriages; farmers from the rural districts, looking uncomfortable yet complaisant in their Sunday

WILLARD GLAZIER, *Peculiarities of American Cities* (Philadelphia, 1885), 503–507.

suits, and trying to take in all there was to see and understand; their wives, old-fashioned and countrified in their dress, and with a tired look upon their faces, which this week given up to idleness and sight-seeing could not quite dispel; sporting men, easily recognizable by their flashy dress and "horsey" talk; gamblers and blacklegs by the score, whose appearance and manners were too excessively gentlemanly to pass as quite genuine, and whose gains during the week were probably larger and more certain than those of any other class; western men, with their patois, borrowed apparently from the slang of every nation on the globe; Southerners, with their long hair, slouched hats and broad accent; river hands, whose most noticeable accomplishments seemed to be disposing of tobacco and inventing new oaths; Negroes, whose facile natures entered heartily into the occasion . . . ; eastern men, with the Yankee intonation; Germans, in great numbers, patronizingly endorsing their adopted country, and selling lager beer with stolid content; Irishmen, whose preference was whisky, and who were ever ready for fun or a fight; beggars, plying their vocation with an extra whine, adopted to conceal an unwonted tendency to cheerfulness; magnates, who looked pompous and conscious of their own importance, but who were jostled and pushed with the democratic disregard for rank and station which characterizes an American crowd.

.   .   .   .

The fair grounds of the St. Louis Agricultural and Mechanical Association are three miles northwest of the Court House, and embrace eighty-five acres handsomely laid out and containing extensive buildings. The Amphitheatre will seat 40,000 persons. The street cars leading to these grounds were at all times filled with people, and in addition there was a constant procession of carriages, wagons and carts, going and returning. Within the enclosure the dense throng surged and swayed like a human whirlpool. The displays in the agricultural and mechanical departments were something astonishing. . . .

In art the East as yet exceeds the West. . . . St. Louis has no picture gallery worthy the name, but excells in scientific and educational institutions.

The Mercantile Library, at the corner of Fifth and Locust

streets, contains 50,000 volumes, and its hall is decorated by paintings, coins and statuary. . . .

Besides the library there is a public school library of 38,000 volumes; an Academy of Science, founded in 1856, with a large museum and a library of 3,000 volumes; and a Historical Society, founded in 1865, with a valuable historical collection. Washington University, organized in 1853, embraces the whole range of university studies except theology. With it is connected the Mary Institute, for the education of women, the Polytechnic School, and the Law School. The public school system of St. Louis is one of the best in the country, and its school-houses are commendably fine. . . .

The hotels . . . will compare favorably, in point of attendance, comfort and elegance, with any in the country. Horse cars traverse the city in every direction, rendering all points easily accessible, and carriages are in waiting at the depots and steamboat landings. Ferries ply continually to East St. Louis, on the Illinois shore, from the foot of Carr street, north of the bridge, and from the foot of Spruce street, south of it, the two points of departure being about a mile apart.

. . . .

22 The Culture of New Orleans in the 1880's

Between 1800 and 1860 New Orleans ranked fifth in population among the cities of the nation. Before the completion of the Erie Canal and the coming of the railroad, the city that received produce and goods from the entire Mississippi and Ohio river valleys had high hopes that it would surpass even New York in size. But this was not to be. New Orleans grew steadily but not spectacularly— no small accomplishment due to a debilitating climate and problems of public health.

Few American cities retained the cultural tone set by

their early inhabitants as long or as distinctively as did
New Orleans. Its commercial life, like the economic life
of other American cities, was rejuvenated about 1880
after virtually a decade of hard times. The ship channel
at the mouth of the Mississippi was deepened in the
1870's; by 1883 New Orleans was tied to the West and
the North by railroads; in 1892 trolley cars replaced
horse cars in the city. But the other side of New Orleans
life, its cultural aspect, lost few of the leisurely Creole
ways that have always made it unique among our cities.
It is this part of New Orleans life that is described here
by Charles Dudley Warner (1829–1900), essayist, editor,
and novelist, who for many years was editor of the Hartford, Connecticut, *Courant*. Several books resulted from
Warner's five trips to Europe and his travels in this country. On Warner see the *Dictionary of American Biography*.

On New Orleans and Southern cities in this period see
E. W. Parks, "Southern Towns and Cities," in W. T.
Couch (ed.), *Culture in the South* (Chapel Hill, 1934),
ch. 23, and C. V. Woodward, *Origins of the New South,
1877–1913* (Baton Rouge, 1951), ch. V.

NEW ORLEANS IS THE MOST COSMOPOLITAN OF PROVINCIAL CITIES.
Its comparative isolation has secured the development of
provincial traits and manners, has preserved the individuality of
the many races that give it color, morals, and character, while its
close relations with France—an affiliation and sympathy which
the late war has not altogether broken—and the constant influx
of Northern men of business and affairs have given it the air of a
metropolis. To the Northern stranger the aspect and the manners
of the city are foreign, but if he remains long enough he is sure
to yield to its fascinations, and become a partisan of it. It is not
altogether the soft and somewhat enervating and occasionally

CHARLES DUDLEY WARNER, *Studies in the South and West, with
Comments on Canada* (New York, 1889), 44–48, 53–55,
58–62.

treacherous climate that beguiles him, but quite as much the easy terms on which life can be lived. There is a human as well as a climatic amiability that wins him. No doubt it is better for a man to be always braced up, but no doubt also there is an attraction in a complaisance that indulges his inclinations.

Socially as well as commercially New Orleans is in a transitive state. The change from river to railway transportation has made her levees vacant; the shipment of cotton by rail and its direct transfer to ocean carriage have nearly destroyed a large middle-men industry; a large part of the agricultural tribute of the Southwest has been diverted; plantations have either not recovered from the effects of the war or have not adjusted themselves to new productions, and the city waits the rather blind developments of the new era. The falling off of law business, which I should like to attribute to the growth of common-sense and good-will is, I fear, rather due to business lassitude, for it is observed that men quarrel most when they are most actively engaged in acquiring each other's property. The business habits of the Creoles were conservative and slow; they do not readily accept new ways, and in this transition time the American element is taking the lead in all enterprises. The American element itself is toned down by the climate and the contagion of the leisurely habits of the Creoles, and loses something of the sharpness and excitability exhibited by business men in all Northern cities, but it is certainly changing the social as well as the business aspect of the city. . . .

For the old civilization had many admirable qualities. With all its love of money and luxury and an easy life, it was comparatively simple. It cared less for display than the society that is supplanting it. Its rule was domesticity. I should say that it had the virtues as well as the prejudices and the narrowness of intense family feeling, and its exclusiveness. But when it trusted, it had few reserves, and its cordiality was equal to its *naïveté*. The Creole civilization differed totally from that in any Northern city; it looked at life, literature, wit, manners, from altogether another plane; in order to understand the society of New Orleans one needs to imagine what French society would be in a genial climate and in the freedom of a new country. Undeniably, until recently, the Creoles gave the tone to New Orleans. And it was the French culture, the French view of life, that was diffused. The young ladies mainly were educated in convents and French schools. This education had womanly agreeability and matrimony in view, and the graces of social life. . . . French was a study and a possession, not a fashionable accomplishment. . . . There was . . . in the old New Orleans life something nobler than the spirit of plutocracy. The Creole middle-class population had, and has yet, captivating *naïveté*, friendliness, cordiality.

But the Creole-influence in New Orleans is wider and deeper than this. It has affected literary sympathies and what may be called literary morals. In business the Creole is accused of being slow, conservative, in regard to improvements obstinate and reactionary, preferring to nurse a prejudice rather than run the risk of removing it by improving himself, and of having a conceit that his way of looking at life is better than the Boston way. His literary culture is derived from France, and not from England or the North. And his ideas a good deal affect the attitude of New Orleans towards English and contemporary literature. The American element of the town was for the most part commercial, and little given to literary tastes. That also is changing, but I fancy it is still true that the most solid culture is with the Creoles, and it has not been appreciated because it is French, and because its point of view for literary criticism is quite different from that prevailing elsewhere in America. It brings our American and English contemporary authors, for instance, to comparison, not with each other, but with French and other Continental writers. And this point of view considerably affects the New Orleans opinion of Northern literature. In this view it wants color, passion; it is too self-conscious and prudish, not to say Puritanically mock-modest. I do not mean to say that the Creoles as a class are a reading people, but the literary standards of their scholars and of those among them who do cultivate literature deeply are different from those at the North. We may call it provincial, or we may call it cosmopolitan, but we shall not understand New Orleans until we get its point of view of both life and letters.

In making these observations it will occur to the reader that they are of necessity superficial, and not entitled to be regarded as criticism or judgment. But I am impressed with the foreignness of New Orleans civilization, and whether its point of view is right or wrong, I am very far from wishing it to change. It contains a valuable element of variety for the republic. We tend everywhere to sameness and monotony. New Orleans is entering upon a new era of development, especially in educational life. The Toulane University is beginning to make itself felt as a force both in polite letters and in industrial education. And I sincerely hope that the literary development of the city and of the South-west will be in the line of its own traditions, and that it will not be a copy of New England or of Dutch Manhattan. It can, if it is faithful to its own sympathies and temperament, make an original and valuable contribution to our literary life.

.   .   .   .

One does not need to go into the past of New Orleans for the picturesque; the streets have their peculiar physiognomy, and "character" such as the artists delight to depict is the result of the extraordinary mixture of races and the habit of out-door life. The long summer, from April to November, with a heat continuous, though rarely so excessive as it occasionally is in higher latitudes, determines the mode of life and the structure of the houses, and gives a leisurely and amiable tone to the aspect of people and streets which exists in few other American cities. The French quarter is out of repair, and has the air of being for rent; but in fact there is comparatively little change in occupancy, Creole families being remarkably adhesive to localities. The stranger who sees all over the French and the business parts of the town the immense number of lodging-houses—some of them the most stately old mansions—let largely by colored landladies, is likely to underestimate the home life of this city. New Orleans soil is so wet that the city is without cellars for storage, and its court-yards and odd corners become catch-alls of broken furniture and other lumber. The solid window-shutters, useful in the glare of the long summer, give a blank appearance to the streets. This is relieved, however, by the queer little Spanish houses, and by the endless variety of galleries and balconies. . . .

The glimpses of street life are always entertaining, because unconscious, while full of character. It may be a Creole court-yard, the walls draped with vines, flowers blooming in hap-hazard disarray, and a group of pretty girls sewing and chatting, and stab-

bing the passer-by with a charmed glance. It may be a cotton
team in the street, the mules, the rollicking driver, the creaking
cart. It may be a single figure, or a group in the market or on the
levee—a slender yellow girl sweeping up the grains of rice, a
colored gleaner recalling Ruth; . . . the broad-faced women in
gay bandannas behind their cake-stands; a group of levee hands
about a rickety table, taking their noonday meal of pork and
greens; . . . the black stalwart vender of tin and iron utensils,
who totes in a basket, and piled on his head, and strung on his
back, a weight of over two hundred and fifty pounds; and Negro
women who walk erect with baskets of clothes or enormous bun-
dles balanced on their heads, smiling and "jawing," unconscious
of their burdens. These are the familiar figures of a street life as
varied and picturesque as the artist can desire.

New Orleans amuses itself in the winter with very good theatres,
and until recently has sustained an excellent French opera. It has
all the year round plenty of *cafés chantants*, gilded saloons, and
gambling-houses, and more than enough of the resorts upon which
the police are supposed to keep one blind eye. . . .

New Orleans has never been called a "strait-laced" city; its Sunday is still of the Continental type; but it seems to me free from
the socialistic agnosticism which flaunts itself more or less in Cincinnati, St. Louis, and Chicago; the tone of leading Presbyterian
churches is distinctly Calvinistic, one perceives comparatively little
of religious speculation and doubt, and so far as I could see there
is harmony and entire social good feeling between the Catholic
and Protestant communions. Protestant ladies assist at Catholic
fairs, and the compliment is returned by the society ladies of the
Catholic faith when a Protestant good cause is to be furthered by a
bazaar or a "pink tea." Denominational lines seem to have little to
do with social affiliations. There may be friction in the management of the great public charities, but on the surface there is
toleration and united good-will. The Catholic faith long had the
prestige of wealth, family, and power, and the education of the
daughters of Protestant houses in convent schools tended to allay
prejudice. Notwithstanding the reputation New Orleans has for
gayety and even frivolity—and no one can deny the fast and
furious living of ante-bellum days—it possesses at bottom an old-
fashioned religious simplicity. . . .

But whatever way we regard New Orleans, it is in its aspect, social tone, and character *sui generis;* its civilization differs widely from that of any other, and it remains one of the most interesting places in the republic. Of course, social life in these days is much the same in all great cities in its observances, but that of New Orleans is markedly cordial, ingenuous, warm-hearted. I do not imagine that it could tolerate, as Boston does, absolute freedom of local opinion on all subjects, and undoubtedly it is sensitive to criticism; but I believe that it is literally true, as one of its citizens said, that it is still more sensitive to kindness.

.   .   .   .

23 Indianapolis, A City of Homes, 1904

By the close of the nineteenth century many Middle Westerners prided themselves on their orderly, prosperous, middle-class towns and cities. Drawn from this attitude and written by a man who loved Indianapolis is the following portrait by Meredith Nicholson. In Nicholson's opinion, and in the view of his fellow townsman Booth Tarkington, the people of Indianapolis led the "typical American" life. The city then held about 170,000 inhabitants and was a true regional capital due to the interurban streetcar lines connecting it with surrounding towns.

Nicholson (1866–1947) was an Indiana essayist and poet, whose *Hoosier Chronicle* (1912) was a semi-autobiographical work. In the 1930's he served in diplomatic posts in South America.

On Indianapolis see Frederick D. Kershner, Jr., "A Social and Cultural History of Indianapolis, 1860–1914" (unpublished Ph.D. dissertation, University of Wisconsin, 1950).

INDIANAPOLIS—LIKE JERUSALEM, "A CITY AT UNITY WITH IT-
SELF," where the tribes assemble, and where the seat of judgment is established—is in every sense the capital of all the Hoosiers. With the exception of Boston and Providence, it is the
largest state capital in the country; and no other American city
without water communication is as large. It is distinguished primarily by the essentially American character of its people. The
total foreign-born population of Indianapolis at the last census
was only 17,000; whereas Hartford, which is only half the size
of Indianapolis, returned 23,000, Rochester, with 7000 fewer people, returned 40,000; and Worcester, in a total of 118,000, reported 37,000 as foreign-born. A considerable body of Germans
and German-Americans have contributed much to the making of
the city; but the town has been passed over by the Swedes, Poles,
and Bohemians that are to be reckoned with in many American
cities. There are, however, 5000 Negro voters in the city. Indianapolis is marked again by the stability of its population. A large
percentage of the householders own their homes; and a substantial body of labor is thus assured to the community.

. . . It is of record that the first mention [in 1821] of the name
Indianapolis in the legislature caused great merriment. The town
was laid out in broad streets, which were quickly adorned with
shade trees that are an abiding testimony to the foresight of the
founders. Alexander Ralston, one of the engineers employed in
the first survey, had served in a similar capacity at Washington,
and the diagonal avenues, the generous breadth of the streets, and
the circular plaza at the monument are suggestive of the national
capital. The urban landscape lacks variety: the town is perfectly
flat, and in old times the mud was intolerable, but the trees are a
continuing glory.

. . . The young capital was a converging point for a slender
stream of population that bore in from New England, and a
broader current that swept westward from the Middle and Southeastern states. There was no sectional feeling in those days. Many
of the prominent settlers from Kentucky were Whigs, but a
newcomer's church affiliation was of far more importance than

MEREDITH NICHOLSON, "Indianapolis, A City of Homes," *Atlantic Monthly*, XCIII (June, 1904), 836–845.

his political belief. Indianapolis was charged in later years with a lack of public spirit, but with reference only to commercial matters. There has never been a time when a hearing could not be had for any undertaking of philanthropy or public education.

The effect of the Civil War upon Indianapolis was immediate and far-reaching. It emphasized through the centralizing there of the state's military energy the fact that it was the capital city,— a fact which until that time had been accepted languidly by the average Hoosier countryman. The presence within the state of an aggressive body of sympathizers with Southern ideas directed attention throughout the country to the energy and resourcefulness of Morton, the war governor, who pursued the Hoosier Copperheads relentlessly, while raising a great army to send to the seat of war. Again, the intense political bitterness engendered by the war did not end with peace, or with the restoration of good feeling in neighboring states, but continued for twenty-five years more to be a source of political, and, markedly at Indianapolis, a cause of social irritation. . . .

A panic is a great teacher of humility, and the financial depression that fell upon the country in 1873 drove the lesson home remorselessly at Indianapolis. . . . The memory of the hard times lingered long at home and abroad. A town where credit could be so shaken was not, the Eastern investor declared, a safe place for further investments; and in many quarters Indianapolis was not forgiven until an honest, substantial growth had carried the lines of the city beyond the *terra incognita* of the boom.

Many of the striking characteristics of the people are attributable to those days, when the city's bounds were moved far countryward, to the end that the greatest possible number of investors might enjoy the ownership of town lots. The signal effect of this dark time was to stimulate thrift and bring a new era of caution and conservatism; for there is a good deal of Scotch-Irish in the Hoosier, and he cannot be fooled twice with the same bait. During the period of depression the town lost its zest for gayety. It took its pleasures a little soberly; it was notorious as a town that welcomed theatrical attractions grudgingly, though this attitude must be referred back also to the religious prejudices of the early comers. . . . So conservatism became the city's rule of life. The panic of 1893 caused scarcely a ripple, and the typical Indianapolis business man to this day is one who minds his barometer carefully.

Indianapolis was a town that became a city rather against its will. It liked its own way, and its way was slow; but when the calamity could no longer be averted, it had its trousers creased and its shoes polished, and accepted with good grace the fact that its population was approximately two hundred thousand, and that it had crept to a place comfortably near the top in the list of bank clearances. A man who left Indianapolis in 1880, returned in 1900 —the Indianapolitan, like the cat in the ballad, always goes back; he cannot successfully be transplanted—to find himself a stranger in a strange city. Once he knew all the people who rode in chaises; but on his return he found new people abroad in smart vehicles; once he had been able to converse on topics of the day with a passing friend in the middle of Washington Street; now he must duck and dive, and keep an eye on the policeman if he would make a safe crossing. He was asked to luncheon at a club; in the old days there were no clubs, or they were looked on as iniquitous things; he was taken to look at factories which were the largest of their kind in the world. At the railroad yards he saw machinery being loaded for shipment to Russia and Chili; he was told that books published at Indianapolis were sold in New York and Boston, Toronto and London, and he was driven over asphalt streets to parks that had not been dreamed of before his term of exile.

Manufacturing is the great business of the city. There are nearly two thousand establishments within its limits where manufacturing in some form is carried on. . . . It is not only a good place in which to make things, but a point from which many things may be sold to advantage. Jobbing flourished before manufacturing became a serious factor. The jobbers have given the city an enviable reputation for enterprise and fair dealing. When you ask an Indianapolis jobber whether the propinquity of St. Louis, Cincinnati, Chicago, and Cleveland is not against him, he answers that he meets his competitors every day in many parts of the country and is not afraid of them.

Indianapolis is not like other cities of approximately the same size. It is not the native who says so, but the visitor from abroad, who is puzzled by a difference between the Hoosier capital and

Kansas City, Omaha, and Denver, or Minneapolis and St. Paul. It has perhaps more kinship with Cincinnati than with any other Western city. Most Western towns try to catch the step of Chicago, but Indianapolis has never suffered from any such ambition; so the Kansas City man and the Minneapolis man visit Indianapolis and find it slow, while the Baltimore or Washington or Hartford visitor wonders what there is about the Hoosier capital that reminds him of his own city.

Indianapolis is a place of industry, thrift, and comfort, and not of luxury. Its social entertainments were long of the simplest sort, and the change in this respect has come only within a few years, —with the great wave of growth and prosperity that has wrought a new Indianapolis from the old. . . . Business men no longer go home to dinner at twelve o'clock and take a nap before returning to work; and the old amiable habit of visiting for an hour in an office where ten minutes of business was to be transacted has passed. A town is at last a city when sociability has been squeezed out of business and appointments are arranged a day in advance by telephone.

The distinguishing quality of Indianapolis is its simple domesticity. The people are home-loving and home-keeping. In the early days . . . the people stayed at home perforce; and when the railroad reached them they did not take readily to travel. A trip to New York is still a much more serious event, considered from Indianapolis, than from Denver or Kansas City. . . . The more the Hoosier travels, the more he likes his own town. . . .

The Hoosiers assemble at Indianapolis in great throngs with slight excuse. In addition to the sixteen railroads that touch there, newly constructed interurban traction lines have lately knit new communities into sympathetic relationship with the capital. You may stand in Washington Street and read the names of all the surrounding towns on the big interurban cars that mingle with the local traction traffic. . . .

Unlike many other American cities, Indianapolis has never been dominated by a few rich men. . . . It is probably fair to say that there are more large fortunes in the much smaller towns of Dayton or Columbus, Ohio, than in Indianapolis, where a quarter of a million dollars is enough to make a man conspicuously rich.

.   .   .   .

The narrow margin between the great parties in Indiana has made the capital a centre of incessant political activity. The geographical position of the city has also contributed to this, the state leaders and managers being constant visitors. Every second man you meet is a statesman; every third man is an orator. The largest social club in Indianapolis exacts a promise of fidelity to the Republican party, and within its portals chances and changes of men and measures are discussed tirelessly. And the pilgrim from abroad is not bored with talk of local affairs; not a bit of it! The nation's future is at once disclosed to him. If, however, he wishes to obtain a Godkinian forecast, he can be accommodated at the University Club grillroom, where a court of destructive critics meets daily at high noon. . . .

. . . The Indianapolis public schools owe their marked excellence and efficiency to their complete divorcement from political influence. This has not only assured the public an intelligent and honest expenditure of school funds,—and the provision is generous,—but it has created a corps spirit among the city's 750 teachers, admirable in itself, and tending to cumulative benefits not yet realized. . . . The superintendent of schools has absolute power of appointment, and he is accountable only to the commissioners, and they in turn are entirely independent of the mayor and other city officers. Positions on the school board are not sought by politicians. The incumbents serve without pay, and the public evince a disposition to find good men and keep them in office.

.   .   .   .

If you do not meet an author at every corner, you are at least never safe from the man that reads books. In a Missouri River town, a stranger must listen to the old wail against the railroads; at Indianapolis he must listen to politics, and possibly some one will ask his opinion of a sonnet, just as though it were a cigar. . . .

.   .   .   .

The Hoosier capital has always been susceptible to the charms of oratory. Most of the great lecturers in the golden age of the American lyceum were welcomed cordially at Indianapolis. The Indianapolis pulpit has been served by many able men, and great store is still set by preaching. . . .

. . . The women of Indianapolis built for themselves in 1888 a building—the Propylæum—where many clubs meet; and they have been the mainstay of the Indianapolis Art Association. . . . The Indianapolis Woman's Club is thirty years old.

. . . It is a city that brags less of its freight tonnage than of its public schools; but it is proud of both. At no time in its history has it been indifferent to the best thought and achievement of the world; and what it has found good it has secured for its own. . . .

---

24   Wealth and Poverty in New York City, 1890's

The even tenor of life in Middle Western cities like Indianapolis at the end of the nineteenth century stands in sharp contrast to life at that time in our great metropolitan centers. There a larger population meant a more cosmopolitan culture as well as people living at economic extremes. The smaller cities of course were not free of the problems of poverty or slums or crime or ethnic adjustments, but the great cities, especially those that received the millions of new Americans from Europe, were faced with these issues in greater magnitude.

Ward McAllister (1827–1895), social arbiter of "the 400" elite members of New York City's high society, briefly depicts the grand balls, important features in the customs of Manhattan's wealthy residents throughout the last quarter of the nineteenth century. McAllister was a Georgian who made his fortune in a law practice in San Francisco before beginning his social career at Newport, Rhode Island, and New York City. On McAllister see the *Dictionary of American Biography*.

At the other extreme in their standards of living were the far greater number of New Yorkers who are described here in two pieces by Jacob Riis (1849–1914). Riis came to New York City from Denmark in 1870 and

made his way through journalism as a police reporter on
the *New York Tribune* (1877–1888) and the *Evening
Sun* (1888–1899). He constantly exposed tenement life
in Manhattan and became famous here and abroad as the
"great emancipator" of the slums. The degraded conditions that Riis fought were not new to New York. Eighteen years before Riis used the title "How the Other Half
Lives," the phrase was used as a subtitle of a series of
illustrated articles on "Our Homeless Poor," published in
Frank Leslie's Illustrated Newspaper in 1872. And there
had been a law regulating tenement houses in Manhattan
in 1867, followed by stronger laws in 1879, 1887, 1895,
and in 1901, when some real reforms were achieved.

One indication of the rapidity with which the problems of slum and tenement housing were thrust upon
New York City is found in the fact that from a population of 1,209,500 in 1880, the number of New Yorkers
rose to nearly 3,500,000 in 1900. Much of this increase
was due to the movement of country and small town
people to the city. But between 1880 and 1884 alone
nearly two million foreign immigrants arrived in New
York port. Of course not all of them remained in New
York City: in 1881 the cash value of railroad tickets sold to
immigrants at the Castle Garden depot was over $5,000,-
000. Yet in 1890, thirty-nine percent of the New York-
Brooklyn population was foreign-born. And four out of
every five people of greater New York in 1890 were immigrants or children of immigrants. On Riis see the *Dictionary of American Biography*.

On New York City at this time see Moses Rischin,
The Promised City: New York's Jews, 1870–1914 (Cambridge, Massachusetts, 1962); J. G. Wilson (ed.), *Memorial History of . . . New York* (New York, 1893),
vol. III, ch. XV; Bayrd Still, *Mirror for Gotham* (New
York, 1956), ch. 8; Roy Lubove, *The Progressives and
The Slums: Tenement House Reform in New York City,
1890–1917* (Pittsburgh, 1962).

IMAGINATION WAS THEN WHAT I REQUIRED TO CONCEIVE AND CARRY OUT some new enterprise in the way of a subscription New Year's ball, to surpass anything I had ever before given.

The most difficult rooms to decorate are those at Delmonico's; but this establishment is unequaled in London or Paris in that it gives under its roof incomparable balls, banquets, and dinners. So we resolved that talent, taste, and money should be expended in an effort to design and give there a superb ball. The house had the advantage of having a large square room, all that was required for a dance of three to four hundred people. On this occasion we were to have seven hundred, and for so large a number we had to provide two *salles de danse*. The upper supper room we turned into a conservatory. Its ceilings were low, but covering them with creeping plants, making around the entire room a dado of banks of flowers and the walls themselves decorated with plaques of roses, introducing the electric light and throwing its jets through all the foliage, we had an improvised bower of flowers and plants that tempted all to wander through, if not to linger in it in admiration of the artistic skill which produced such a result. One room we converted, with Vantine's assistance, into a perfect Japanese interior. Once in it, we felt transported to that country. Here were served tea and Japanese confections, and over all shone the electric light with charming effect. The *salon* known as the Red Room had its walls decorated with sheaves of wheat, in which nestled bunches of *Marechale Neil* roses, the background of scarlet bringing these decorations out strikingly. This, with a new floor, was converted into a *salle de danse*. The large hall into which all these rooms opened was superb, for on all sides of it, from floor to ceiling, were hung the finest Gobelin tapestries of fabulous value. To obtain their use we had to telegraph to Paris, and were required to insure them for a large sum. Servants in light plush livery, pumps, and silk stockings, with powdered hair, stood on either side to direct the guests. Having the whole house, we supped in both restaurant and café, and as we had given an unlimited order had an elaborate and exquisite supper.

WARD MCALLISTER, *Society as I Have Found It* (New York, 1890), 374–381.

For a small ball of seven hundred people, I have always felt, and
still feel, that this New Year's Ball, as given at Delmonico's, was
in every sense of the word the handsomest, most complete, and
most successful thing of the kind that I have ever attempted in
New York City, and I find I am not alone in this opinion. It was
as much a feast for the eye as the elaborate supper was for the
palate, being complete in every detail, luxurious in adornment,
as to its rooms—and epicurean in its feasting.

New York society had now become so large that it seemed
necessary to solve at once what, to us, has long been a problem,
i.e. where we could bring general society together in one large
dancing-room; for though you may have a dozen rooms thrown
open, you will always find that all rush to the room where there
is dancing. Where then could we get a room where all could at
one and the same time be on the floor? It occurred to me that the
Metropolitan Opera House had, in its stage and auditorium, such
a room, and if we could only divest it of its characteristics, it
would be what we wanted.

Satisfying ourselves that we could accomplish this, we formed
a Committee of Three and entered on this new enterprise. Artists,
who have with ability painted small pictures, may venture on
larger canvas. We had succeeded in giving balls of seven hundred and four hundred people. Why not have a similar success
on a larger scale? Had our ideas been properly carried out, this
ball would have been twice the success it was. The defects were
evident, but when seen it was too late to remedy them. The artificial ceiling, cleverly planned to shut out the galleries, was not
completed, the electric lights were not shaded as they should have
been, and the music stands, ordered by the authorities to be elevated, were unsightly, and marred the brilliant effect we had
studied to produce. All else received more praise than criticism.

The four most striking points of this ball were, first, the reception of over twelve hundred people as at a private house by
three of our most brilliant and accomplished society ladies; again,
what may be termed the *Quadrille d'Honneur* of that ball, which
was the different sets of the Sir Roger de Coverly, danced by the
most distinguished ladies of this city, the "nobs" and the "swells"
on this occasion uniting; the supping of over twelve hundred peo-

ple at one time at small tables, and the cotillion ably led by one
of our distinguished State Senators, a man in himself representing
family, wealth, and political position.

.   .   .   .

Before leaving this ball, I must mete out due praise to the man
who could so successfully care for so large a number of people at
supper at one time, and give credit to the good and effective
work done by the three hundred well-trained, liveried servants
scattered through the house, understanding their work and per-
forming it admirably. This ball was given as a New Year's Ball on
the 2d of January, 1890. . . .

WHERE MULBERRY STREET CROOKS LIKE AN ELBOW WITHIN HAIL
OF THE OLD DEPRAVITY OF THE FIVE POINTS, is "the Bend,"
foul core of New York's slums. . . . Never was change more
urgently needed. Around "the Bend" cluster the bulk of the tenements that are stamped as altogether bad, even by the optimists
of the Health Department. Incessant raids cannot keep down the
crowds that make them their home. In the scores of back alleys,
of stable lanes and hidden byways, of which the rent collector
alone can keep track, they share such shelter as the ramshackle
structures afford with every kind of abomination rifled from the
dumps and ash-barrels of the city. . . .

In the street, where the city wields the broom, there is at least
an effort at cleaning up. There has to be, or it would be swamped
in filth overrunning from the courts and alleys where the rag-
pickers live. It requires more than ordinary courage to explore
these on a hot day. The undertaker has to do it then, the police
always. Right here, in this tenement on the east side of the street,
they found little Antonia Candia, victim of fiendish cruelty,
"covered," says the account found in the records of the Society
for the Prevention of Cruelty to Children, "with sores, and her

JACOB RIIS, *How the Other Half Lives: Studies among the
Tenements of New York* (New York, 1890), 55, 61–65,
67–68, 166–168.

hair matted with dried blood." Abuse is the normal condition of "the Bend," murder its everyday crop, with the tenants not always the criminals. In this block between Bayard, Park, Mulberry, and Baxter Streets, "the Bend" proper, the late Tenement House Commission counted 155 deaths of children * in a specimen year (1882). Their per centage of the total mortality in the block was 68.28, while for the whole city the proportion was only 46.20. The infant mortality in any city or place as compared with the whole number of deaths is justly considered a good barometer of its general sanitary condition. Here, in this tenement, No. 59½, next to Bandits' Roost, fourteen persons died that year, and eleven of them were children; in No. 61 eleven, and eight of them not yet five years old. According to the records in the Bureau of Vital Statistics only thirty-nine people lived in No. 59½ in the year 1888, nine of them little children. There were five baby funerals in that house the same year. Out of the alley itself, No. 59, nine dead were carried in 1888, five in baby coffins. . . . The general death-rate for the whole city that year was 26.27.

These figures speak for themselves, when it is shown that in the model tenement across the way at Nos. 48 and 50, where the same class of people live in greater swarms (161, according to the record), but under good management, and in decent quarters, the hearse called that year only twice, once for a baby. The agent of the Christian people who built that tenement will tell you that Italians are good tenants, while the owner of the alley will oppose every order to put his property in repair with the claim that they are the worst of a bad lot. Both are right, from their different stand-points. It is the stand-point that makes the difference—and the tenant.

What if I were to tell you that this alley, and more tenement property in "the Bend," all of it notorious for years as the vilest and worst to be found anywhere, stood associated on the tax-books all through the long struggle to make its owners responsible, which has at last resulted in a qualified victory for the law, with the name of an honored family, one of the "oldest and best," rich in possessions and in influence, and high in the councils of

---

* *The term child means in the mortality tables a person under five years of age. Children five years old and over figure in the tables as adults.*

the city's government? It would be but the plain truth. Nor would it be the only instance by very many that stand recorded on the Health Department's books of a kind that has come near to making the name of landlord as odious in New York as it has become in Ireland.

.   .   .   .

Well do I recollect the visit of a health inspector to one of these tenements on a July day when the thermometer outside was climbing high in the nineties; but inside, in that awful room, with half a dozen persons washing, cooking, and sorting rags, lay the dying baby alongside the stove, where the doctor's thermometer ran up to 115°! Perishing for the want of a breath of fresh air in this city of untold charities! Did not the manager of the Fresh Air Fund write to the pastor of an Italian Church only last year * that "no one asked for Italian children," and hence he could not send any to the country?

.   .   .   .

. . . In the stifling July nights, when the big barracks are like fiery furnaces, their very walls giving out absorbed heat, men and women lie in restless, sweltering rows, panting for air and sleep. Then every truck in the street, every crowded fire-escape, becomes a bedroom, infinitely preferable to any the house affords. A cooling shower on such a night is hailed as a heaven-sent blessing in a hundred thousand homes.

Life in the tenements in July and August spells death to an army of little ones whom the doctor's skill is powerless to save. When the white badge of mourning flutters from every second door, sleepless mothers walk the streets in the gray of the early dawn, trying to stir a cooling breeze to fan the brow of the sick baby. There is no sadder sight than this patient devotion striving against fearfully hopeless odds. Fifty "summer doctors," especially trained to this work, are then sent into the tenements by the Board of Health, with free advice and medicine for the poor. Devoted women follow in their track with care and nursing for the sick. Fresh-air excursions run daily out of New York on land and water; but despite all efforts the grave-diggers in Calvary

* See City Mission Report, February, 1890, page 77.

work over-time, and little coffins are stacked mountain-high on
the deck of the Charity Commissioners' boat when it makes its
semi-weekly trips to the city cemetery.

Under the most favorable circumstances, an epidemic, which
the well-to-do can afford to make light of as a thing to be got
over or avoided by reasonable care, is excessively fatal among the
children of the poor, by reason of the practical impossibility of
isolating the patient in a tenement. The measles, ordinarily a
harmless disease, furnishes a familiar example. Tread it ever so
lightly on the avenues, in the tenements it kills right and left. . . .
The records showed that respiratory diseases, the common heritage of the grippe and the measles, had caused death in most
cases, discovering the trouble to be, next to the inability to check
the contagion in those crowds, in the poverty of the parents and
the wretched home conditions that made proper care of the sick
impossible. . . .

That ignorance plays its part, as well as poverty and bad hygienic surroundings, in the sacrifice of life is of course inevitable.
They go usually hand in hand. . . .

::::::::::::::::

JACOB BERESHEIM WAS FIFTEEN WHEN HE WAS CHARGED WITH
MURDER. It is now more than three years ago, but the touch
of his hand is cold upon mine, with mortal fear, as I write. Every
few minutes, during our long talk on the night of his arrest and
confession, he would spring to his feet, and, clutching my arm as
a drowning man catches at a rope, demand with shaking voice,
"Will they give me the chair?" The assurance that boys were not
executed quieted him only for the moment. Then the dread and
the horror were upon him again.

Of his crime the less said the better. It was the climax of a
career of depravity that differed from other such chiefly in the
opportunities afforded by an environment which led up to and
helped shape it. My business is with that environment. The man
is dead, the boy in jail. But unless I am to be my brother's jail

JACOB RIIS, *A Ten Years' War: An Account of the Battle with
the Slum in New York* (Boston and New York, 1900),
139–148, 150–151, 160.

keeper, merely, the iron bars do not square the account of Jacob with society. Society exists for the purpose of securing justice to its members, appearances to the contrary notwithstanding. . . .

We shall take Jacob as a type of the street boy on the East Side, where he belonged. What does not apply to him in the review applies to his class. But there was very little of it indeed that he missed or that missed him.

He was born in a tenement in that section where the Tenement House Committee found 324,000 persons living out of sight and reach of a green spot of any kind, and where sometimes the buildings, front, middle, and rear, took up ninety-three per cent. of all the space on the block. Such a home as he had was there, and of the things that belonged to it he was the heir. The sunlight was not among them. . . . Very early the tenement gave him up to the street. The thing he took with him as the one legacy of home was the instinct for the crowd . . .

To the lawlessness of the street the home opposes no obstacle, as we have seen. Until very recently the school did not. It might have more to offer even now. There are, at least, schools where there were none then, and so much is gained; also, they are getting better, but too many of them, in my unprofessional judgment, need yet to be made over, until they are fit to turn out whole, sound boys, instead of queer manikins stuffed with information for which they have no use, and which is none of their business anyhow. It seemed to me sometimes, when watching the process of cramming the school course with the sum of human knowledge and conceit, as if it all meant that we distrusted nature's way of growing a man from a boy, and had set out to show her a shorter cut. . . .

But Jacob Beresheim had not even the benefit of such schooling as there was to be had. He did not go to school, and nobody cared. There was indeed a law directing that every child should go, and a corps of truant officers to catch him if he did not; but the law had been a dead letter for a quarter of a century. There was no census to tell what children ought to be in school, and no place but a jail to put those in who shirked. Jacob was allowed to drift. From the time he was twelve till he was fifteen, he told me, he might have gone to school three weeks,—no more.

Church and Sunday school missed him. I was going to say that they passed by on the other side, remembering the migration of the churches uptown, as the wealthy moved out of, and the poor into, the region south of Fourteenth Street. But that would hardly be fair. They moved after their congregations; but they left nothing behind. . . .

What the boy's play has to do with building character in him Froebel has told us. Through it, he showed us, the child "first perceives moral relations," and he made that the basis of the kindergarten and all common-sense education. That prop was knocked out. New York never had a children's playground till within the last year. . . .

Such fun as he had he got out of lawbreaking in a small way. In this he was merely following the ruling fashion. Laws were apparently made for no other purpose that he could see. Such a view as he enjoyed of their makers and executors at election seasons inspired him with seasonable enthusiasm, but hardly with awe. A slogan, now, like that raised by Tammany's late candidate for district attorney,—"To hell with reform!"—was something he could grasp. Of what reform meant he had only the vaguest notion, but the thing had the right ring to it. Roosevelt preaching enforcement of law was from the first a "lobster" to him, not to be taken seriously. . . .

Jacob's story ends here, as far as he is personally concerned. The story of the gang begins. So trained for the responsibility of citizenship, robbed of home and of childhood, with every prop knocked from under him, all the elements that make for strength and character trodden out in the making of the boy, all the high ambition of youth caricatured by the slum and become base passions,—so equipped he comes to the business of life. As a "kid" he hunted with the pack in the street. As a young man he trains with the gang, because it furnishes the means of gratifying his inordinate vanity, that is the slum's counterfeit of self-esteem. Upon the Jacobs of other days there was a last hold,—the father's authority. Changed conditions have loosened that also. There is a time in every young man's life when he knows more than his father. It is like the measles or the mumps, and he gets over it, with a little judicious firmness in the hand that guides. It is the misfortune of the slum boy of to-day that it is really so, and that he knows it. His father is an Italian or a Jew, and cannot even speak the language to which the boy is born. He has to depend on him in much, in the new order of things. . . .

The gang is a distemper of the slum that writes upon the generation it plagues the recipe for its own corrective. It is not the night stick, though in the acute stage that is not to be dispensed with. Neither is it the jail. To put the gang behind iron bars affords passing relief, but it is like treating a symptom without getting at the root of the disease. Prophylactic treatment is clearly indicated. The boy who flings mud and stones is entering his protest in his own way against the purblind policy that gave him jails for schools and the gutter for a playground, that gave him dummies for laws and the tenement for a home. He is demanding his rights, of which he has been cheated,—the right to his childhood, the right to know the true dignity of labor that makes a self-respecting manhood. The gang, rightly understood, is our ally, not our enemy. Like any ailment of the body, it is a friend come to tell us of something that has gone amiss. The thing for us to do is to find out what it is, and set it right.

.   .   .   .

25   Chicago Trade and Commerce, 1890-1913

Like New York City, Chicago experienced a sharp rise in the number of its immigrants from Europe in the 1880's. While New York was receiving Irish, English, Germans, Russians, and Italians, Chicago was taking in more Scandinavians, Bohemians, Poles, and Canadians. When immigration was cut off during World War I and many Chicago workers went into the military services, some 65,000 Negroes migrated to Chicago from the South to take jobs. In 1890 Chicago's population passed the million mark. By 1930 the city would have over 3,000,000 people.

Around the turn of the century our major American cities were also extending their leadership in the nation's commercial, financial, and merchandising affairs. In 1897 the linking of elevated railways around the commercial center of Chicago gave this area its famous name, The Loop.

The "pure business" aspect of Chicago life is here described by three writers. On C. D. Warner see Reading 22. Franklin Head (1835–1914) was born in New York and came to Chicago to practice law and to serve there as executive in insurance companies and as a director of the Chicago Exposition of 1893. Julian Street (1879–1947) was a native Chicagoan who became a journalist and author.

On Chicago in this period see B. L. Pierce, *A History of Chicago*, vol. III (New York, 1957), chs. XIII-XIV; Edith Abbott, *The Tenements of Chicago 1908–1935* (Chicago, 1936); and W. I. Thomas and F. Znaniecki, *The Polish Peasant in Europe and America*, vol. II (New York, 1958), part III.

IN 1888 CHICAGO IS A MAGNIFICENT CITY. Although it has been incorporated fifty years, during which period its accession of population has been rapid and steady—hardly checked by the devastating fires of 1871 and 1874—its metropolitan character and appearance is the work of less than fifteen years. There is in history no parallel to this product of a freely acting democracy: not St. Petersburg rising out of the marshes at an imperial edict, nor Berlin, the magic creation of a consolidated empire and a Cæsar's power. The north-side village has become a city of broad streets, running northward to the parks, lined with handsome residences interspersed with stately mansions of most varied and agreeable architecture, marred by very little that is bizarre and pretentious—a region of churches and club-houses and public buildings of importance. The west side, the largest section, and containing more population than the other two divisions combined, stretching out over the prairie to a horizon fringed with villages, expanding in three directions, is more mediocre in build-

C. D. WARNER, *Studies in the South and West* (New York, 1889), 184–187, 191.

ings, but impressive in its vastness; and the stranger driving out
the stately avenue of Washington some four miles to Garfield Park
will be astonished by the evidences of wealth and the vigor of the
city expansion.

But it is the business portion of the south side that is the miracle
of the time, the solid creation of energy and capital since the fire
—the square mile containing the Post-office and City Hall, the
giant hotels, the opera-houses and theatres, the Board of Trade
building, the many-storied offices, the great shops, the club-houses,
the vast retail and wholesale warehouses. This area has the advantage of some other great business centres in having broad
streets at right angles, but with all this openness for movement,
the throng of passengers and traffic, the intersecting street and
cable railways, the loads of freight and the crush of carriages, the
life and hurry and excitement are sufficient to satisfy the most
eager lover of metropolitan pandemonium. Unfortunately for a
clear comprehension of it, the manufactories vomit dense clouds
of bituminous coal smoke, which settle in a black mass in this part
of the town, so that one can scarcely see across the streets in a
damp day, and the huge buildings loom up in the black sky in
ghostly dimness. . . . No other city in the Union can show business warehouses and offices of more architectural nobility. The
mind inevitably goes to Florence for comparison with the structures of the Medicean merchant princes. One might name the
Pullman Building for offices as an example, and the wholesale
warehouse of Marshall Field, the work of that truly original
American architect, Richardson, which in massiveness, simplicity
of lines, and admirable blending of artistic beauty with adapt-
ability to its purpose, seems to me unrivalled in this country. . . .

Leaving the business portion of the south side, the city runs in
apparently limitless broad avenues southward into suburban villages and a region thickly populated to the Indiana line. The
continuous slightly curving lake front of the city is about seven
miles, pretty solidly occupied with houses. The Michigan Avenue of 1860, with its wooden fronts and cheap boarding-houses,
has taken on quite another appearance, and extends its broad way
in unbroken lines of fine residences five miles, which will be six
miles next summer, when its opening is completed to the entrance
of Washington Park. I do not know such another street in the

world. In the evening the converging lines of gas lamps offer a prospective of unequalled beauty of its kind. . . .

. . . The cost of the Michigan Avenue drive was two hundred thousand dollars a mile. The cost of the parks and boulevards in each of the three divisions is met by a tax on the property in that division. The tax is considerable, but the wise liberality of the citizens has done for the town what only royalty usually accomplishes—given it magnificent roads; and if good roads are a criterion of civilization, Chicago must stand very high. But it needed a community with a great deal of daring and confidence in the future to create this park system.

One in the heart of the city has not to drive three or four miles over cobble-stones and ruts to get to good driving-ground. When he has entered Michigan Avenue he need not pull rein for twenty to thirty miles. . . .

Perhaps there never was before such an opportunity to study the growth of an enormous city, physically and socially, as is offered now in Chicago, where the development of half a century is condensed into a decade. In one respect it differs from all other cities of anything like its size. It is not only surrounded by a complete net-work of railways, but it is permeated by them.

———————————

THE MOST NOTICEABLE FEATURE OF THE HEART OF CHICAGO IS ITS SIZE. The business of this city, covering an area of one hundred and eighty-one square miles, is substantially all done or managed in an area something less than thirty-five hundred feet square. The city has some thirty large banking establishments, nearly all of which would be embraced in a circle with a radius of nine hundred feet. Within this circle, too, would be included the principal office buildings. The concentration of business into so small an area has its advantages in convenience of communication, which seems thus far sufficient to prevent its spreading to any considerable extent to other parts of the city. This concentration, however, leads to excessive crowding of the streets and sidewalks, amounting to a serious hindrance to travel. Compared

FRANKLIN HEAD, "The Heart of Chicago," *The New England Magazine*, new series, VI (July, 1892), 555–556, 558–561.

with many of the busiest Chicago streets, the most crowded avenues of New York or Boston are meagrely peopled, and those of
Philadelphia are a desert waste. . . .

After the great fire, the city ordinances for a time practically
prohibited the erection of buildings exceeding four or five stories
in height, and the business district was largely covered with
structures of this class. The idea underlying the building laws
was that no building should be so high as to be beyond easy reach
of the appliances for the extinguishment of fires. When the erection of fire-proof buildings was commenced, greater heights were
allowed, and since that time many of the buildings erected twenty
years ago have been torn down to be replaced by the ten to
twenty-four story structures of to-day. In other cases, where the
foundations and walls were sufficient, additional stories have been
placed upon the older buildings. Within the present year, some of
the buildings, which five or six years ago were considered the
finest buildings in the city, have been torn down, and the entire
cost of the original building sacrificed, that its site might be occupied by a building adapted to the present wants of the city.
Of the office buildings, the one known as the Rookery is at this
time the largest, 3,800 people being employed within it. Several
of the other office buildings house 2,000 people and upwards.

Chicago is the business centre and commercial metropolis of
more than 25,000,000 people, and it is scarcely an exaggeration to
say that the business of this number of people is transacted upon
this space, 3,500 square feet. This is the grain market of the continent; for, although Duluth, Milwaukee, and some other points
ship large amounts of grain, yet the bulk of this grain is owned
and marketed by Chicago men and Chicago capital. Omaha, Kansas City, and several other western towns have vast establishments
for the curing and packing of meats, yet these establishments are
owned in Chicago, and their products are marketed from that
point.

Chicago is now and always has been a city of young men. Even
now, when the city has passed its semi-centennial, very few of its
active men of affairs are past middle life. . . . New York possesses immeasurably greater accumulated wealth than Chicago,
having garnered, doubtless, a greater number of dollars than Chicago has cents; yet it is easier, in behalf of a public measure for

the good or glory of the city, to raise dollars in Chicago than
cents in New York. There is in Chicago almost no inherited
wealth. The capital is thus far largely in the hands of those who
have accumulated it, and they seem to realize that the city and
its marvellous growth and opportunities have been factors in their
success, and are willing to recognize their public obligations. The
Armour Mission, with its Kindergarten, Manual Training and
other schools . . . will doubtless preserve the memory of its
founder long after his wonderful commercial achievements have
been forgotten. The new University of Chicago, the endowment
of which has been so munificently commenced by Mr. Rocke-
feller, has for its site a large and valuable tract of land donated
by Mr. Field; while the hand and purse of Mr. Pullman are
ever open for every worthy cause.

.   .   .   .

The architecture of the business centre of Chicago is not of
especial excellence. The building of twenty years ago was of
thick and substantial walls and deep-set windows, the interior
necessarily somewhat dark and gloomy. The latter idea is to make
the walls as thin as is consistent with safety, the windows large
and numerous, and the interior as light and airy as possible.

The concentration of the city's business into so small an area
has enormously increased the value of real estate in this favored
locality. Lots upon the business streets are usually from 100 to
150 feet in depth, and, as a rule, prices are fixed by the front foot
rather than by the square foot, as is the usage in some of our eastern cities. It is but a few years since the first sale of land at $1,000
per front foot was recorded, and the most hopeful of our real
estate dealers conceded that the price was excessive and that it
would be long before this valuation would be exceeded; but
within the last two years several sales and leases have been made
based upon a valuation as high as $10,000 per front foot, and even
at this valuation it is claimed that the property when improved
with the best style of lofty office or mercantile building will earn
a reasonable interest upon its cost. High rentals would seem to be
a serious drawback in lines of business open to general competition; yet merchants appear to find it to their advantage to pay

the extravagant rents necessitated by the high price of central property, rather than to remove to equally commodious quarters half a mile distant at one-tenth the annual rental. One reason of this may be that all the four hundred miles of intramural lines of transportation, in the way of horse-car, cable, and elevated roads, terminate in the business centre of the city, and thus bring the customers of the merchants from all parts of the city to their very doors.

In construction, no deep basements or sub-cellars are practicable, as the city is built upon land but a few feet above the level of Lake Michigan. It stands upon a bed of clay of varying thickness and density, which is a most unsatisfactory material upon which to place foundations. The best method yet devised is to cover substantially the whole area of the building with pads of steel and cement. Steel rails are placed parallel with each other and six or eight inches apart, the spaces between them filled with cement, another similar course placed above these and at right angles to the first, and so on for four or five courses. Buildings upon this foundation settle but little and settle uniformly, so that no damage is done to the walls. The method used elsewhere in swampy locations, of driving pile foundations, has not been satisfactory in Chicago. The Government Building for the Post-Office and Federal Courts is built upon piles, and while it has been completed for many years, is constantly settling, and its absolute collapse seems imminent. A local statistician of unchallenged accuracy has computed that, at its present rate of travel toward China, the highest point of the roof will, in sixty years, be forty feet below the level of Lake Michigan, which would necessitate the employment of submarine divers for the entire clerical force of the Post Office and the removal of the Federal Courts to other quarters, except during the trial of cases in admiralty.

.   .   .   .

Chicago is a city wherein are represented divers nationalities, and many of these have papers published in their native tongues, with wide circulation among their especial clientage. There are also several religious journals, ably edited and having a wide denominational circulation, as well as sundry others depicting the social life and gossip of the town, and multitudes of weekly papers, agricultural or devoted to the interests of special lines of trade.

The city has also in its business district the general offices of all the great railway systems west of Chicago, representing nearly one-third of the railway mileage in the United States. Thousands of clerks are employed in these offices, where the transportation facilities for twenty-five million people are regulated, wrangled over, and controlled.

Chicago is the largest lumber market in the world, and the offices of the hundreds of lumbermen and lumber companies are found within this same limited area. Here, too, is the Chicago Board of Trade Building, an architectural monstrosity, in and about which are hundreds of offices occupied by the members of the Board. Here is transacted the bulk of the vast business of the city in grain and provisions, as well as probably one hundred times as much in fictitious trades, through puts, calls, options, or futures, through which instrumentalities the Chicago man of speculative tendency gambles in the specialties of the market, as his Eastern brother bets upon the prospective value of railway or industrial stocks or bonds. Near by are the numerous offices of the Columbian World's Fair, from which go forth daily thousands of letters and circulars to arouse the interest of the world in the coming Exposition of the arts and industries of all nations.

The arrivals and clearances of vessels at Chicago exceed in number those of the port of New York, although not equal to New York in tonnage, and in the business district are the offices of all the great marine transportation companies.

.   .   .   .

The dozen leading hotels of the city are also located in the crowded business centre. No worker in this district has time to go to his home for lunch. The hotels, even when kept on the American plan, have *café* annexes, and these, with the clubs and scores of restaurants, are thronged for an hour or two in the middle of each day. Multitudes of saloons are also scattered throughout this district. . . .

In the same limited area are also the half dozen principal theatres and opera houses. Amusements both good and bad are liberally patronized, but it is to the credit of our population that dramatic artists like Henry Irving and Booth, and singers like Patti and Materna play longer engagements and to larger audiences in Chicago than in any other American city. Like credit is fairly earned from the fact that, as has often been publicly stated by Mr. Phelps, our late Minister to England, Chicago supports by far the largest and most complete retail bookstore in the world.

The City and County Buildings occupy a square in this crowded quarter. Here hundreds of faithful as well as unfaithful public servants are busily at work, or actively avoiding work, and in and about the vast buildings throng the grimy crowd of idlers and vagabonds, to whom courts and public offices are ever a fascinating resort.

The enormous business transacted in Chicago by its great jobbers of groceries, hardware, and metals is familiar to all those interested in such affairs.

∷∷∷∷∷∷∷

O F COURSE WE VISITED MARSHALL FIELD'S.
The very obliging gentleman who showed us about the inconceivably enormous buildings, rushing from floor to floor, poking in and out through mysterious, baffling doors and passageways, now in the public part of the store where goods are sold, now behind the scenes where they are made—this gentleman seemed to have the whole place in his head—almost as great a feat as knowing the whole world by heart.

"How much time can you spare?" he asked as we set out from the top floor, where he had shown us a huge recreation room, gymnasium, and dining room, all for the use of the employees.

"How long should it take?"

"It can be done in two hours," he said, "if we keep moving all the time."

"All right," I said—and we did keep moving. Through great rooms full of trunks, of brass beds, through vast galleries of furni-

JULIAN STREET, *Abroad at Home: American Ramblings, Observations, and Adventures of Julian Street* (Garden City, 1926), 150–152.

ture, through restaurants, grilles, afternoon tea rooms, rooms full
of curtains and coverings and cushions and corsets and waists and
hats and carpets and rugs and linoleum and lamps and toys and
stationery and silver, and Heaven only knows what else, over
miles and miles of pleasant, soft, green carpet, I trotted along be-
side the amazing man who not only knew the way, but seemed
even to know the clerks. Part of the time I tried to look about me
at the phantasmagoria of things with which civilization has en-
cumbered the human race; part of the time I listened to our
cicerone; part of the time I walked blindly, scribbling notes,
while my companion guided my steps.

Here are some of the notes:

Ten thousand employees in retail store—— Choral society,
two hundred members, made up of sales-people—— Twelve baseball teams in retail store; twelve in wholesale; play during season,
and, finally, for championship cup, on "Marshall Field Day"——
Lectures on various topics, fabrics, etc., for employees, also for
outsiders: women's clubs, etc.—— Employees' lunch: soup, meat,
vegetables, etc., sixteen cents—— Largest retail custom dress-
making business in the country—— Largest business in ready-
made apparel—— Largest retail millinery business——Largest retail shoe business—— Largest branch of Chicago public library
(for employees)—— Largest postal sub-station in Chicago——
Largest—largest—largest!

Now and then when something interested me particularly we
would pause and catch our breath. Once we stopped for two or
three minutes in a fine schoolroom, where some stock-boys and
stock-girls were having a lesson in fractions—"to fit them for
better positions." Again we paused in a children's playroom,
where mothers left their youngsters while they went to do their
shopping, and where certain youngsters, thus deposited, were
having a gorgeous time, sliding down things, and running around
other things, and crawling over and under still other things.
Still again we paused at the telephone switchboard—a switchboard large enough to take care of the entire business of a city of
the size of Springfield, the capital of Illinois. And still again we
paused at the postal sub-station, where fifty to sixty thousand
dollars' worth of stamps are sold in a year, and which does as

great a postal business, in the holiday season, as the whole city of Milwaukee does at the same period.

<hr />

26   Minneapolis and St. Paul in 1892

First settled in 1839 and advantageously situated for river traffic just below the falls of the Mississippi River, St. Paul developed as a commercial center throughout the middle years of the nineteenth century. Minneapolis began its growth after the Civil War as a center for lumber and flour milling. Like Indianapolis, Minneapolis was also a "city of homes." But the makeup of population in the two cities was different: in 1890 seven eighths of the people of Indianapolis were native born, whereas in that year in Minneapolis, the Scandinavian capital of the country, two-fifths of its population (60,500) were foreign born. By the 1890's the twin cities of Minneapolis and St. Paul developed into a regional capital for the entire newer Northwest. Together they had a population of close to 300,000 inhabitants, and at the time this article was written the two cities had just closed a decade of heated rivalry for the lead in population. The regional leadership of these two cities was similar to the economic and cultural place that Kansas City or Dallas and Fort Worth or Denver held in other areas of our maturing West.

The tone of urban "boosterism" in the following description of the two cities is typical of many magazine pieces on various cities in the 1880's. Before long the satisfied view of American cities would give way to the devastating criticisms of muckraking journalists. Julian Ralph (1853–1903) was for twenty years a journalist with Charles A. Dana's New York *Sun*. He was commissioned by *Harper's Magazine* in 1891–1893 to travel throughout the United States to write articles like the following. On Ralph see the *Dictionary of American Biography*.

On Minneapolis and St. Paul at this time see T. C. Blegen and P. D. Jordan, *With Various Voices: Recordings of North Star Life* (St. Paul, 1949), 234–240; W. W. Folwell, *A History of Minnesota*, vol. III (St. Paul, 1926), ch. VIII and appendix 12. Contrast this selection with Lincoln Steffens' exposure of political corruption in Minneapolis in 1903; reprinted in Arthur and Lila Weinberg; *The Muckrakers* (New York, 1961), 6–21.

To begin with minneapolis, the larger of the two cities, let me introduce the town as that one which seems to me the pleasantest and most nearly perfect place for residence of all the cities I have seen in my country. St. Paul is in the main so nearly like Minneapolis that a slight sense of injustice comes with the writing of those words: yet St. Paul lacks some of the qualities which Minneapolis possesses, and the words must stand. Both cities have arisen amid park-like surroundings, both rejoice in the possession of the lovely Mississippi (for it is a most beautiful river up there), and both are largely made up of dwelling districts which fascinate the very soul of a man from the solid, pent-up cities of the East. But in one minor respect Minneapolis triumphs in being thoroughly consistent with her ruling trait, and at that particular point St. Paul fails. That is to say, Minneapolis is ample and broad and roomy in her business district, while St. Paul is in that quarter narrow, compact, huddled, and old-fashioned.

I cannot force Minneapolis to challenge the world to produce her equal, but it seems to me that it will be difficult to find another influential trading and manufacturing city that is so peculiarly a city of homes. It was after riding over mile after mile of her streets and boulevards, and noting the thousands of separated cottages, each in its little garden, that I came to a locality wherein there were a few—a very few—apartment-houses. They were not

Julian Ralph, "The Capitals of the Northwest," *Harper's New Monthly Magazine*, LXXXIV (March, 1892), 578, 581–583.

what we in New York call "tenement-houses," for the poor
seemed superior to the evil, and lived in their own tiny boxes;
they were flat-houses for families few in members and indolent
by nature. These were so very few that the array of dwellings
took on an extraordinary importance. Try, then, to fancy the
pleasure and surprise with which I read in the city directory,
afterward, a statement that the city's 164,738 inhabitants occupy
32,026 dwellings. If there were 921 more dwellings there would
be one to every five persons, which is to say one to each family.

As these houses are in the main owned by their tenants, the city
presents a spectacle of communal dignity, self-respect, and comfort that distinguishes it even in a greater degree than Philadelphia is distinguished among our Atlantic seaboard cities. It was
pleasing to hear in the neighboring city of St. Paul, where nearly
the same conditions prevail, that when the citizens go to the City
Hall to ask for places in the public service, or to demand their
rights, they often draw themselves up to their full height and say,
"I am a tax-payer," by way of preface to a statement of their
wishes. The man who carries that pride in his breast, and who
goes home to a house whose every side offers windows to the
light and air, should be as nearly a complete and perfect individual
as it is possible for the more or less artificial conditions of life in
a city to produce. Of such individuals is the great bulk of the
population of Minneapolis composed.

.   .   .   .

To give an idea of the extent of the principal industries of the
Flour City, let me say, roughly, that her saw-mills cut 343,000,000
feet of lumber, 162,000,000 shingles, and half as many laths in
1890; that in the upper Mississippi region four billion feet of
forest trees were cut down, and that the city received 45,000,000
bushels of wheat, and shipped 12,000,000 bushels away. The city
has an assessed valuation of $138,000,000, and nine millions of
dollars of banking capital. It boasts a public-school system that is
everywhere held to be unexcelled, and a function of the government is the maintenance of a library of 47,000 volumes, housed
in a noble building, and having two circulating branches connected with it. In the extent of its circulation of books this library
is the seventh in the country. . . .

But the growth of the manufacturing interests is the most important feature of the development of this city. It is rapidly fitting itself to become the main source of supplies for the most opulent farming region in America, and among recent additions to the list of her industries may be noted a knitting-mill; a piano factory; a linen mill; tub and pail, carriage, and macaroni factories; a manufactory for wood-carving machinery, in connection with a street-car construction company; a smelter for reducing Montana silver ore; a stove-works; and additions to the facilities for making boots and shoes, woollens, lumber, and flour. The difference in freight rates enables the manufacturers of the twin cities to hold their own against Chicago in the trade with the Northwest, and they have their drummers in all the cities and villages of the region.

The street-car service in Minneapolis is as nearly perfect as that of any city. Within a year, when the extensions now planned are completed, it will be without a rival in this respect. The electrical system which depends on overhead trolleys is in use there. The cars are elegant and spacious, and run upon 70 miles of tracks. They are propelled at a speed of 8 miles an hour in the city, and at 12 to 14 miles outside. They have run to Lake Harriet in 20 minutes, which is at the rate of 15 miles an hour, and they have made the journey to St. Paul (10½ miles), including ordinary stops, in 32 minutes. At the end of this year the system will embrace 130 miles of tracks.

To the mind that is accustomed to judge of Eastern towns, St. Paul is more city-like than Minneapolis. Its business portion . . . is such a compact mass of solid blocks and little streets that it might almost have been a ward of Boston transplanted in the West. One sees the same conditions in Portland, Oregon, but they are rare in the West, where the fashion is to plan for plenty of elbow-room. If we were to imagine the twin cities personified, we would liken Minneapolis to a vigorous rustic beauty in short skirts; while St. Paul we would describe as a fashionable marriageable urban miss, a trifle stunted and lacking color and plumpness, but with more style and worldly grace than her sister. As to which should have the preference, there will be views as differing as the two towns. . . . For my part, I find it so hard to decide between them that I am not going to try. Every man to his taste, say I. Minneapolis has done wondrous work for the future; St. Paul has done more for present improvement than any other city in the West that I have seen.

The twins are very like or very unlike in other respects, according as you look at them. Minneapolis is very American and St. Paul is very mixed in population. She has sixty-five per cent. of foreigners in her make-up, and the Teutons predominate—in the form of Norwegians, Swedes, Danes, and Germans. There are Irish and Poles, French Canadians and Bohemians, there also, and the Irish and Irish Americans are conspicuous in the government. St. Paul is usually Democratic; Minneapolis is generally Republican.

In eight years St. Paul has made tremendous strides away from the habits and methods of civic childhood. . . . The annual growth of the city by the addition of new buildings has long kept up to a remarkable standard. For two years—1888 and 1889—St. Paul was fourth in the list of American cities in this respect. Last year (1890) the permits issued were for 3174 buildings, planned to cost nine and a half millions of dollars. But the wonder ceases after the relation of the twin cities to the rich Northwest is understood. St. Paul is the meeting-point of twenty-eight railroads that crisscross that region. . . .

. . . St. Paul does not lack all elegance and ornament of the highest and most modern order. In one boulevard, called Summit Avenue, it possesses one of the noblest thoroughfares, and the nucleus of one of the most impressive collections of great mansions, in the country. Euclid Avenue, Cleveland, has long ceased to lead the rich residence streets of the nation, for Chicago has more than one finer street of the same character, and so has Buffalo, and so has New York since Riverside Avenue has begun to build up. None of these has the beauty which the Hudson River and its Palisades lend to Riverside Avenue, but a good second to it is Summit Avenue, St. Paul. From its mansions, rising upon a tall bluff, the panorama of a great and beautiful country-side is commanded.

27 Lectures, Libraries, and Dining Out in New York City around 1910

The level of popular culture in large cities has been gauged in many ways: by a city's facilities for mass education, by the reading matter available to its people, by the manner of entertainment in the city, and even by the degree of cosmopolitanism in its dining establishments. Although they can hardly do justice to this urban theme, the following two short selections depict some of the means for popular culture in New York City during the years before the first World War. In this era cities throughout America were conscientiously trying to improve their mass cultural level.

Delos Wilcox (1873–1928) devoted a lifetime to the study of city government and municipal franchises. On his life see the *Dictionary of American Biography*.

Edward Hungerford (1875–1948) was a journalist who became one of our early public relations experts for various transportation companies.

On popular culture in urban America see A. M. Schlesinger, Sr., *The Rise of the City, 1878–1898* (New York, 1933), chs. VI–X; and Blake McKelvey, *The Urbanization of America, 1860–1915* (New Brunswick, New Jersey, 1963), chs. 11–16.

O NE OF THE MOST NOTABLE BRANCHES OF THE WORK CARRIED ON BY THE BOARD OF EDUCATION is the system of free evening lectures which had its origin in a special act of the legislature passed in 1888. The lecture system flourished in old New York prior to consolidation, and was extended to all the boroughs of

DELOS F. WILCOX, *Great Cities in America, Their Problems and Their Government* (New York, 1910), 158–161.

the greater city in 1901. During the winter of 1907-1908 lectures were delivered in 178 lecture centres by a staff of 663 lecturers before 5572 audiences, with a total attendance of 1,208,336 people. The subjects of the lectures cover the whole field of literature, science, art, and descriptive geography. These lectures constitute a "University for the People," and their wonderful development under the intelligent and enthusiastic care of Dr. Henry M. Leipziger entitles him to a permanent place of honor in the annals of American civic progress.

The New York Public Library, the Brooklyn Public Library, and the Queensborough Public Library are separate corporations controlled by boards of trustees upon which the city is represented by the mayor, the comptroller, and the president of the board of aldermen. The people thus have the advantages of free libraries and have the chance to contribute largely to their support out of the proceeds of taxation, but the city has only an advisory voice in their management. The employees of the libraries, numbering 700 or 800, are not a part of the municipal civil service.

The building now under construction in Bryant Park at the corner of Fifth Avenue and Forty-second Street, at the site of the old reservoir, when completed, will be one of the most magnificent library buildings in the world. The land was furnished and the building is being erected by the city of New York. The library that will be housed in this building is the consolidated New York Public Library formed in 1895 by the union of the Astor, Lenox, and Tilden foundations. . . . The library has grown rapidly until at the close of the year 1908 there was a total of 1,722,237 books and pamphlets available for the use of readers. . . . By the end of 1908 twenty-eight Carnegie branch libraries had been opened in these three boroughs and construction was in progress on four other sites.

∴∴∴∴∴∴∴∴∴∴∴∴

DINNER IS NEW YORK'S REAL FUNCTION OF THE DAY. And dinner in New York means five million hungry stomachs demanding to be filled. The New York dinner is as cosmopolitan as the

EDWARD HUNGERFORD, *The Personality of American Cities* (New York, 1913), 48–50.

folk who dwell on the narrow island of Manhattan and the two other islands that press closely to it. The restaurant and hotel dinners are as cosmopolitan as the others. Of course, for the sake of brevity, if for no other reason, you must eliminate the home dinners—and read "home" as quickly into the cold and heavy great houses of the avenue as into the little clusters of rooms in crowded East Side tenements where poverty is never far away and next week's meals a real problem. And remember, that to dine even in a reasonably complete list of New York's famous eating places—a new one every night—would take you more than a year. At the best your vision of them must be desultory.

Six o'clock sees the New York business army well on its way toward home—the seething crowds at the Brooklyn bridge terminal in Park Row, the overloaded subway straining to move its fearful burden, the ferry and the railroad terminals focal points of great attractiveness. To make a single instance: take that division of the army that dwells in Brooklyn. It begins its march dinnerward a little after four o'clock, becomes a pushing, jostling mob a little later and shows no sign of abatement until long after six. Within that time the railroad folk at the Park Row terminal of the old bridge have received, classified and despatched Brooklynward, more than one hundred and fifty thousand persons—the population of a city almost the size of Syracuse. And the famous old bridge is but one of four direct paths from Manhattan to Brooklyn.

Six o'clock sees restaurants and cafés alight and ready for the two or three hours of their really brisk traffic of the day. There are even dinner restaurants downtown, remarkably good places withal and making especial appeal to those overworked souls who are forced to stay at the office at night. There are bright lights in Chinatown where innumerable "Tuxedos" and "Port Arthurs" are beginning to prepare the chop-suey in immaculate Mongolian kitchens. But the real restaurant district for the diner-out hardly begins south of Madison square. There are still a very few old hotels in Broadway south of that point—a lessening company each year—one or two in close proximity to Washington square. Two of these last make a specialty of French cooking—their *table d'hôtes* are really famous—and perhaps you may fairly say when you are done at them that you have eaten at the best restaurants in all New York. From them Fifth avenue runs a straight course to the newer hotels far to the north—a silent brilliantly lighted street as night comes "with the double row of steel-blue electric lamps resembling torch-bearing monks" one brilliant New York writer has put it. But before the newest of the new an intermediate era of hotels, the Holland, the nearby Imperial and the Waldorf-Astoria chief among these. The Waldorf has been from the day it first opened its doors—more than twenty years ago—New York's really representative hotel. Newer hostelries have tried to wrest that honor from it—but in vain. It has clung jealously to its reputation. The great dinners of the town are held in its wonderful banqueting halls, the well-known men of New York are constantly in its corridors. It is club and more than club—it is a clearing-house for all of the best clubs. It is the focal center for the hotel life of the town.

There is an important group of hotels in the rather spectacular neighborhood of Times square—the Astor, with its distinctly German flavor, and the Knickerbocker which whimsically likes to call itself "the country club on Forty-second street" distinctive among them. And ranging upon upper Fifth avenue, or close to it, are other important houses, the Belmont, the aristocratic Manhattan, the ultra-British Ritz-Carlton, the St. Regis, the Savoy, the Netherland, the Plaza, and the Gotham. In between these are those two impeccable restaurants—so distinctive of New York and so long wrapped up in its history—Sherry's and Delmonico's.

Over in the theatrical brilliancy of Broadway up and down from Times square are other restaurants—Shanley's, Churchill's, Murray's—the list is constantly changing. A fashionable restaurant in New York is either tremendously successful—or else . . . they are telephoning for the sheriff. And the last outcome is apt more to follow than the first. For it is a tremendous undertaking to launch a restaurant in these days.

.   .   .   .

Part Six

Urban Reform

28 Businessmen and Corruption in St. Louis around 1900

At the beginning of the twentieth century political corruption was not new to American cities; but the politically progressive reformers who observed, reported, and attacked urban wrongs acted as if it were. They were vigorous in their reporting, undismayed by the great efforts necessary to erase social evil, and generally optimistic. For them America was still a new country, and its ills could and would be cured. Perhaps one key to progressive political thought in this period is that the muckrakers, the people who wrote the literature of exposure from around 1902 to 1912, were read and believed.

The pieces reprinted in this section are such an important part of American political history that they scarcely need an introduction; yet in the way they confront and describe the political problems of urban America they are clearly a part of the story of our cities. Lincoln Steffens (1866–1936) wrote the first two articles partly reprinted here for *McClure's Magazine* between 1902 and 1905. (The first article was written in collaboration with a St. Louis journalist, Claude Wetmore.) Steffens came from a prosperous San Francisco family, and, after higher studies at the University of California and in Germany, he became, like Jacob Riis (see Reading 24), a police reporter in New York City for the *Evening Post*, where, again like Riis, he was influenced toward reform by Theodore Roosevelt. In 1901 he joined *McClure's Magazine*, a low-priced and lively journal that also had on its staff Ida Tarbell and Ray Stannard Baker, his fellow muckrakers. His articles for *McClure's* were later collected for publication in his book, *The Shame of the Cities* (New York, 1904). With the passing of the muckraking period by 1912 Steffens went on to engage in reform briefly in Boston, to dabble in socialism and in "applied" Christianity, and to observe and champion the Mexican Revolution of 1914 and the Russian Revolution of 1917. His famous *Autobiography* (1931) describes men and events of the First World War era. On Steffens see the *Dictionary of American Biography*.

On the urban reformers of the muckraking period in general see Louis Filler, *Crusaders for American Liberalism* (New York: Collier Books, 1961); John Chamberlain, *Farewell to Reform* (New York, 1932); Harvey Swados, *Years of Conscience: The Muckrakers* (New York: Meridian Books, 1962); and Arthur and Lila Weinberg, *The Muckrakers* (1961).

THE CORRUPTION OF ST. LOUIS CAME FROM THE TOP. The best citizens—the merchants and big financiers—used to rule the town, and they ruled it well. They set out to outstrip Chicago. The commercial and industrial war between these two cities was at one time a picturesque and dramatic spectacle such as is witnessed only in our country. Business men were not mere merchants and the politicians were not mere grafters; the two kinds of citizens got together and wielded the power of banks, railroads, factories, the prestige of the city, and the spirit of its citizens to gain business and population. And it was a close race. Chicago, having the start, always led, but St. Louis had pluck, intelligence, and tremendous energy. It pressed Chicago hard. It excelled in a sense of civic beauty and good government; and there are those who think yet it might have won. But a change occurred. Public spirit became private spirit, public enterprise became private greed.

> CLAUDE H. WETMORE and LINCOLN STEFFENS, "Tweed Days in
> St. Louis," *McClure's Magazine*, XIX (October, 1902),
> 577–580, 586.

Along about 1890, public franchises and privileges were sought, not only for legitimate profit and common convenience, but for loot. Taking but slight and always selfish interest in the public councils, the big men misused politics. The riffraff, catching the smell of corruption, rushed into the Municipal Assembly, drove out the remaining respectable men, and sold the city—its streets, its wharves, its markets, and all that it had—to the now greedy business men and bribers. In other words, when the leading men began to devour their own city, the herd rushed into the trough and fed also.

So gradually has this occurred that these same citizens hardly realize it. Go to St. Louis and you will find the habit of civic pride in them; they still boast. The visitor is told of the wealth of the residents, of the financial strength of the banks, and of the growing importance of the industries, yet he sees poorly paved, refuse-burdened streets, and dusty or mud-covered alleys; he passes a ramshackle fire-trap crowded with the sick, and learns that it is the City Hospital; he enters the "Four Courts," and his nostrils are greeted by the odor of formaldehyde used as a disinfectant, and insect powder spread to destroy vermin; he calls at the new City Hall, and finds half the entrance boarded with pine planks to cover up the unfinished interior. Finally, he turns a tap in the hotel, to see liquid mud flow into wash-basin or bath-tub.

The St. Louis charter vests legislative power of great scope in a Municipal Assembly, which is composed of a council and a House of Delegates. Here is a description of the latter by [Mr. Folk's] . . . February grand jury. . . .

"Our investigation, covering more or less fully a period of ten years, shows that, with few exceptions, no ordinance has been passed wherein valuable privileges or franchises are granted until those interested have paid the legislators the money demanded for action in the particular case. Combines in both branches of the Municipal Assembly are formed by members sufficient in number to control legislation. To one member of this combine is delegated the authority to act for the combine, and to receive and to distribute to each member the money agreed upon as the price of his vote in support of, or opposition to, a pending measure. So long has this practice existed that such members have

come to regard the receipt of money for action on pending measures as a legitimate perquisite of a legislator."

.   .   .   .

The blackest years were 1898, 1899, and 1900. Foreign corporations came into the city to share in its despoliation, and home
industries were driven out by blackmail. Franchises worth millions were granted without one cent of cash to the city, and with
provision for only the smallest future payment; several companies which refused to pay blackmail had to leave; citizens were
robbed more and more boldly; pay-rolls were padded with the
names of non-existent persons; work on public improvements
was neglected, while money for them went to the boodlers.

Some of the newspapers protested, disinterested citizens were
alarmed, and the shrewder men gave warnings, but none dared
make an effective stand. Behind the corruptionists were men of
wealth and social standing, who, because of special privileges
granted them, felt bound to support and defend the looters. Independent victims of the far-reaching conspiracy submitted in
silence, through fear of injury to their business. Men whose in-
tegrity was never questioned, who held high positions of trust,
who were church members and teachers of Bible classes, contributed to the support of the dynasty,—became blackmailers,
in fact,—and their excuse was that others did the same, and that
if they proved the exception it would work their ruin. The
system became loose through license and plenty till it was as wild
and weak as that of Tweed in New York.

.   .   .   .

Mayor Ziegenhein, called "Uncle Henry," was a "good fellow," "one of the boys," and though it was during his administration that the city grew ripe and went to rot, his opponents talked
only of incompetence and neglect, and repeated such stories as
that of his famous reply to some citizens who complained because
certain street lights were put out: "You have the moon yet—
ain't it?"

When somebody mentioned Joseph W. Folk for Circuit Attorney the leaders were ready to accept him. . . .

"Very well," he [Folk] said, at last, "I will accept the nomination, but if elected I will do my duty. There must be no attempt to influence my actions when I am called upon to punish law-breakers."

The committeemen took such statements as the conventional platitudes of candidates. They nominated him, the Democratic ticket was elected, and Folk became Circuit Attorney for the Eighth Missouri District.

Three weeks after taking the oath of office his campaign pledges were put to the test. A number of arrests had been made in connection with the recent election, and charges of illegal registration were preferred against men of both parties. Mr. Folk took them up like routine cases of ordinary crime. Political bosses rushed to the rescue. Mr. Folk was reminded of his duty to his party, and told that he was expected to construe the law in such a manner that repeaters and other election criminals who had hoisted Democracy's flag and helped elect him might be either discharged or receive the minimum punishment. The nature of the young lawyer's reply can best be inferred from the words of that veteran political leader, Colonel Ed Butler, who, after a visit to Mr. Folk, wrathfully exclaimed, "D—n Joe! he thinks he's the whole thing as Circuit Attorney."

The election cases were passed through the courts with astonishing rapidity; no more mercy was shown Democrats than Republicans, and before winter came a number of ward heelers and old-time party workers were behind the bars in Jefferson City. He next turned his attention to grafters and straw bondsmen with whom the courts were infested. . . .

. . . Other cities are to-day in the same condition as St. Louis before Mr. Folk was invited in to see its rottenness. Chicago is cleaning itself up just now, so is Minneapolis, and Pittsburg recently had a bribery scandal; Boston is at peace, Cincinnati and St. Paul are satisfied, while Philadelphia is happy with the worst government in the world. As for the small towns and the villages, many of these are busy as bees at the loot.

St. Louis, indeed, in its disgrace, has a great advantage. It was exposed late; it has not been reformed and caught again and again, until its citizens are reconciled to corruption. But, best of all, the man who has turned St. Louis inside out, turned it, as it were, upside down, too. In all cities, the better classes—the business men—are the sources of corruption; but they are so rarely pursued and caught that we do not fully realize whence the trouble comes. Thus most cities blame the politicians and the ignorant and vicious poor.

Mr. Folk has shown St. Louis that its bankers, brokers, corporation officers,—its business men are the sources of evil, so that from the start it will know the municipal problem in its true light. With a tradition for public spirit, it may drop Butler and its runaway bankers, brokers, and brewers, and pushing aside the scruples of the hundreds of men down in blue book, and red book, and church register, who are lying hidden behind the statutes of limitations, the city may restore good government. . . .

---

29   Tom Johnson in Cleveland, 1905

See the headnote to Reading 28. On Cleveland in this period see Elbert J. Benton, *Culture Story of an American City, Cleveland* (Cleveland, 1943), ch. 13.

IT SEEMS TO ME THAT TOM JOHNSON IS THE BEST MAYOR OF THE BEST-GOVERNED CITY IN THE UNITED STATES. . . .

. . . The best evidence of the "goodness" of this government is the spirit of the men in it. They like their work; they like to talk about their work; theirs is a sense of pride and preoccupation such as I never felt in any other American municipal government. The members of the administration are of all classes, but they get together, they and their wives, and they talk shop, shop, shop. The Mayor's levees are the most popular. Everybody goes there, evenings and Sundays, and it is Cleveland, Cleveland, Cleveland, till an outsider is bored to death. Say what you will, pick flaws

LINCOLN STEFFENS, "Ohio: A Tale of Two Cities," *McClure's,* XXV (July, 1905), 302, 305–311.

as you may and as I could, Tom Johnson has proved what I never heard him say he hoped to prove: He has proved that it can be made a joy to serve one's city.

. . . .

Tom Johnson is the "business man for mayor" that business men have been prophesying so long must come along some day to give us a "good business administration of a city government," and, now that he has come, Business hates him because he has given Cleveland not only good government, but representative government; not only clean streets, but clean tax lists; he has stopped not only blackmail, but bribery; he tackled not only low-down petty police and political graft, but high-toned, big, respectable, business graft, both legitimate and illegitimate. Tom Johnson is a reformed business man. His reform began at home; he reformed himself first, then he undertook political reform; and his political reform began with the reform of his own class. And that is Tom Johnson's sin.

. . . .

When some men go in for yachting, or the Senate, and give money to charity and churches, colleges and libraries, Tom Johnson gave himself and his money to politics, to municipal reform as the mayor of Cleveland. And as a mayor he knew what he was about.

His platform as a candidate was equal taxation and "three-cent fares with universal transfers" on the street railways; "good" government was a side issue; he threw that in. His idea was to make that city government represent and serve all its people. That doesn't sound bad, but applied by an expert big business man who knew just where the System lay and who reached for it with ability and humor, Mayor Johnson's simple idea had mixed and terrible consequences.

. . . .

Let's run down there again to see what [George B.] Cox has done since 1898 to make Cincinnati the model Ohio city. He has 'Russianized' it. His voting subjects are all down on a card catalogue, they and their children and all their business, and he

lets them know it. The Democratic Party is gone. Cox has all
the patronage, city, county, state and Federal, so the Democratic
grafters are in Cox's Republican Club. . . . He picks ward leaders, and they deliver the votes. The citizens have no choice of
parties, but they must get out and vote. Cox is good to some
of them. If they knuckle under, he puts respectable men up for
the school board. He has little use for schools; not much graft
in them; except to cut down their appropriations in favor of
fatter departments, and as a place to try respectable men. If they
take orders on the school board, Cox tries them higher up, and
he has a-plenty. The press is not free. The *Post* and the *Citizens'
Bulletin*, the last a weekly organ of the smallest but one of the
most enduring groups of reformers in America—these are the
only papers that ever speak out honestly for the public interest.
Official advertising, offices for the editors, public service stock
and political prospects for the owners, hold down the rest. It is
terrible. The city is all one great graft; Cox's System is the most
perfect thing of the kind in this country, and he is proud of it.

.   .   .   .

So, when Cox says only one divides the graft in Cincinnati, he
probably means that one man can dispose as he will of all of it,
police, political, and financial, as the examples cited indicate, but
he has to let all sorts of men in on it. And he does. And that is
his best hold on the graft. They talk in Cincinnati, as they do in
Philadelphia, of apathy. Apathy! Apathy is corruption. Cincinnati and Philadelphia are not asleep; they are awake, alive. The
life is like that of a dead horse, but it is busy and it is contented.
If the commanding men, of all the natural groupings of society,
were not interested in graft, no city would put up with what
satisfies Cincinnati. For Cincinnati is not unhappy. . . .

The rest are in it for profit or—fear. The bums get free soup;
the petty criminals "get off" in court; the plain people or their
relatives get jobs or a picnic or a friendly greeting; the Germans
get their beer whenever they want it; the neighborhood and
ward leaders get offices and graft; "good" Democrats get their
share of both; shopkeepers sell to the city or to politicians or
they break petty ordinances; the lawyers get cases, and they
tell me that the reputation of the bench is such that clients seek

lawyers for their standing, not at the bar, but with the ring; the
banks get public deposits and license to do business; the public
utility companies get franchises and "no regulation;" financiers
get canals, etc., they "get blackmailed," too, but they can do
"business" by "dividing up"; property owners get low assess-
ments, or high; anybody can get anything in reason, by standing
in. And anybody who doesn't "stand in," or "stand by," gets
"nothing but trouble." And there is the point that pricks deepest
in Cincinnati. Cox can punish; he does punish, not with physical
cruelty, as a Czar may, but by petty annoyances and "trouble,"
and political and business ostracism. The reign of Cox is a reign
of fear. The experience that made my visits there a personal hu-
miliation was the spectacle I saw of men who were being pun-
ished; who wanted to cry out; who sent for me to tell me facts
that they knew and suffered and hated; and these men, after leading me into their back offices and closing the door, dared not
speak. They had heard that I was shadowed, and they were afraid.
Afraid of what? They were afraid of their government, of their
Czar, of George Cox, who is not afraid of them, or of you or of
me. Cox is a man, we are American citizens, and Cincinnati has
proved to Cox that Americans can be reduced to craven cowards.

.   .   .   .

Now, is it clear why Mayor Johnson, came to run for governor of Ohio? He had to. The System, beaten in Cleveland, had
retreated to the state and there, with its legislature, its courts and
its other cities, it was preparing to crush him and conquer Cleveland. . . .

. . . Dayton is bad and glad of it; "we hope to be as 'good' as
Cincinnati some day," one of its rulers told me. Southern Ohio is
pretty low. But the spirit of the late Mayor Jones lives in Toledo,
and though its citizens have to present "petitions in boots" to get
it, they do get representative government. And in Cleveland, we
have, as I write, this spectacle: Two street-railway men, Mayor
Johnson representing the city, President Andrews his stock-
holders, negotiating in public for the disposition of the street-
railway system. There is no excitement, no bad feeling, no suspicion of boodle or corruption. Some franchises have expired,
others are falling in; all must be renewed. Mayor Johnson op-

poses any renewal except upon terms which will bring to the city
two things: First, the removal of the street railways out of politics; second, the benefit, in the form of reduced fares, [of] im-
proved service, or profits, of all that increase of earnings which
will come with the natural growth of the city. Mr. Andrews says
this is fair, so it is all a question of terms. . . .

So the cynics lie who say that capital has to corrupt a democratic government to get a "square deal" from the people. Such
men as Horace Andrews, an honest conservative, and Tom Johnson, a patient liberal, could settle Cleveland's street-railway problem, they and the people they both trust. But will they? Their
spirit would settle all our political problems. But will it? . . .

The forces of evil, beaten in the city, hold the state. The forces
of good, winning in Cleveland, fighting in Toledo, hopeful in
Cincinnati, to hold their own, must carry Ohio. Ohio,—the whole
state—has to make the choice, the choice we all have to make:
Cleveland or Cincinnati. The Herricks and Dicks and false "Fire
Alarms" won't do; we cannot "stand pat." It is the square deal,
or bribes and brickbats; Horace Andrews or Mark Hanna; Tom
Johnson or George Cox, all over the United States.

30   The Commuter and the Conductor in Pittsburgh, 1910

The problems of urban transit relief were frequently tied
to city politics. Riders on commuter trains and in common carriers in our cities have complained of their tribu-
lations since Jacksonian days. But this vignette of a Pittsburgh commuter in the days of urban reform politics
seems to sum up the entire history of the commuter.

On Hungerford see Reading 27 headnote: on a modern
bus rider's grievances see Jacques Barzun, *God's Country
and Mine* (Boston, 1954), 241–244.

THE FACT THAT PITTSBURGH MEN LIVE OUTSIDE OF PITTSBURGH goes to give her the fourth largest suburban train service in the country. Only New York, Boston and Philadelphia surpass her in this wise. Even San Francisco has less. One hundred and fifty miles to the northwest is Cleveland, the sixth city in the country and outranking Pittsburgh in population. There is not a single distinctive suburban train run in or out of Cleveland. From one single terminal in Pittsburgh four hundred passenger trains arrive and depart in the course of a single business day and ninety-five percent of these are for the sole benefit of the commuter.

So congested have even these railroad facilities become that the city cries bitterly all the while for a transit relief and experts have been at work months and years planning a subway to aid both the steam roads and the overworked trolley lines. At best it is no sinecure to operate the trolley cars of Pittsburgh. Combined with narrow streets, uptown and downtown, are the fearful slopes of the great hills. It takes big cars to climb those hills, let alone haul the trailers that are a feature of the Pittsburgh rush-hour traffic. When the New Yorker sees those cars for the first time he looks again. They are chariots of steel, hardly smaller than those that thread the subway in his daily trip to and from Harlem, and when they come toward him they make him think of locomotives. The heavy car gives a sense of strength and of hill capability. But the company staggers twice each day under a traffic that is far beyond its facilities—and it staggers under its political burdens.

For it is almost as much as your very life is worth to "talk back" to a street car conductor in Pittsburgh. The conductor is probably an arm of the big political machine that holds that western Pennsylvania town as in the hollow of its hand. The conductors get their jobs through their alderman, and they hold them through their alderman. So if a New York man forgets that he is four hundred and forty miles from Broadway, and gets to asserting his mind to the man who is in charge of the car let him look out for trouble. Chances are nine to one that he will be

EDWARD HUNGERFORD, *The Personality of American Cities* (New York, 1913), 175–177.

hauled up before a magistrate for breaking the peace, and that another arm of the political machine will come hard upon him.

A man, who was a life-long resident of Pittsburgh, once made a protest to the conductor of a car coming across from Allegheny. The passenger was in the right and the conductor knew it. But he answered that protest with a volley of profanity. If that thing had happened in a seaboard town, the conductor's job would not have been worth the formality of a resignation. In Pittsburgh a bystander warned—the passenger—and he saved himself arrest by keeping his mouth shut and getting off the car.

But the Pittsburgh man had not quite lost his sense of justice, and so he hurried to a certain high officer of the street railroad company. When he came to the company's offices he was ushered in in high state, for it so happened that the born Pittsburgh man was a director of that very corporation. It so happens that street railroad directors do not ride—like their steam railroad brethren —on passes, and the conductor did not know that he was playing flip-flap with his job.

"You'll have to fire that man," said the director, in ending his complaint. "If that had happened at the club I would have punched him in the head."

The big man who operated the street railroad looked at the director, and smiled what the lady novelists call a sweet, sad smile.

"Sorry, Ben," said he, "but I know that man. He's one of Alderman X_____'s men, and if we fired him X_____ would hang us up on half a dozen things."

Do you wonder that in the face of such a state of things transit relief comes rather slowly to Pittsburgh?

_31_   Judge Ben Lindsey's Denver, 1915

The problem of juvenile delinquency has been for centuries a part of the history of cities. Within a decade
from the time when Jacob Riis (see Reading 24) con-
fronted delinquency and crime in the tenement districts

of New York City, Benjamin Barr Lindsey (1869–1943) became judge of the juvenile court in Denver, Colorado. From 1901 to 1927 Lindsey publicized and promoted the features of his court, and he became an international authority on juvenile delinquency. He was responsible for the passage of contributory laws on delinquency, which held parents responsible for their delinquent children. Lindsey later was judge of the Superior Court in California. See his autobiography, *The Dangerous Life* (1931).

On the author of this description of Denver, Julian Street, see the headnote to Reading 25.

PERHAPS BECAUSE OF THE UNFAVORABLE FIRST IMPRESSION I HAD RECEIVED IN KANSAS CITY, I had expected Denver, being farther west, to have a less finished look. Furthermore, I had been reading Richard Harding Davis's book, "The West Through a Car Window," which, though it told me that Denver is "a smaller New York in an encircling range of white-capped mountains," added that Denver has "the worst streets in the country." Denver is still by way of being a miniature New York, with its considerable number of eastern families, and its little replica of Broadway café life, as well; but the Denver streets are no longer ill paved. Upon the contrary, they are among the best paved streets possessed by any city I have visited. . . .

Another feeling of my first ten minutes in Denver was one of wonder at the city's flatness. That part of it through which we passed on the way to the Brown Palace Hotel was as flat as Chicago, whereas I had always thought of Denver as being in the mountains. However, if flat, the streets looked attractive, and I arrived at the proudly named caravansary with the feeling that Denver was a fine young city.

Meeting cities, one after another, as I met them on this journey, is like being introduced, at a reception, to a line of strangers. A glance, a handshake, a word or two, and you have formed an

JULIAN STREET, *Abroad at Home* (Garden City, New York, 1926), 380–387, 391–394.

impression of an individuality. But there is this difference: the individual at the reception is "fixed up" for the occasion, whereas the city has but one exterior to show to every one.

That the exterior shown by Denver is pleasing has been, until recently, a matter more or less of accident. The city was laid out by pioneers and mining men, who showed their love of liberality in making the streets wide. There is nothing close about Denver. She has the open-handed, easy affluence of a mining city. She spends money freely on good pavements and good buildings. Thus, without any brilliant comprehensive plan she has yet grown from a rough mining camp into a delightful city, all in the space of fifty years.

. . . The discovery of gold in California brought a new influx of men to Colorado—though the part of Colorado in which Denver stands was then in the territory of Kansas, which extended to the Rockies. Many of the pioneers were men from eastern Kansas, and hence it happened that when the mining camps of Auraria and St. Charles were combined into one town, the town was named for General James W. Denver, then Governor of Kansas.

Kansas City and Denver are about of an age and are comparable in many ways. The former still remains a kind of capital to which naturally gravitate men who have made fortunes in southwestern oil and cattle, while the latter is a mining capital. Of her "hundred millionaires," most have been enriched by mines, and the story of her sudden fortunes and of her famous "characters" makes a long and racy chapter in American history, running the gamut from tragedy to farce. And, like Kansas City, Denver is particularly American. Practically all her millionaires, past and present, came of native stock, and almost all her wealth has been taken from ground in the State of Colorado.

.   .   .   .

In 1870 . . . Denver got its first railroad: a spur line from Cheyenne; in the 80's it got street cars; to-day it has the look of a city that is made—and well made. But, as I have said before, that has, hitherto, been largely a matter of good fortune. Denver's youth has saved her from the municipal disease which threatens such older cities as St. Louis and St. Paul: hardening of the arteries of traffic. . . .

Consider these few random items taken from the credit side of her balance: She is one of the best lighted cities in the land. She has the commission form of government. (Also, as you will remember, she has woman suffrage, Colorado having been the first State to accept it.) Her Children's Court, presided over by Judge Ben B. Lindsey, is famous. She has no bread line, and, as for crime, when I asked Police Inspector Leonard De Lue about it, he shook his head and said: "No; business is light. The fact is we ain't got no crime out here." Denver owns her own Auditorium, where free concerts are given by the city. Also, in one of her parks, she has a city race track, where sport is the only consideration, betting, even between horse owners, having been successfully eliminated. Furthermore, Denver has been one of the first American cities to begin work on a "civic center." Several blocks before the State Capitol have been cleared of buildings, and a plaza is being laid out there which will presently be a Tuileries Garden, in miniature, surrounded by fine public buildings, forming a suitable central feature for the admirable system of parks and boulevards which already exists.

.   .   .   .

The mountains directly west of Denver form a barrier which has forced the main lines of transcontinental travel to the north and south, leaving Denver in a backwater.

. . . The great difficulty has always been the crossing of the divide. The city of Denver has now come forward with the Moffat tunnel project, and has extended her credit to the extent of three million dollars, for the purpose of helping the railroad company to build the tunnel. It will be more than six miles long, and will penetrate the Continental Divide at a point almost half a mile below that now reached by the road, saving twenty-four miles in distance and over two percent. in grade. The tunnel is now under construction, and will, when completed, be the longest railroad tunnel in the Western Hemisphere. The railroad company stands one-third of the cost, while the city of Denver undertakes two-thirds. When completed, this route will be the shortest between Denver and Salt Lake by many miles.

Nor is Denver giving her entire attention to her railway line. The good-roads movement is strong throughout the State of Colorado. Last year two million dollars was expended under the

direction of the State Highway Commission—a very large sum
when it is considered that the total population of the State is not
a great deal larger than that of the city of St. Louis.

.   .   .   .

Denver, in her general architecture, is more attractive than certain important cities to the eastward of her. Her houses are, for
the most part, built solidly of brick and stone, and more taste
has been displayed in them, upon the whole, than has been shown
in either St. Louis or Kansas City. Like Kansas City, Denver has
many long, tree-bordered streets lined with modest homes which
look new and which are substantially built, but there is less monotony of design in Denver.

.   .   .   .

It is impossible to consider Denver without considering Judge
B. Lindsey—although I may say in passing that I was urged to
perform the impossible in this respect.

Opinion with regard to Judge Lindsey is divided in Denver.
It is passionately divided. I talked not only with the Judge himself, but with a great many citizens of various classes, and while
I encountered no one who did not believe in the celebrated Juvenile Court conducted by him, I found many who disapproved
more or less violently of certain of his political activities, his
speech-making tours, and, most of all, of his writings in the magazines which, it was contended, had given Denver a black eye.
. . . The charge that the Judge had injured Denver by "knock-
ing" it in his book was used against him freely in the 1912 and
1914 campaign, but he was elected by a majority of more than
two to one. He is always elected. He has run for his judgeship ten
times in the past twelve years—this owing to certain disputes as
to whether the judgeship of the Juvenile Court is a city, county,
or state office. But whatever kind of office it is, he holds it firmly,
having been elected by all three.

At present the Judge is engaged in trying to complete a code
of laws for the protection of women and children, which he
hopes will be a model for all other States. This code will cover
labor, juvenile delinquency, and dependency, juvenile courts,
mothers' compensation, social insurance (the Judge's term for a

measure guaranteeing every woman the support of her child, whether she be married or unmarried), probation, and other matters having to do with social and industrial justice toward mother and child. It is the Judge's general purpose to humanize the law, to cause temptations and frailties to be considered by the law, and to make society responsible for its part in crime.

.   .   .   .

He speaks of his causes quietly but very earnestly, and you feel, as you listen to him, that he hardly ever thinks of other things. There is something strange and very individual about him.

"The story of one American city," he said to me, "is the story of every American city. Denver is no worse than the rest. Indeed, I believe it is a cleaner and better city than most, and I have been in every city in every State in this Union."

Part Seven

Cities between the World Wars

32 Pittsburgh and Detroit in the 1920's

In 1880 only New York City had a population of 1,000,-000; from 1890 to 1920 the census showed three cities (New York, Chicago, and Philadelphia) with a million or more people. In 1930 five cities (New York, Chicago, Philadelphia, Detroit, and Los Angeles) were ranked in this class. By 1930 there were eight American cities with a population of 500,000 to 1,000,000; twenty-four cities with 250,000 to 500,000 people; and fifty-six cities with 100,000 to 250,000 people. By 1940 56 per cent of the American people lived in urban areas of a population of 2500 or more.

American cities came of age in the nineteenth century, but we became, in a statistical sense, an urban nation in the twentieth century. Clearly, however, rural traditions and three centuries of agrarian life, most of it in an unsettled continent, could hardly make us, in the cultural sense, an "urban" people overnight.

The business prosperity of the 1920's gave an economic lift to many American cities. Typical of the "boosting" attitude toward the newer cities of mass production in an automobile age, with its disparagement of an older industrial city, is the following article by French Strother (1883–1933). It reflects the attitude of those who in good times cannot see the ills still present in American urban society: contrary to Strother's contention, there were indeed tenements in Detroit in the 1920's. And Strother's image of benevolently paternalistic industrial management in Detroit was rudely shattered within only seven years by the unrest that accompanied the founding of the CIO. In 1920 Pittsburgh's population was 600,000, while Detroit had close to a million people.

Strother was for many years (1904–1907, 1912–1926) on the staff of the magazine, *World's Work*. And throughout the 1920's he was administrative assistant to Herbert Hoover.

On Detroit in this era see Arthur Pound, *Detroit, Dynamic City* (New York, 1940), chs. XXVIII–XXX.

PITTSBURGH WAS OUR FIRST GREAT INDUSTRIAL CITY. Detroit, chronologically, is our second great industrial city. Both rose like magic upon the rushing tide of development of an industry —the one upon coal and steel, the other upon the motor car. Both grew from mediocrity to greatness in the short span of the working life of one generation. Pittsburgh was built by mediæval-minded men, upon feudal foundations. Detroit was built by modern-minded men, upon new conceptions. The contrast in the results is startling.

. . . .

During the years from 1907 to 1912, Pittsburgh was subjected to a "social survey" by the Russell Sage Foundation. Though partially financed by Pittsburghers, this survey was regarded by most of the best people there as an impertinence and an affront. The investigators found that half the working people of Pittsburgh were living on the border-line of destitution, that their wages were barely enough to provide food and shelter to men of strong bodies who could keep going under the strain of twelve hours daily of hard manual labor, under a system of management that drove them to the limit of production. They found a large part of the population of Pittsburgh living in tenements, getting their drinking water by pumping it from shallow wells by hand, disposing of human sewage in open privies, two and three families living in one room, other families living in unlighted cellars. They found the schools of Pittsburgh managed by eighty school boards,

FRENCH STROTHER, "What Kind of a Pittsburgh is Detroit?" *The World's Work*, LII (October, 1926), 635–639.

one in every ward, each taxing its little neighborhood, amenable to no financial accounting, and providing local "education" without relation to any central system of teaching control. They found the children with no place to play but the streets. They found Pittsburgh with the highest typhoid death-rate, the highest infant death-rate, and one of the highest pneumonia death-rates in America. And they found the workers hopeless of improving their condition. They did not dare to belong to a trade union. Political redress was impossible, for politics, too, belonged to the employers.

Pittsburgh to-day is somewhat improved. Sanitation has been provided for the whole city, and the death-rate has gone down. A central board of education controls all the schools, and in buildings and instruction Pittsburgh has joined the modern world. National public opinion, not local public opinion, has forced the United States Steel Corporation to install the three-shift eight-hour day in its continuous processes.

But in little else have conditions changed. Half the employees of the Steel Corporation work in non-continuous processes that are feeders to the continuous processes. These men still work on the twelve-hour basis, and as work is slack or rushed, the twelve-hour day may mean ten hours or it may mean fourteen. Tenements that were photographed for the survey of 1907 as "horrible examples" of over-crowding, can be photographed to-day, still occupied as human rabbit-warrens. Wages in Pittsburgh, though increased in money, have not relatively increased in purchasing power. A high percentage of the working population still lives on the verge of destitution. The school buildings are closed when teaching is finished, and the school-yards likewise. The few public playgrounds are about one fifteenth adequate to the needs. Boys who have no other time or place for healthful, organized play, may not play baseball on Sunday on the vacant lots—they will be arrested if they try it. Their fathers have no place in which to meet and discuss politics or civic problems—and anyhow, it is not safe for mere workingmen in Pittsburgh to give public expression to their views on politics or civic problems. Civic pride, in the sense in which this term expresses itself in Boston or Los Angeles or Detroit—in democratic achievements for the well-being of the people, growing out of their own initiative and produced out of their free common council—this kind of civic pride does not exist. Pittsburgh *is* mediæval; and it is characterized by civic apathy, baronial mastery, and a most depressing social atmosphere.

Detroit is a joyous contrast to all this. Detroit has its faults (a recent survey of one special subject declares it to be the most immoral city in America—though to the casual visitor, acquainted as casually with many other cities, this sounds exaggerated), but its faults are the faults of the American people and not of the feudal system. And its civic virtues are legion. Let us here cover the same ground we have covered with Pittsburgh.

About 1905, labor troubles loomed big in Detroit, then just beginning to be a really industrial city. Here, however, the captains of industry took a novel tack. They dreaded the growth of labor unionism. But they did not try to break the unions. They did "beat the unions to it." They went to their men and asked them what their grievances were. They got the usual answer: low wages, long hours, the arbitrary control of the petty boss. The captains did an astonishing thing: they raised wages, reduced hours, and arranged various devices by which the men could get redress from the tyranny of the boss by appeal directly to the owner. To-day labor unionism in Detroit is not much stronger than it is in Pittsburgh—except in the building trades—but it is weak only because the employers freely gave the men more than the union leaders elsewhere ask.

There are no tenements in Detroit. Practically every family lives in an individual frame cottage, with a front yard and a back yard. It is said that this has been possible in Detroit because of the cheap automobile, but the fact is that many more people ride to work on the trolleys (425 miles of track, municipally owned) and the buses (702 motor buses covering 145 miles of streets) than ride in their own cars. Every house in Detroit is connected with the city water main and the city sewer.

The schools of Detroit are not merely good, they are among the best in the world. There are 214 public schools with 5,800 teachers, maintained at a cost of $23,000,000 last year. They have kept pace with the growth of the city, and the city has grown at the rate of two hundred thousand new people a year for several years. The school buildings are used during school hours for instruction. After school hours they are used for art exhibitions, lectures for old and young, neighborhood gatherings for civic discussions and political meetings. Practically all the voting places in Detroit are in the school buildings. The schools are the heart of the civic life of the community, and that civic life is full, free, and various. When school itself is over, the school yard is taken over by the Department of Public Recreation, and a trained organizer of play goes on duty to help the boys and girls of its neighborhood get full use of it for baseball, folk-dancing, anything that can develop the muscles and enlarge the spirit of the child. This department employs 396 outdoor play supervisors and spends $600,000 yearly to operate the playgrounds. These grounds are open from nine in the morning until nine at night, and where tennis is played they are in use as early as five o'clock in the morning.

Detroit has fifty public parks, large and small, covering an area of 3,184 acres. They are used to the limit for public enjoyment. They include playgrounds, ball fields, tennis courts, golf courses —all open every day of the week and all attended by experts whose business is to see that the most people get the most fun out of them. Free popular band concerts are given daily, and at the same time free symphony orchestra concerts are given, in the open air in summer. If you like jazz you can hear it expertly rendered. If you prefer Chaikovski, you can hear his mournful intricacies, rendered under the direction of Ossip Gabrilovich. . . .

Detroit got tired, a number of years ago, of such petty politics as it had. In 1918, it elected James Couzens, now United States Senator, its mayor. He had made a fortune during his business association with Henry Ford, but instead of retiring to enjoy it, he threw himself whole-heartedly into public service in the city government. Under his energetic leadership, Detroit completely made over and modernized its form of government. It wrote a new charter. The old ward system was abolished. The city council now consists of nine members, elected at large. The business of government was divided into a few simple grand divisions. The head of each was made definitely responsible for its success or failure in doing its job. The only department that has not notably succeeded is the Police Department, and here, as usual, the better element of the citizenship is quietly taking a hand and will whip that failure into shape.

The school board of Detroit is also a small body. It does all its work in "committee of the whole." Frank Cody, the superintendent of schools, is primarily a business man, interested in results—educational results. Political influence does not count. No head of any city department has ever been hired or fired for political reasons in the last seven years.

Because wages have been high, Detroit has no real problem of destitution. Such cases as exist are chiefly found among the sixty thousand "floating population," such as wanders in and out of any thriving city. It may look to prompt relief, either from the city Department of Public Welfare, or from the seventy-one charitable organizations of every description that pool their requests for support in the Community Fund, which raised three million dollars last year by public subscription to meet the operating deficits of these privately managed charities. . . .

Detroit has faced the usual dilemma of traffic congestion. Instead of dreaming indefinitely, it has acted. It is spending eighteen million dollars widening its arterial avenues. It is going to spend fifty millions more widening Woodward Avenue and other principal business thoroughfares in the heart of the city, though this means a wholesale condemnation of store and shop fronts and the cutting off of slices of office buildings to make room. . . .

In Pittsburgh, a high percentage of even the generation that made its fortunes there went somewhere else to enjoy them. They moved to New York or Philadelphia or Paris. But in Detroit, Crœsus has made his home where he made his money. . . .

In Detroit, not only have the fathers stayed near the works, but the sons have been made to taste of manual labor. . . . They got a large crop of blisters, and the point of view of the man whose blisters have long since become callouses. Idling for pleasure or "culture" is not the fashion in Detroit. Abundant opportunity for rational pleasure and for the most generous culture is provided in Detroit itself, and these are just as free to the Polish immigrant in Hamtramk as they are to the millionaire's son, and they do actually share them in the evening classes in the art museums, in the performances of the Theater Guild, and in the concerts on Belle Isle.

Much of the difference between Pittsburgh and Detroit is due to Henry Ford, but by no means all. Ford accelerated a progress in industrial management that was already under way. Other industries in other cities had observed that the old system of "telling labor where it got off" was not only bad Americanism but bad business as well. Many corporations tried "welfare work." Henry Ford tried it, for a time. But that form of paternalism, too, is un-American and unbusiness-like, and he dropped it.

Ford then gave the most spectacular demonstration yet given anywhere, that the best management is to pay men enough money so they can afford a good living for themselves and their families, and then to see to it that their work is so arranged that, in decent hours and without indecent pressure, their production is sufficient to make the wages profitable. Ford accepted one obvious fact of life, that labor cannot in good sense be held responsible for its inability to produce efficiently. He accepted the responsibility of management to do the thinking, and he included in that thinking the figuring out of profitable ways of paying good wages for a human day's work. The result is the Ford industries, in which the remarkable thing is not their size but their universal evidences of prevision, planning, thought, and the use of machinery instead of men wherever it is humanly possible to make a machine do the work.

Other employers in Detroit have followed the same line. They, and Ford, need not be credited with angelic altruism of motives, though it is pleasanter to believe, and it is sounder ethics to believe, that unless the motives were good, the wonderfully good effects could not have followed. Crœsus probably *did* change for the better when he moved to Detroit. Crœsus was in process of changing everywhere in America. He had actually learned something in thirty years, or twenty, or ten. He had got a better vision of the rights of man; a better ideal of what business ought to be; a kindlier feeling toward the man less gifted than himself; a more American idea of citizenship and of the duties of business in helping to develop citizens.

·   ·   ·   ·   ·   ·   ·   ·   ·   ·   ·   ·

If you think this is rhapsodizing, go visit Detroit. It will give you a faith in the present and in the future of our industrialized world—in America, at least—that will be worth much to your peace of mind.

---

33   The Great Depression in Chicago

Rural and urban America alike were hit hard by the economic depression of the 1930's. The symptoms of hard times were more easily recognizable in our large cities where bread lines, soup kitchens, jobless apple vendors, and the kind of human misery depicted here by Edmund Wilson, one of America's foremost men of letters, became a sordid chapter in our history. The 1930 census gave Chicago a population of 3,376,438.

For another view of Chicago in this period see Emmett Dedmon, *Fabulous Chicago* (New York, 1953), pt. IV. For urban life generally during the depression see Dixon Wecter, *The Age of the Great Depression* (New York, 1948), ch. VII.

THE SINGLE MEN ARE DRIVEN TO FLOPHOUSES. During the last year—September 30, 1931–September 30, 1932—50,000 have registered at the clearing house. Those who are not residents of Chicago are ordered to leave the city: if they got there by paying their fare, they are given a half-fare which will take them home. Others are sent to the asylum, the poorhouse, the veterans' home; referred to the blind pension, the juvenile court. About 500 men a month are disposed of in this way. The Oak Forest

EDMUND WILSON, *The American Earthquake: A Documentary of the Twenties and Thirties* (New York: Doubleday Anchor Books, 1958), 457–458, 459–463. Reprinted with permission of the author.

poorhouse, called "the Graveyard," has people sleeping in the corridors and turned 19,000 away last year. The rest are directed to the shelters, where they get two meals a day and a bed.

Among the high whitewashed walls of an obsolete furniture factory, the soiled yellow plaster and the scrawled and punctured blackboards of an old public school, the scraped-out offices and pompous paneling of a ghastly old disused courthouse; on the floors befouled with spittle, in the peppery-sweetish stink of food cooking, sulphur fumigations, bug exterminators, rank urinals doctored with creosote—ingredients of the general fetor that more or less prominently figure as one goes from floor to floor, from room to room, but all fuse in the predominant odor of stagnant and huddled humanity—these men eat their chicken-feed and slum amid the deafening clanking of trays and dump the slops in g.i. cans; wait for prize-fights or movies of Tarzan (provided to keep them out of the hands of the Communists or from holding meetings themselves) in so-called "recreation halls," on the walls of which they have chalked up "Hoover's Hotel"— big bare chambers smothered with smoke, strewn with newspapers like vacant lots, smeared like the pavements with phlegm. Here they sit in the lecture seats, squat on the steps of the platform, stretch out on the floor on old papers. . . .

Yet Chicago has apparently been particularly efficient in providing and running these shelters. At best, it is not unlike the life of barracks—but without the common work and purpose which give a certain momentum to even a dull campaign. In the shelters, there is nothing to coöperate on and nothing to look forward to, no developments, no chance of success. The old man is ending his life without a home and with no hope of one; the wage-earner who has hitherto been self-dependent now finds himself dropped down among casuals and gradually acquires their attitude; the young man who comes to maturity during the workless period of the depression never learns the habit of work. (There are few actual hoboes here: the hobo can do better by begging or stealing.)

In so far as they are unable to adapt themselves, they must live under a continual oppression of fear or guilt or despair. One sees among them faces that are shocking in their contrast to their environment here: men who look as if they had never had a day's ill health or done a day's careless work in their lives. Now they jump at the opportunity of spending a day a week clearing the rubbish off vacant lots or cleaning the streets underneath the Loop tracks. This is the only thing that stands between them and that complete loss of independence which can obliterate personality itself—which degrades them to the primal dismal undifferentiated city grayness, depriving them even of the glow of life that has formerly set them off from the fog and the pavements and the sodden old newspapers, rubbing them down to nothing, forcing them out of life.

Yet none of these single-men's shelters produces such an impression of horror as the Angelus Building on South Wabash Avenue, where families of homeless Negroes have taken refuge. This neighborhood was once fairly well-to-do; but at the present time, left behind by the city's growth in other directions, it presents a desolation that is worse than the slums. . . . The Angelus Building looms blackly on the corner of its block: seven stories, thick with dark windows, caged in a dingy mesh of fire-escapes like mattress-springs on a junk-heap, hunched up, hunchback-proportioned, jam-crammed in its dumbness and darkness with miserable wriggling life.

It was built in 1892 and was once the Ozark Hotel, popular at the time of the old World's Fair. In the dim little entrance hall, the smudged and roughened mosaic, the plaster pattern of molding, the fancy black grill of the elevator, most of it broken off, do not recall former splendor—they are abject, mere chips and shreds of the finery of a section now dead, trodden down into the waste where they lie. There is darkness in the hundred cells: the tenants cannot pay for light; and cold: the heating system no longer works. It is a firetrap which has burned several times—the last time several people were burned to death. And, now, since it is not good for anything else, its owner has turned it over to the Negroes, who flock into the tight-packed apartments and get along there as best they can on such money as they collect from the charities.

There are former domestic servants and porters, former mill-hands and stockyard workers; there are prostitutes and hoodlums next door to respectable former laundresses and Baptist preachers. One veteran of the war, once foreman of the Sunkist Pie Company, now lives in cold and darkness with his widowed mother, even the furniture which he had been buying for $285 the outfit and on which he had paid all but the last installment of $50.20, taken away by the furniture company. For light, they burn kerosene lamps, and for warmth, small coal-stoves and charcoal buckets. The water-closets do not flush, and the water stands in the bathtubs.

The children go to play in the dark halls or along the narrow iron galleries of an abysmal central shaft, which, lighted faintly through glass at the top, is foggy and stifling with coal-smoke like a nightmare of jail or Hell. In the silence of this dreadful shaft, sudden breakages and bangs occur—then all is deathly still again. The two top floors have been stripped by fire and by the tenants' tearing things out to burn or sell: apartments have lost their doors and plumbing pipes lie uncovered. These two floors have been condemned and deserted. Relief workers who have visited the Angelus Building have come away so overwhelmed with horror that they have made efforts to have the whole place condemned —to the piteous distress of the occupants, who consider it an all-right-enough place when you've got nowhere else to go. And where to send these sixty-seven Negro families? Brought to America in the holds of slave-ships and afterwards released from their slavery with the chance of improving their lot, they are now being driven back into the black cavern of the Angelus Building, where differing standards of living, won sometimes by the hard work of generations, are all being reduced to zero.

Those who want to keep clear of the jail-like shelters get along as they can in the streets and huddle at night under the Loop or build shacks on empty lots. On whatever waste-places they are permitted to live, the scabby-looking barnacles appear, knocked together from old tar-paper and tin, old car-bodies, old packing boxes, with old stovepipes leaning askew, amid the blackened weeds in the snow and the bones of old rubbish piles. One "Hooverville" on Harrison Street flies a tattered black rag like the flag of despair.

The inhabitants of these wretched settlements chiefly forage from the city dumps, as do many of those whom charity will not help or who for one reason or another will not go to it or for whom the relief they get is inadequate. There is not a garbage-dump in Chicago which is not diligently haunted by the hungry. Last summer in the hot weather, when the smell was sickening and the flies were thick, there were a hundred people a day coming to one of the dumps, falling on the heap of refuse as soon as the truck had pulled out and digging in it with sticks and hands. They would devour all the pulp that was left on the old slices of watermelon and cantelope till the rinds were as thin as paper; and they would take away and wash and cook discarded turnips, onions and potatoes. Meat is a more difficult matter, but they salvage a good deal of that, too. The best is the butcher's meat which has been frozen and has not spoiled. If they can find only meat that is spoiled, they can sometimes cut out the worst parts, or they scald it and sprinkle it with soda to neutralize the taste and the smell. Fish spoils too quickly, so it is likely to be impossible—though some people have made fish-head soup. Soup has also been made out of chicken claws.

A private incinerator at Thirty-fifth and La Salle Streets which disposes of the garbage from restaurants and hotels, has been regularly visited by people, in groups of as many as twenty at a time, who pounce upon anything that looks edible before it is thrown into the furnace. The women complained to investigators that the men took an unfair advantage by jumping on the truck before it was unloaded; but a code was eventually established which provided that different sets of people should come at different times every day, so that everybody would be given a chance. Another dump at Thirty-first Street and Cicero Avenue has been the center of a Hooverville of three hundred people.

34 Towns within Cities: Brownsville and West Bronx

In 1930 the borough of the Bronx in greater New York City had 1,265,258 inhabitants. It was a city within a city, just as many other urban centers have towns within them composed of ethnic residential groups. What it means to grow up in one of these subcities is described in these two selections by William Poster (1916–1960), editor and literary critic, and Ruth Gay, who published a number of articles on the American Jewish scene in *Commentary* under the name of Ruth Glazer.

B UILT UP NEARLY OVERNIGHT ON RUNDOWN FARMLAND, Browns-ville, in the 20's, had come to occupy an area of about two square miles set apart by such natural boundaries as the IRT El on Livonia Avenue, the BMT El on Junius Street, the junction of Pitkin Avenue's macadam with the greensward of Easton Park-way at Howard Avenue, and the Liberty Avenue trolley. It was, I believe, the largest solidly Jewish community in the city. Other reputedly Jewish sections may have contained more Jews than Brownsville's two hundred thousand, but they were likely to be strongly Jewish for only a block or two and then give way to a mixed ethnic pattern. Brownsville was a Jewish island. I would guess that the population was about ninety-five per cent Jewish and four per cent Italian, with a handful of Negroes and a few Polish janitors making up the remainder.

Up to the age of twelve or so, a Brownsville child scarcely saw any members of other groups except for teachers and police-men, and never really felt that the Jews were anything but an overpowering majority of the human race. I don't think my con-temporaries and I believed that the figures who loomed largest in our imagination—say, George Washington, Nathan Hale, Tom Mix, Babe Ruth, and Jack Dempsey—were actually Jewish, but we never clearly thought of them as anything else.

In a period when most of New York's Jews were striving des-perately to become Americanized, perhaps Brownsville's solid Jewishness alone was enough to account for the section's lowly status. But there were other factors. For one thing, circumstances

WILLIAM POSTER, " 'Twas a Dark Night in Brownsville," *Commentary*, 9 (May, 1950), 458–467. Reprinted with the permission of Mrs. Constance H. Poster and with the per-mission of *Commentary*.

seem to have attracted a specific type of Jew out to Brownsville:
I have the impression that the great majority came from the regions of Russia around Minsk, with relatively few of Polish,
Rumanian, or any other origin. By and large, they were an energetic, hustling, robust lot, but rarely possessed of any but the
simplest material ambitions. The desire for respectability or elegance must have been weak in them to begin with, and Brownsville scarcely supplied the soil on which it could thrive. Essentially, the district was the New York center of the *proste yid*,
the "plain Jew," remarkably level-headed, and rarely noteworthy
for imagination or lofty aspirations. Most of the older men had
their occupations in the neighborhood; they were storekeepers,
real estate men, peddlers of fruits and vegetables, the auxiliaries
of these businesses, and those professionals indispenable to the
community.

The most prosperous merchant of Pitkin Avenue and the
poorest potato peddler were likely to live in the same house or
adjacent ones, and to buy most of their food, clothing, and furniture at the same stores—if only out of lack of desire or time to
do otherwise. Brownsvillians, in general, were either so busy or
so unimaginative that "conspicuous waste" or snobbery of any
kind was minimal: when one of them finally did get the idea
and had the leisure and the cash, he migrated to another section. But as long as he stayed in Brownsville, he remained subject
to its prevailing egalitarianism of tone and manners. Likewise, the
children all went to the same schools, and played together in
packs in which the children of the fairly affluent (like myself)
were indistinguishable from those of pushcart venders and junk-
men (like most of my playmates).

In appearance, too, Brownsville was egalitarian, with no very
distinguished residence within its confines, and the streets pretty
much littered and grimy everywhere, though there was considerable space inside and about the buildings, and it did not at all
resemble the congested, malodorous slum districts of Manhattan.
The dwellings were of every variety and looked as though they
had been dropped chaotically from the sky, while the business
establishments gave a curious appearance of systematic arrangement: seven blocks of furniture stores on Rockaway Avenue, so
that a walk down that street was like a girl's domestic daydream
of plushy sofas and gleaming mahogany bedroom suites; five teem-

ing, pungent blocks of pushcarts, groceries, and "appetizing" stores on Belmont Avenue; men's and women's clothing and similar emporia on the ten busy blocks of Pitkin Avenue. A huge six-block square of junkshops, tinsmithies, stables, garages, and miscellaneous small enterprises surrounded these main arteries. How it all rang and clattered and hammered and buzzed and smelled! There wasn't a quiet square yard in the whole district.

For all its reputation, Brownsville in the 20's was scarcely a poverty-stricken neighborhood. The merchants of Pitkin Avenue had prospered in the postwar boom, often accumulating enough surplus capital to open second or third stores or to dabble in real estate (a Brownsville passion). Belmont Avenue flourished on a largely deserved reputation for cheapness and quality that drew customers from a wide area. And while selling vegetables from a pushcart may not have looked very elegant, it was often amazingly lucrative: one peddler was reputed to have three cellars and a fleet of four trucks devoted solely to stocking his cart—which was, indeed, always surrounded by a large group of chaffering *veiblach*.

Junk, rag, and paper dealers, who had gone into business with nothing but a horse and wagon, their bare hands, and inexhaustible patience, expanded their lots, acquired trucks, and even ventured into manufacturing. Stables gave way to garages—alas for the children who in the early 20's could still watch the blacksmiths at their forges and stuff old pocketbooks with horse manure for the unwary! The owner of the local barber shop replaced his flyblown mirrors, hired an extra helper, and to the consternation of the conservatives installed a *zaftig* blond manicurist. The tailor, who could be seen in his undershirt sweating over the pressing machine, hired a regular delivery boy instead of luring us from our games with the promise of big tips. The gabbling flock of carpenters, painters, plumbers, and masons that used to swarm on the corner of Stone and Pitkin Avenues dwindled noticeably on weekdays.

Unemployment, the great blight on the prosperity of the 20's, could not have been too great in Brownsville because nearly everybody was in business for himself. Good food could be had cheap and rent was low. Many families lived in two- or three-story houses that were sturdily constructed, relatively spacious, and comfortably, if primitively, heated by wood or coal stoves

and gas radiators. Free of the high costs of social conformism and
ostentation, Brownsville didn't fare badly.

.   .   .   .

In an odd way and for a brief period, Brownsville fulfilled the
age-old Jewish need for a sanctuary, an escape from the consciousness (if not the fact) of being a minority in exile. To a
child, at any rate, Brownsville was a kind of grimy Eretz Yisrael
without Arabs. Living in a world all Jewish, where no alien group
imposed its standards, the child was secure in his own nature.
What social shame he did feel was simply for his own lack of
shame when, outside the boundaries of Brownsville, he ran up
against those for whom a nervous consciousness of the opinions
of the world had become a badge of superiority.

True, his first vision of the real state of affairs was apt to produce something like a traumatic shock. Indeed, to reach maturity
with anything like a normal relation to society was difficult for
Brownsville's second generation. All that remained functional to
their parents out of the wreck of the European heritage were some
simple physical and prudential precepts and a few copybook maxims. Maturity alone constituted the power of the parent over the
child, for the reciprocal relation by which parents derive strength
from conventions and conventions derive strength from parents
was shattered by the break from Europe, by social change and the
facts of life. Too often the children were the guides in matters of
American language and custom, and the parent could never be
certain that even the most outrageous adolescent behavior did not
issue from some mysterious American norm that his child understood better than he. . . .

Despite his inward anarchy, the life of a Brownsville boy was
as regulated, definite in its objectives, and ritualized as that of a
member of a primitive tribe. Whenever he could wrench himself
free from such chores as eating, sleeping, school, and homework,
all of which he had to be coerced into by force or the threat of
force, he got together with the gang, from which he could never
be excluded unless its psychological or physical hazards were more
than he could endure. And as long as he had sufficient strength
to participate, he was relieved of some of the worst terrors of
childhood. All kinds of attitudes were fixed and ordered for him:

the limits of his territory, his position within the gang, his relations with strangers and with boys of different ages.

Age groups were marked out by a mobile but definite system.
No matter what a boy's age, there was always a group of boys
younger than himself which he called "duh liddle guys" and an
older group which he called "duh big guys." And he himself to
his juniors was a "big guy" and to his seniors a "liddle guy." A
cluster of rights, prerogatives, and attitudes was attached to this
relation which had so powerful a grip that even when one saw a
"big guy" some ten or fifteen years later, some of the old feelings
were automatically revived.

Among the "big guys" were to be found all one's "big brudders" and among the "liddle guys" were to be found the "kid
brudders." It was an absolute obligation of "big brudders" to
protect "kid brudders" and redress any physical injury to them,
even if it was inflicted in fair fight with a peer. At some desperate point in a fight between two boys of equal age, the one
who was losing would threaten his opponent with the might
of the older males of his family. This tactic was orthodox and did
not lessen the status of the individual using it, beyond the natural
drop in status resulting from his defeat. A skillfully used "big brudder" was an advantage paid for by receiving numerous raps on
the head, while a "kid brudder" was on the whole a liability, useful for errands and menial tasks and as a source of admiration, but
altogether too likely to subject his protector to the gratuitous perils
of fights with all the "big guys" whom he happened to antagonize.

:::::::::::::::

W HEN THE WOODLAWN ROAD-JEROME AVENUE EXPRESS RUSHES
OUT OF THE TUNNEL AT 161ST STREET IN THE BRONX, the subway rider catches a glimpse of rows of six-story apartment houses

RUTH GLAZER, "West Bronx: Food, Shelter, Clothing," *Commentary*, 7 (June, 1949), 578–585. Reprinted with permission of Ruth Gay and with the permission of *Commentary*. This selection and the preceding one are also
reprinted in Elliot E. Cohen (ed.), *Commentary on the
American Scene: Portraits of Jewish Life in America*
(New York, 1953).

flanking the elevated tracks on both sides and extending far back into the hinterland. Viewing the crossword puzzle of yellow squares made by the lighted windows block after block, the outlander cannot resist musing profoundly to himself, "Ah, those poor people living out their pallid lives in regimented cells, one above the other." Luckily for him the Bronxite wedged next to him cannot read his thoughts; otherwise he would transfix him with that characteristic glare of the embattled straphanger. Pallid? Ha!

Why, there's more life, vigor, and excitement in one single Bronx apartment house at six o'clock in the evening than in a thousand elm-lined Main Streets on a Fourth of July. Visualize six little girls, none over three and a half feet high, dragging their roller skates up over the marble staircase; two or three fourth-floor mothers trying to summon recalcitrant sons to dinner; the building superintendent, flanked by irate ground-floor tenants, descending on a group of boys playing "association."

To be sure, the returning fathers, crushed by forty minutes in the subway, are extraordinarily noiseless at this hour.

The West Bronx is located in time midway between the Lower East Side (or the East Bronx) and West Side Manhattan. It is a community whose residents seem occupied full time in discovering the wonderful things produced by the world that can be had for even the moderate amount of money at their disposal. In so doing, they have created a style of living all their own.

Take any of the main arteries that mark the topography of the West Bronx—170th Street, Burnside Avenue, University Avenue, the Upper Concourse, Fordham Road. What streets anywhere can match them for sheer number in food stores, ice-cream parlors, delicatessens, restaurants, specialty shops for women and children, haberdasheries, and that special institution of the area, the "hardware" store, which maintains only the most distant kinship with establishments elsewhere engaged in selling nuts, bolts, gardening tools, and other such items. These "hardware" stores are crammed with every conceivable ingenious brightly colored gadget for the kitchen—painted bread boxes, the newest thing in shelving, 22-carat warranted gold-plated china tea sets, chromium Chanukah candelabra, ruby glass luncheon-sets, toasters, broilers, mixers, and a whole window of bottles, sterilizers, infant china and silverware, and complicated devices for warming baby food. For the West Bronx is nothing if not a *crèche*. . . .

Whereas on other days the patronizing of the various food stores is a matter requiring only an ordinary degree of acumen, tact, and watchfulness, a certain air of solemnity settles over the West Bronx on Thursday. Thursday is devoted to shopping for the weekend, since Friday is given over to cooking and cleaning so that Saturday can be the day of rest ordained on Mount Sinai. Even emancipated young housewives have been caught up in the tyranny of this custom. This is the day when the housewife descends to do battle with the butcher in earnest. Small purchases during the week of "a few veal cutlets" or "a piece liver" can be regarded as minor skirmishes. The one point that must be firmly grasped is that one does not buy meat from a butcher, one negotiates. One lives in a state of armed truce.

The young bride, for example, goes through a long period of training before she dares ask for so much as a single lamb chop. This rigorous course includes elements both scientific and psychological. To know the cuts of meat derived from the cow, the calf, and the lamb is, of course, primary. (For to what end all this fencing if one simply gives away one's hand by asking for two pounds of meat for pot roast?) Even more important are the little professional tricks suspected of every butcher by every well-versed housewife. This information is generally delivered *sotto voce* as the butcher disappears to get the cut of meat requested; viz., "If he asks you what you want it for, tell him you want to broil it. It's *his* business that you want to use it for chopped meat?" or "Make sure when you ask for *mittle* chuck, that he doesn't give you single chuck."

This masked antagonism, this deep-lying mutual suspicion between the kosher butcher and his customer, is symbolized by the customarily empty showcase. The only function of this elaborate testimonial to refrigeration seems to be to set a restraining barrier, a neutral zone, between the two contending parties. Every piece of *flanken*, every shoulder steak must be custom-cut, and each piece of meat is held up for inspection with the furtive glances, the special avowals which only a butcher knows how to utter. Occasionally a timid young woman will attempt to influence his mysterious choice as he disappears into the refrigerator. "A small piece of calf's liver," she'll say, "I hope it'll be good. It's for the baby." To dissipate the illusion that the prospective cut is not already predestined, the butcher will respond, "Whaddya mean 'good'? Would I give you a piece of liver that isn't good?" Is there a reply?

Unlike other stores, too, there is a leisurely, almost club-like atmosphere here as the women gather of a Thursday morning. Then the butcher holds court, announcing his opinions on the world, commenting on departing customers. There are no small private conversations between neighbors. No. There is an easy general public discussion and everyone is included. "Well, Mr. Pizetsner" (not "Sam," as she might say to the grocery-store man), will begin an older and more favored customer, "and how are your sons these days?" "All right, thank God; the new business in Flatbush is doing fine." "So, how do you like living in Brooklyn, Mr. Pizetsner?" "Well, it's not so bad. We have our own house. . . ." "It must be a terrible trip for you every day. How come you don't move the store to Brooklyn?" "Listen," says the butcher, as he prepares to quarter a chicken, "everyone says the same thing. My wife wants me to give up the business. (*chop*) The boys have a good spot for me there. (*chop*) But you know what I say . . . ? (*The cleaver is suspended.*) I tell 'em, I couldn't give up my business here. Where would I ever find such customers? They're not customers. They're dolls!" (*chop, chop*) Really, could you buy in the A&P?

In view of the breathtaking variety of food which confronts his eyes and nose as he walks down any one of the main streets, the incautious observer might well conclude that Lucullan feasts are concocted each evening in Bronx kitchens and that Bronx housewives are culinary paragons. Nothing, alas, could be further from the truth. Quantity, perhaps, or wholesomeness, yes (or maybe). But variety—never. . . .

Bronx style extends to clothing, too, for undeniably there *is* a Bronx style, the result of an appreciation for, even a reveling in rich fabrics, in sumptuous textures, in elaborate folds, in dense colors, and in complex designs. This emerges in the extravagant hats, the weighty fall of a dress, the dark and brilliant nail polish, and the sculptured, appliquéd, and platformed shoes.

Even men can taste a little of this sheer exuberance of costume, now that it has been semi-legalized as "California style." They can have silky gabardines (just a bit more silky than Brooks Brothers would approve), smooth, rich flannel shirts, of an altogether different nature from the scratchy, plaid, woodsman's type, and brilliant, broadly knotted ties. And so—a suit is not a suit, but an experience, just as a fur coat is the achievement of a decade of yearning. It would be a shame if people didn't notice.

For Sunday afternoons the men have developed a special style suitable for airing the baby, milling about on the Concourse, visiting relatives in the neighborhood, and not inappropriate for local parties or poker sessions. This costume, often the cause of hidden, or sometimes energetically expressed, distress on the part of the wife, enables the Bronx husband to indulge his liking for informality (no tie), color (!), and comfort (sport shirt). With the aid and abetment of local haberdashers, the men have gained their first victory in a decade over the delicate sensibilities of Bronx taste which draws a sharp distinction between what is proper for everyday and what is required for occasions. The women, however, will not be deterred from their knowledge that Sunday is the day to be straitened by corsets, pinched by shoes, hobbled by skirts, and burdened by furs.

The role of the Concourse in Bronx life, like its geographical location, is central. Its once aristocratic buildings have become shabby and it no longer has its former prestige. But as the longest and broadest avenue in the Bronx it is still a name to conjure with. Do you desire a pastoral afternoon? At one end of the Concourse there is a small but intricate park, complete with bandstand and Sunday afternoon concerts. Or perhaps your taste fancies a walk on civilized pavements. There is the middle section where one may see and be seen. And at its far end is the big shopping center that is almost the lodestar of Bronx life. Here the best furniture and clothing stores display their brightest wares so that the young may gaze and be educated and the old may sigh and envy.

But the architecture of the Bronx is basically characterized by the long sober lines of six-story apartment houses, built some twenty to thirty years ago, running in a northerly and southerly direction, intersecting the main avenues. The majority of these edifices are built in a plain, unpretentious style vaguely suggesting Italian Renaissance fortresses. In harmony with their solid construction are the gloomy but magnificent hallways that even the marauding hands of three or four generations of children have not been able to disfigure. There are black-and-white tiled floors, laid out in formal patterns to resemble marble; there are gilded, pilastered walls, heavy mirrors, tables and chairs of an indefinite but regal historical period, and rococo flambeaux on the walls, unfortunately requiring the prosaic aid of electricity. The arrangement and interior architecture of the apartments also suggest palace chambers. The entrance to a meanly proportioned living room, for example, will be guarded by two elaborate French doors; the walls imitate wood paneling; the floors are parqueted; once again, there are flambeaux on the walls. Most buildings front directly on the street, but many, built on a larger scale, have center courts frequently ornamented by a pirouetting nymph or a cupid cut in stone.

The "new" houses of the Bronx (some are more than fifteen years old) are all built in a uniform "modern" style, with white or cream brick façade, casemented windows, and chromium-decorated doorways. Their interiors are likewise constructed smoothly, with a minimum of doorways, mouldings, and decoration. Despite their great number, these houses always seem exceptional, and, somehow, frivolous, appearing at random among the "regular" apartment houses, and practically never in solid blocks.

The sobriety and regularity of the life of the West Bronx is suggested more by the even and dull architecture of the side streets than by the color and movement of the shopping avenues. This regularity is enforced by the schedule of the head of the family; when he must get up to go to work, when he returns—this sets the boundaries of the day. Few of the housewives can afford to break the pattern with club meetings and charitable activities; most are completely absorbed by the creatures of their own creation—home, children, their style of living. Only the children, and particularly the adolescents among them, are free. Probably the children are little different outwardly from other city children. The girls play with their dolls, or mimic their mothers, or rather awkwardly play in street games. Once out of the confines of their apartments, the boys rush around the streets in packs, dressed uniformly during most of the year in plaid shirts and corduroy trousers. At play, both groups are rather anonymous. But the adolescents are another story.

When the weather is warm and pleasant, numerous islands of greenery, groupings of stone benches, and even little parks seem to appear in almost every area of the West Bronx. During the day the benches are occupied principally by mothers with baby carriages, old men talking with their friends, and old ladies sunning themselves. In the early evening these areas lose their calm. The benches are still occupied by the old, but perched on the iron railings or standing about in knots in out-of-the-way corners are groups of teen-age boys and girls. Gradually the darkness begins to seethe with their laughter and talk. Those still unattached wander casually but tensely up and down the paths hoping to be invited into a "crowd." The girls here are young, carefully made up, carefully dressed, very wise, and terribly shy and afraid, for all their outward brazenness. The boys are very bold in their new power. It is up to them to set the tone of the group, to tease the girls, to make wisecracks about the passers-by, while the girls "just die laughing." The "crowd" is free-floating in space and time. What relation can it have to a stifling apartment, to dowdy mothers, to school, to relatives? It is disembodied excitement; night after night the girls and boys are drawn by it to the same spot.

---

35   Washington in 1941

No one who was in Washington during the second World War can forget its crowded conditions, the thousands of workers in and out of uniform, the queues, the inadequate transportation facilities. Our capital city in 1940 had a population of 663,091. Two decades later it had increased by only 100,000 people. Some of Washington's wartime flavor is recaptured in this article, written on the eve of America's entry into the war. But the longer lasting prob-

lems of space, of urban planning, and of racial adjustment
that have long been with Washington, as well as with
other cities, are memorably described in this piece by
Alden Stevens, who lived in Washington during the late
1930's and later became a designer and a writer for television shows.

WASHINGTON THE CAPITAL IS A SYMBOL OF DEMOCRACY AND
AMERICA. Washington the city is a symbol of almost everything that sincere and thoughtful men know is wrong with
democracy and America. Washington the Capital is the hope of
world freedom; Washington the city is overcrowded, badly
housed, expensive, crime-ridden, intolerant, with inadequate
transportation, schools, and health facilities. It staggers under
a dilapidated and hopeless governmental organization, and its
problems are rapidly getting worse. It is the most undemocratic
city in America.

The metropolitan district has grown in population from 621,-
000 in 1930 to more than a million to-day. No American city of
comparable size has shown anything like this expansion. It is
much greater than that which Washington experienced during the
years of the First World War. More than 5,000 new federal workers are pouring into Washington every month; and with them an
estimated 4,000 to 6,000 others—members of their families and
employees of the private concerns which serve the Capital.

At times the Union Station is so jammed that no red-caps can
be had, and strangers carrying their bags thread their way
through the crowds to the taxi stand, where it is not uncommon
to stand in line twenty minutes waiting for a cab. (The taxi business is so rushed that many government clerks supplement their
earnings by driving cabs in their off hours.) Lines in front of
ticket windows are sometimes so long that trains leave while
would-be passengers are frantically attempting to buy tickets.

ALDEN STEVENS, "Washington—Blight on Democracy: Plain
Talk about our Capital City," *Harper's Monthly Magazine*, 184 (December, 1941), 50–58. Reprinted with permission of the author.

A summary of current D.C. statistics is a grab basket of all-time highs. Two hundred and twenty thousand federal employees now work there. The government pay roll was up to $33,-000,000 in August. Building permits for the metropolitan area are being issued at 1,500 a month. 1940 brought 82,500 outsiders to 208 conventions, another record. Retail trade is over $400,-000,000 a year. Bank deposits are $440,000,000—the largest in history. The District government's budget will reach $54,000,000 in 1942. And so on. There are more automobiles, more new homes, more hotel rooms, more telephones, and more bars than ever before. There is also more crime, more disease, more congestion, and more poverty.

Washington society is having the same continuous field day it had in 1917. The parties are bigger and brighter. Hostesses compete excitedly for the new crop of dollar-a-year men and their families (the "defense people" they are called) with an intensity never in evidence over the New Dealers, few of whom had either social standing or money. Newcomers to the Capital are amazed at the indifference of many merchants who are selling so much they do not seem to care about either making sales or giving satisfaction, and at the shoulder-shrugging carelessness of laundries, cleaners, and auto-repair men, who are so busy that they seem glad to lose a customer.

To provide desk space for the 5,000 new employees a month the government has taken over stables, ripped seats out of old theaters and installed partitions and desks in the auditoriums, conjured up "temporary" buildings, and has even used tents. It has taken over old residences and new apartment houses—some of the latter before they were even finished. For a time Leon Henderson's OPACS had a kitchen and a bath for every suite of offices. As this goes to press there are persistent rumors, faintly denied, that the new Statler Hotel will be taken over by the government as soon as it is finished. All this in a city where many families of eight and ten live in a single basement room; where four and five single workers share a room, and twenty may share a bath in a rooming house; where some workers even sleep in shifts in the same sort of "hot beds" for which Harlem is famed.

It is true that there are furnished rooms available; some for single occupancy, some for double or more than double. The

Housing Registry office has more than 3,000 listed. These will do for single workers, though the best that can be said for most of them is that they are kept clean and can be slept in. There are apartments vacant too—at prices most defense workers couldn't meet if their entire income went into rent. There is a desperate shortage of small, moderately priced apartments suitable for families with incomes under $1,500—and half the people who work for the government in Washington make less than this. So incoming workers must leave their families behind, and must double up with other new workers and try to cut their living expenses enough to send something home. The number who do this is reflected in the 2,000,000 postal money orders totalling $23,000,000 that went out of Washington last year—more in proportion to the population than from any other U.S. post office.

Rents have gone up, though fear of regulation by hard-boiled Leon Henderson has kept them from skyrocketing as they did in 1917. It has been common practice to jam three people into rooms which formerly held one or two; and at little or no reduction per person. Thus a room which brought $40 a month as a single will now be found bringing $37.50 to $40 from each of two or three occupants.

The crush in hotel space, always worst in the spring, is not so bad as I write, but Statler would not be building Washington's largest hotel, with 850 transient rooms, if there weren't a good chance of filling it. The Washington Hotel Association insists there is no room shortage, refuses to cancel or even discourage conventions, and publishes impressive figures to prove its point. Visitors who must, time after time, search for another hotel after finding their chosen house full remain unconvinced.

Scattered like measles in all parts of the city, surrounded by fairly respectable-looking red-brick houses, are Washington's famous alley dwellings—1,700 multiple houses almost every one of which should be torn down, but now more crowded than ever. The Alley Dwelling Authority since its establishment in 1934 has made great strides toward rehousing alley residents, but the defense boom is making it almost impossible to demolish any kind of housing because of the impossibility of finding quarters for the residents. Yet here and elsewhere in Washington are

15,000 dwelling places without inside toilets, menacing an already precarious health situation. Here is the fountainhead of Washington's ill-health and crime, and the work of eliminating them should not stop even for defense, lest their very continued presence make defense more difficult.

Five years ago Washington's hospitals were overloaded. Three years ago a report of the U.S. Public Health Service called for immediate provision of 850 additional beds, 110 new public health nurses, at least 3 health centers, and various other expansions of health facilities. Since then about 300 additional beds have been provided, a few public-health nurses have been hired, one health center has been built. Meanwhile Washington's population has risen 25 per cent and the recommendations themselves are now out of date and insufficient. Within limits, public health is a purchasable commodity; the city that spends the most gets the best results. The American Public Health Association recommends an annual expenditure of $2.50 per capita in Washington *as a minimum;* the hard-working health officers now have only $1.27 available, and as the population grows the amount per capita drops accordingly. One hundred and fifty public-health nurses are trying to do the work of 300. The tuberculosis rate has been beaten down effectively in the past few years, but it is still 89 per 100,000—almost twice the national rate.

The Washington Criminal Justice Association states that in 1940, 5,961 reported major crimes resulted in only 1,167 convictions—a poor record. Defense seems to have brought with it a real crime wave, and there is general agreement that 1941's figures will look even worse. . . .

Schools have been overcrowded for years and some of them have double shifts. Lack of teachers prevents any more being so operated. Even though a large proportion of new Washington workers are childless or do not bring their children with them, the new influx has strained facilities dangerously. Before the Tolan Committee on Interstate Migration this spring Superintendent Ballou stated that at least ten new buildings were necessary, with a large increase in the teaching staff.

The building of transportation facilities in any city necessarily lags behind its growth. Washington has some fine new streamlined streetcars that move almost silently, inch by inch, sand-

wiched between ancient creaky vehicles suggestive of remodeled
horse cars from perhaps the Cleveland Administration. Buses are
modern enough but most of them are small, and nearly as many
government workers come to work by private auto as manage
to sardine themselves into the public facilities. Taxis are cheap,
but only cheap enough to be used by about 1 per cent of U.S.
workers on their way to the office.

In this city where the inadequacy of the public transportation
system makes it necessary for 35 per cent of government workers to get to their offices by automobile there is garage space
for less than 10 per cent of the registered cars. The rest stand
on the street all night, except on some streets during the winter
months when "No Parking—Snow Removal" signs are put up,
though there is hardly any snow and practically no snow-removal
equipment. The streets are narrowed by lines of parked cars all
night and glutted with snail-pace traffic all day. The traffic reg-
ulations are the most complicated that experienced motorists can
call to mind. Some streets are one-way southbound from 7:30–
9:15 A.M., northbound from 4–6 P.M on week days and from
12–1:30 on Saturdays; two-way at other times. Rates in parking
lots run as high as 25 cents an hour, a prohibitive amount for
low-income workers to spend daily. There are actually government clerks who come to work at 6 A.M to find a parking space,
and eat a box breakfast and read newspapers until eight! The
traffic death toll is not high and has been kept about static in
recent years by the simple method of slowing traffic down practically to a walk, a device which anybody could think up and
which does little credit to the traffic management officers of the
District. A new underpass under Thomas Circle helps automo-
bilists but drives pedestrians nearly crazy by its complicated system of neon "Walk" and "Don't Walk" lights.

Yet the present crisis, brought about by America's need to re-
arm, is only a sudden turn for the worse in a chronic Washington situation. In 1917 people were sleeping on billiard tables
and under counters. The city has never taken its problem
seriously or truly come to grips with it. Congress seems to have
the feeling that next year federal expenses are going to be cut to
the bone and most of these people will be going home and there

won't be any problem any more. This hardly seems likely in the fall of 1941.

. . . .

So far the problem of getting enough office space has been solved mainly by taking over living space, though a new War Department building is functioning now, and another, the largest building in the world, is planned. The new Social Security Building was filled with defense offices before it was finished, and the Social Security Board never got a chance at it. Temporary buildings have been thrown up in sixty days within sight of "temporary" buildings dating from the First World War, and more are coming. These latest shacks look to the casual observer even more temporary than the 1918 models, but they'll probably last just as long, for they'll be needed.

Decentralization is being talked about, and the Federal Home Loan Bank Board has been moving 1,200 employees to New York, while the Department of Agriculture plans to move about the same number out to near-by Maryland. Now if two such moves are consummated *during the same month* it means that a total of about 2,400 employees will leave Washington. In that same month about 5,000 will come into the Capital, effecting a net increase of 2,600! At least this is better than an increase of 5,000.

Private builders put up 5,500 dwelling units in the first half of 1941. Government defense housing agencies are working on about 3,700 more, including a 250-room dormitory for single women which is being built by private interests with a government loan. It sounds like a lot of housing, but at least 50,000 people, half of them government workers, came into the city in the same period.

From the number of streets that are torn up one might get the impression that a great deal is being done to solve Washington's traffic difficulties. Compared with the work that needs doing, as revealed this summer by a comprehensive government highway survey, it is hardly a scratch. This report calls for a $44,-000,000 program of street-widening, grade-separation, new bridges and other highway improvements. So far there seems little reason to expect such a program to be pushed through un-

til it is thoroughly outdated, which will not be long hence as
things are going now. . . .

II

All these things constitute really the simpler problems of
Washington. Far more difficult will be the putting at ease of
Washington's soul.

Here in the Capital of a nation which fought a war round the
slogan of "No taxation without representation!" taxes are under
the control of Congress, and Washington is not represented in
Congress. And if the tax rate is low it is because essential services are pinched and inadequate.

Here in the Capital of a nation dedicated to the proposition that
all men are created equal, one-third of the residents are forbidden
the theaters and the restaurants of the principal business area, are
effectively blocked in their search for employment, are commonly charged two to three times as much rent as the other two-
thirds are equivalent accommodations, and are hated and feared
because they do not like it. In the South the Negro is kept rigidly
in what the whites say is his place; but his place is made somewhat more tenable by a tradition of paternalism and a sort of
code of responsibility and justice, however arbitrary. In the big
cities of the North he is far more free to go where he will and
find what employment he can. There is no paternalism, but there
is a certain amount of granted independence and even a shadow
of equality in the right to vote and in employment opportunities.
But Washington combines the worst features of North and
South; here is neither the paternalism of Atlanta and Tuscaloosa
nor the relative freedom of Chicago and New York. Negroes
who have lived in many parts of the country say that nowhere
else in America is there such bitter mutual race hatred. The
Washington *Afro-American* calls the city a "cesspool of racial
intolerance."

Negroes are being forced out even from their traditional jobs
as waiters and hotel workers, and the chances for private employment are even slimmer than those in the Federal government,
which officially does not discriminate; but except for some few
"co-ordinators of race relations" and the like, you will find colored

people only as messengers, elevator operators, and building-service workers. The Washington Urban League reports cases of Negroes who had taken and passed Civil Service examinations and were called by telegram to the Capital from as far away as New Orleans to take emergency defense jobs; when they arrived, and their color was discovered, they got the "we'll let you know" treatment and were stranded penniless in Washington. Even in the local penal institutions, occupied by two to three times as many blacks as whites, there seem to be almost no jobs for Negroes. Yet Washington wonders why two-thirds of its relief cases are black and two-thirds of its crimes are committed by Negroes. When Leadbelly, the Negro folk-singer, accompanies himself on the twelve-string guitar and sings:

> Home of the brave, land of the free
> I don't want to be mistreated by no bourgeoisie,
>   Lord, it's a bourgeois town!

> Tell all the colored folks to listen to me,
> Don't try to buy no home in Washington, D.C.
>   'Cause it's a bourgeois town!

> Eeee—it's a bourgeois town
> I got the bourgeois blues,
> Gonna spread the news all round!

—he echoes the sentiments of one-third of Washington's population.

Here in the Capital of democracy no citizen has a vote, for those who maintain residence in a State and vote by mail cannot be called citizens of Washington.

Washington once had the vote. In the beginning it was the general assumption that citizens of the Capital were as good as anybody else. The charter of 1820 provided for election of a mayor and other officials and was in effect until 1871, when Congress abolished it and set up a new District government with a governor and eleven-man council selected by the President and approved by the Senate. Even then Washingtonians were permitted to elect yearly 22 members of a "House of Delegates."

This government lasted until 1874. It was a great public-works period for Washington, with U.S. Grant as President, and streets were paved and trees planted. The Capital was changed from a

mudhole to a modern city, but it all looked highly irregular to
Congress, which was shocked at the expense although of course
it had appropriated the money. There was an investigation of
District affairs, charges of graft and corruption flew fast and
thick, and when the smoke had cleared away the last vestige of
suffrage in the District had been removed, and Washington was
ruled by a three-man commission strictly under the thumb of
Congress. There have been only very minor changes in this set-up
in the past sixty-five years.

Now the Constitution gives Congress the right "to exercise exclusive legislation in all cases whatsoever over such district. . . ."
This has traditionally meant that Congress was to have complete
and in effect absolute administrative control. It has never worked
out well. As early as 1831 (when the city of Washington still
retained the power to elect some of its own officials) President
Andrew Jackson spoke to Congress:

". . . It was doubtless wise in the framers of our constitution
to place the people of this District under the jurisdiction of the
General Government, but to accomplish the objects they had in
view it is not necessary that this people should be deprived of
all the privileges of self-government. Independently of the difficulty of inducing the representatives of distant States to turn
their attention to projects of laws which are not of the highest
interest to their constituents, they are not individually nor in
Congress collectively well qualified to legislate over the local concerns of this District. Consequently its interests are much neglected. . . ."

President Jackson, or anyone, could make the same speech to-
day. It describes with rare succinctness what has always been the
matter with Washington, and what is the matter with it now.
Two Congressional committees concerned with other matters
and lacking both responsibility to the District and understanding of its problems, are running the show. As it happens, they
are unusually good committees at present. Pat McCarran, Nevada
Democrat, is the active chairman of the Senate committee, and
he has repeatedly indicated a sincere interest in the District. He
has even said that it ought to have suffrage, though it is hard to
see what he is doing about getting it. . . .

If anything, the present high leadership of these committees proves conclusively that there ought to be a complete change. If the present members can't run Washington effectively no Congressional committees can. Things have more often than not been much worse. Washingtonians still grimace when they think of the days not very long ago when Tom Blanton ran things.

Except in such emergency situations as the present, members of Congress live in Washington only a few months a year, and most of them find it convenient to live in hotels. They are detached from the life and problems of the community and extremely busy with other matters, as they should be. Senator McCarran, for instance, is also on the very important Appropriations Committee, as well as the Judiciary, Irrigation and Reclamation, Post Offices and Post Roads, and Public Lands and Surveys Committees. Jennings Randolph, who heads the House District Committee, serves also on the Civil Service, Labor, Roads, and Mines and Mining Committees.

III

Washington needs a strong man to take up her cause and get her straightened out. But who can do it? If a Senator or Representative should fight hard for a new deal for the District he would need to spend full time on the job. And what would his constituents say? They would say, "The so-and-so doesn't give a whoop about us; he lives in Washington and that's all he cares about. We'd better get somebody else to represent us."

Many experts on government have studied the District set-up during the past fifty years and published recommendations for improvement. Dr. Laurence F. Schmeckebier of the Brookings Institution, one of our ablest students of government, offered a first-class blueprint in 1929. A "Citizens' Efficiency Committee" offered another in 1937. In 1939 Griffenhagen and Associates, a firm of public-administration specialists, hired by the Congress and paid out of District funds, turned in a most acceptable report on what should be done. Congress has listened to all these experts somewhat as an indulgent father listens to a precocious child of two, and has then forgotten them. It is much easier to peck away at the problem, setting up a new committee here and a new Board there, appointing a co-ordinator of this and that, submitting some harassed District official to a third-degree if he suggests that the District is badly in need of something. As a result, local government in the District is carried on almost as much by Federal government bureaus as it is by the District's own, and nearly every Federal department is concerned with some part of the District's affairs. The F.B.I., the Secret Service, the National Park Service, and the D.C. Metropolitan Police all take a hand in policing and crime investigation. The Bureau of the Budget, the Comptroller of the Currency, and the General Accounting Office of the Federal government share the handling of financial matters with the District's Board of Accountancy, Office of the Auditor, Budget Officer, and Disbursing Officer.

It is beyond human comprehension to understand where the duties of one office stop and those of another begin; to know what is handled by the District's own government and what is handled for the District by one of the regular bureaus of the Federal government. . . .

. . . Democracy is fighting for its existence in the world, and there are better things for our legislators to do than furrow their brows over every purchase of chalk or extension of a sewer line in Washington.

It may be said that this is no time for such an upheaval. On the contrary, it is exactly the time for it. If democracy is to survive it has got to make itself more efficient. We cannot any longer afford the anachronistic, wasteful, and undemocratic hodgepodge that now runs the District of Columbia.

The planners of Washington, from L'Enfant to Frederic A. Delano, have had a mania for monumental stage settings. The Lincoln Memorial cost $3,000,000. The Washington Monument was cheaper at $1,500,000; but the new Jefferson Memorial will cost another $3,000,000. The Tomb of the Unknown Soldier and the Memorial Amphitheater cost over $1,000,000. Mr. Mellon sank $15,000,000 into his art gallery. We seem to have no difficulty getting plenty of money for theatrical effects. It should not be impossible to spend at least comparable amounts for a modern subway, cleaning up the housing situation, putting up adequate schools and health facilities, and for making Washington a decent place to live for people with low incomes, which would include 90 per cent of the people who live there. The effect on morale, especially the morale of the disgusted men and women who work for the government and have to put up with Washington as it stands, would be enormous.

.   .   .   .

There is a reason more compelling than the Capital's own needs for planning Washington for use rather than for show. Other American cities have long had a habit of copying what is done here. Philadelphia's new boulevards are very reminiscent of Capital roadways. St. Louis has a new and excellent waterfront development similar in many respects to Potomac Park. Nearly every State capitol looks like a small edition of the national Capitol. The hundreds of monumental new post offices and other public buildings that have sprung up from Fresno to Bangor in the past few years show the nation's dependence on Washington's architectural fashion. Make Washington a modern, slumless, livable city and watch others follow.

Fortunately other American cities have not aped Washington's local government. They couldn't of course as it stands. But suppose Washington set up a thoroughly competent, democratic city administration, designed and run by experts. Such a pattern might point the way, and help rid other cities of the inefficiency and graft they suffer now.

Washington has many good and patriotic citizens who have been butting their heads against the stone wall of Congressional indifference year after year, trying to improve government and housing and to get suffrage and representation. They are baffled and beaten. There are others called "Cave Dwellers" who were born and raised in Washington and who do not care very much. Some of them would rather not have suffrage for the District —they fear the Negro vote, or they fear interference with the established real estate interests which are so profitable as things stand, or they simply do not care.

It is not for the Cave Dwellers, nor even for the District's progressive and more public-spirited citizens, that America must rise in wrath and demand a new government and a new soul for Washington—there are few of them and they manage to get along. It is for Democracy the Faith and America the Dream. By cleaning up Washington we do not necessarily wash away the sins and flaws inside Democracy. Without a new soul for Washington, however, Democracy cannot have a new soul. If we cannot, here in this one symbolic place, rid ourselves of intolerance, poverty, and disease, what may the critics of Democracy say? If we cannot here set up a model, a full-scale futurama of what a democratic city should be in government, plan and spirit, can we do this elsewhere?

··

36   Wartime San Francisco in 1943

Although in 1940 the city of San Francisco had only 634,000 people, the metropolitan district of San Francisco-Oakland in 1940 had close to one and a half million people. During the second World War thousands more would pour into this metropolitan area from farms and country towns as they did into the wartime arsenal cities of Seattle, Detroit, Boston-Portsmouth, Baltimore, or San Diego. As a result some of the largest migrations in American history, from east to west and from south to north, occurred in the 1940's. The effects of a wartime change in residence and a change in occupation for millions of Americans are still being felt.

··

THE IMPACT OF SAN FRANCISCO AT WAR comes like the kick of a big gun to anyone who hasn't seen it since Pearl Harbor. Fighting men have taken over the city as did the Vigilantes of old. They have geared its life, colored its streets, inspired its people.

LA VERNE BRADLEY, "San Francisco: Gibraltar of the West Coast," *The National Geographic Magazine*, LXXXIII (March, 1943), 279–280, 290–291, 295, 299–300, 306–308. International copyright by the National Geographic Society. Reprinted with permission of the Society.

Troops, guns, bayonets, motor units, ships, supplies—on the move. Soldiers, marines, mines, nets, bayonets, barrages, barbed wire—on guard. "It is absolutely forbidden to cross this line." "No cameras or field glasses, please." "Men in uniform—welcome!"

If for a moment you lose yourself in old smells, sounds, memories, fighter planes come screaming down the skyline and, lifting you right up on your toes, almost clip off the top of the old Ferry Building to remind you that this is 1943—and a *city at war!*

Helmeted, bullet-belted patrols guard every bridgehead, river mouth, slip landing, seemingly harmless road entrances, tunnels, railroad crossings, barren hills.

.   .   .   .

You hear the rivet guns and hammer presses of shipyards; the screech of braked wheels grating on steel rails as oil moves in thousands of tank cars from refineries; the roar of blast furnaces; the thunder of Army trucks speeding by under guard—10, 20, 30—filled with soldiers.

You see hills being leveled as giant shovels slap at their sides like fly swatters. You see new towns rising from reclaimed swamps and dust holes.

You look across fields of barrage balloons suspended awkwardly in midair like tail-heavy sausages.

Finally, you look across to the Golden Gate where, against a low sun, a line of blue, heavily burdened ships is slowly steaming out.

.   .   .   .

The Navy has here the Mare Island Navy Yard, the new Alameda Naval Air Station, a blimp base, supply depots, drydocks, and training centers.

All other activities are subordinated to the moving of troops and supplies, defending the harbor, maintaining port facilities, and supporting new war industries. During the early months of the war San Francisco cleared more military supplies than all other United States ports combined.

In peacetime 25,000 replacement troops cleared this port every

year to relieve men garrisoned overseas. Today, figures with-
held, one can only watch and wonder at the numbers as soldiers
in full kit swing onto rows of dark blue ships.

Laughing, sweating, swearing, shoving, they pour over gang-
ways and packing boxes.

The fog brushes by like wisps of steam. The low basses of the
fog horns repeat their monotones on the Bay. The smell of fish
and sea rises from the water front.

Some of these soldiers have had a few days or hours in town.
Others, fresh from staging areas, have just pulled off a blacked-
out train.

Only a few familiar objects tell them where they are. Nothing
tells them where they are going.

For the thousands of men who pass through that Golden Gate,
it is their last glimpse of America for many months; it holds all
their parting memories.

.   .   .   .

But the San Francisco Bay area doesn't belong entirely to the
Army.

Mare Island was the first spot in America to get the news about
Pearl Harbor. With its powerful radio station it intercepted Kim-
mel's historic message to the Pacific Fleet which ended with "This
is no drill." The news was flashed to Washington and read to
President Roosevelt by Secretary Knox before an official com-
muniqué reached the Navy Department. . . .

A medley of unholy discords rises from the shipyards, machine shops, drydocks, warehouses, and other centers of ship-
building and ship-repair activity on this small Manhattan-like
island in the north end of the Bay. Shipfitters, pattern makers,
molders, painters, flange turners, electricians mill about in pur-
poseful confusion, eventually losing themselves in the crushing
crowds of a changing shift. . . .

Three hundred special buses carry thousands of Mare Island
workers to and from the mainland and neighboring Bay cities.
Workers commute from as far away as Sacramento and San Jose.
Noncommuters are housed in barracks and emergency dwellings
sprawled all over the dusty hills surrounding Vallejo. Rows and

rows of new buildings file up and down the undulating landscape. They look like cookie boxes with holes punched in them.

On sidings, in special clearings, behind billboards—wherever
room can be found—trailers are bunched together like frightened
beetles.

Vallejo, "The Naval City," and Richmond, with its petroleum
industry and shipyards, have caught the main overflow of new
war worker residents. Normal suburban towns before the emergency, they now operate on a stepped-up 24-hour schedule.
Rippling rayon banners around movie houses announce, "Open
all night." Workers give parties by the shift. Bands frequently
begin to play at five and six o'clock in the morning.

Old sections of Vallejo's main street, usually quiet at night,
now twinkle with lights and entertainment. Jeeps piled high with
sailors and soldiers go roaring up the street, as civilians crowd
and cheer—and try to get on, too. New restaurants and hot-dog
stands along the highway advertise the boom.

.   .   .   .

San Francisco's crowded Chinatown has changed since Pearl
Harbor. On the surface this is hardly noticeable. . . .

The clacking of the abacus where accounts are being added;
the windows filled with carved teak and ivory, silks and jade,
candied ginger, coconut shreds, and lichee nuts; fish shops of incredible variety and aroma; little Chinese women in black trousers and soft slippers; old men in skullcaps and long coats—all
these remain.

But underneath the old familiar scenes there have been far-
reaching changes. Traditions have gone overboard with the rise
of a new wartime generation.

Some six thousand men have left their old jobs in Chinatown
to go into shipyards. . . .

As for the armed services, more than three thousand boys from
Chinatown have either been called up or have enlisted, and about
three-fourths of the colony's doctors and dentists are on their
way. . . .

International colonies have been part of San Francisco since
the first windjammers raked in through the Golden Gate. It does

not surprise a San Franciscan even now to turn his radio to an Italian program and hear men of an enemy tongue selling bonds for American defense. . . .

The impassioned loyalty of many local Italian leaders to the war cause has made a good impression on the city. They have worked unsparingly to see that there would be no doubt as to the sympathies of their people.

War work, hospitality work, volunteer service work, and a wartime city at play have made changes in San Francisco's old way of life. Business is not going on as usual.

The Government in its decentralization plan has sent many important war boards and agencies to this area. Bring in 250,000 people as a resident war population, and watch the natives warm up for action. Tell the tourist to "See California *after* the War!" and notice the transformation in a land which in one year absorbed $200,000,000 in transient trade.

The problem now is to keep everyone away from San Francisco who hasn't a direct connection with the war effort. Railroads plead with people not to waste space, not to expect the usual service, not to come at all unless they have to.

Change and no change. San Francisco is the same enchanting thing it ever was.

Stand on Telegraph Hill, from where, when the city was young, men used to semaphore the approach of a ship through the Golden Gate. Feel the clean coolness of the sea breezes salting your face, racing your heart. Catch the scents of a thousand things, for this is a city of intoxicating smells. The pungent burned-cookie odor of roasting coffee from under the west end of the Bay Bridge; the vinous scents from the wineries of the North Beach section; the yeasty tang of French and Italian bakeries; the heavy smell of chocolate from the Ghirardelli plant.

The water front sends up its full aroma of steaming lobsters and frying bass or sole. A hundred corner stands waft the fragrance of gardenias. The salty draughts of sea air mix with the scent of eucalyptus from the hills.

Here is the same tradition of things well done. Excellent food exquisitely served; symphony, concert, and opera beautifully produced; museums and art galleries unchanged by war measures, only more crowded, more alive.

Physical changes tell mainly of military restrictions.

No more Embarcadero for the civilian; no more the disorganized congress of freight trains, trucks, vans, taxies whirling in confusion along the water front. No more Kodachroming red lobsters, pink shrimps, and bronzed fisherfolk along Fisherman's Wharf. No pictures of bridges, buildings, skylines, communications, military movements, ships, supplies, natural resources.

No driving out through the Presidio along El Camino del Mar to the Palace of the Legion of Honor; you go by way of town now, perhaps past Sea Cliff with its beautiful homes boarded up or blacked-out, or frequently "For Sale." No sitting in a window at the Cliff House watching the moonlight play on huge waves breaking against Seal Rocks.

By Army proclamation everything visible from the sea has been totally blacked out and every bright light for 150 miles inland has been dimmed.

.   .   .   .

The San Franciscan is at heart a Bohemian. Though engrossed in his wartime work, he will seize every opportunity to enjoy the savor of life—to watch the passing show.

He can, and does, still dine in the tradition of almost any country. As whim dictates, he may stop for a cocktail of tiny shrimps at Fisherman's Wharf, then cross the Bay to Trader Vic's for a *Tiare Tahiti* and sweet-and-sour spareribs served in a Polynesian bamboo garden.

He may stand on a quiet street and listen to the familiar whir of cables running under his feet—or travel by one of them to the top of a steep hill just to watch the rippling panorama of the city swaying under its myriad banners.

Here flags fly from the tops of buildings more often than from the fronts. The land of constant breezes keeps them always unfurled.

The San Franciscan who knows and loves these things may still listen for the evening Angelus or the noon bells from St. Patrick's; but now the chimes which once played only religious hymns ring out with "From the Halls of Montezuma."

He may drive out to Coit Tower for the exhilarating view of sea and bay. But instead of looking down on a yacht basin preparing for a regatta, he sees a water front charged with the complicated activities of war.

He watches heavy, self-possessed ships plying a bay that is restless, fitful, wary of the strange things that have been done to her, the strange nets strung over her, the strange craft that ride her.

He looks up to see a sharp, startling skyline suddenly fade into the softness of a tulled fog, a shaft of sunlight break through the white bank and strike down to great blue warships lying motionless on a gray bay. He sees the contrast of peace and war.

Yet these are but the froth and sparkle and battle raiment of San Francisco at war. It is the deeper spirit of the city which defies definition and is the real birthright of her sons.

It is the very greatness of her that has caused the West and the Far East, perhaps the whole world, to look this way and wonder what will happen to Frémont's beautiful "Chrysopylae"—to this Golden Gate which has always been the symbol of the Setting Sun.

Part Eight

<hr>

Cities of Today

<hr>

37 Society and Community in Boston in the 1940's

Rarely does a social scientist capture the historic flavor and significance of parts of a great city as does Walter Firey, Professor of Sociology at the University of Texas, in this selection. The 1940 census just before this study was made reported the city of Boston as having 770,816 people. In the decade of the 1940's the city's population increased by only 31,000, and the census of 1960 showed the city with a decrease of 13 per cent from the population of 1950, slipping to 697,197. Since there was concurrently a rise in the population of the surrounding towns outside the central city, Boston demonstrated the post-World War II "flight to the suburbs" as did many another American city.

On the development of modern Boston see Sam B. Warner, Jr., *Streetcar Suburbs: The Process of Growth in Boston, 1870–1900* (Cambridge, 1962); and W. M. Whitehill, *Boston: A Topographical History* (Cambridge, 1959), chs. VI–VIII.

BEACON HILL. After mentioning the various notables who have lived on Beacon Hill one resident concludes: "Indeed, nearly

WALTER L. FIREY, JR., *Land Use in Central Boston* (Cambridge, Massachusetts: Harvard University Press, Copyright, 1947, by The President and Fellows of Harvard College), 96–100, 102–104, 106–109, 111–112, 114–115, 263, 267–271, 314–317, 320. Reprinted by permission of the publishers.

every house on the Hill has some precious association with letters
or art." [1] That these are genuine expressions of sentiments, which
truly enter into the motivation of certain people to seek residence
on the Hill, is disclosed in remarks made by a few of the older
residents. Generally these persons do not "wear their hearts upon
their sleeves" and frank, affective statements are not easy to
get. One lady, prominent in the Beacon Hill Association, and
whose forebears as well as some contemporary relatives also lived
on the Hill, spoke with pride of the rooms she occupied. In her
words: "I like living here for I like to think that a great deal of
historic interest has happened here in this room." [2] Other residents
pointed with pride to their Bulfinch staircases, or to their faded
purple window panes,[3] and in other ways revealed the values
which they attach to their homes. In a very real sense such values
are "motives" which have, along with other considerations,
prompted the people who share them to maintain residence on
Beacon Hill. The expressive function of living in a symbolically
significant area is particularly evident in cases of this sort.

It is a point of pride to a Beacon Hill resident if he can boast
that he was born on the Hill or at least grew up there. An even
greater prestige attaches to a continuity of family residence in the
neighborhood. Even today several descendants of the families
who originally developed the Hill continue to live there. . . . [4]

Not only do several residents of the Hill . . . have a continuity of local pedigree, but many of the dwellings have their

[1] *Abbie Farwell Brown*, *"Beacons Still on Beacon Hill,"* Christian Science
Monitor, *December 23, 1922.*

[2] *Miss Marian C. Nichols, of Mount Vernon street.*

[3] *These purple panes possess a special significance, since they were made of
glass shipped from England early in the 1800's. Owing to defects the
glass turned purple in the course of a few years. These purple panes have
become symbols of the venerability of certain houses and are a point of
pride to the occupants of those dwellings. Some residents have put artificial purple panes in their windows, but these are known to all old
residents and antiquarians for what they are and they possess none of the
symbolic significance of the "real" purple panes. The phenomenon, triv-
ial as it may seem, reveals rather well the purely symbolic, non-intrinsic
character of the meanings which certain aspects of Beacon Hill and its
residences possess.*

[4] *Allen Chamberlain*, Beacon Hill, its Ancient Pastures and Early Mansions
(*Boston: 1925*), *p. 5.*

own "pedigrees," and this is a matter of great pride to the occupants of such houses. As one writer puts it: "Hardly a site but
has its legend, whether it be a stately mansion with courtyard
and fountain, or a drab boarding-house soon to be reclaimed." [5]
This is no fortuitous phenomenon confined to Beacon Hill but
is part of a pattern typical of upper class Yankee families elsewhere in New England. In a study of Newburyport, Massachusetts, Warner and Lunt found that certain dwellings, occupied by upper class families and symbolizing the status of their
occupants, possessed their own "lineages." Such houses were pervaded by "the spiritual presence of the ancestors" and as such
linked their occupants with sacred traditions and memories of
the past.[6] A very large proportion of Beacon Hill houses possess
such lineages, and they bestow a corresponding status upon
whatever families currently live in them. One house is known as
the Otis House, another as the Charles Francis Adams House,
another as the Alcott House—not that families having those names
now reside in them, but simply that the memory of earlier
notables has become identified with and symbolized by the houses
they once occupied. . . .

Sometimes young couples of good family but for the time
being living on a shoestring will rent moderately priced apartments in converted Beacon Hill houses. Thus, without too great
expense to themselves they are able to live in a socially acceptable
neighborhood and thereby symbolize their class position. . . .
Apart from these types of residents there are not a few elderly
spinsters, frequently living on depleted patrimonies, who maintain residence on Beacon Hill primarily because their home was
a part of their inheritance and they could ill afford to live anywhere else. Yet another group of upper class families use their
Beacon Hill homes only as winter domiciles, spending the rest of
the year on their suburban or country estates. Finally, as we have
already indicated, there is on Beacon Hill a large population of
clerical workers, both single and newly married. Such people are
above all interested in inexpensive living quarters that are accessible to their places of work. Rational considerations thus pre-

[5] *Abbie Farwell Brown,* The Lights of Beacon Hill, *p. 11.*
[6] *W. Lloyd Warner and Paul S. Lunt,* The Social Life of a Modern Community *(New Haven: 1941), p. 107.*

ponderate in their choice of a neighborhood in which to live. Yet, even among this group there is a surprisingly real appreciation of the "reputation" enjoyed by Beacon Hill. As one young married woman observed: "For young people who are working it's quite the thing to live on Beacon Hill—especially for girls." Office girls who reside on the Hill feel a certain distinction through living there. They are also able to enhance their popularity on such occasions as the Christmas Eve Carols when they may hold open house for their friends.

.   .   .   .

There exists with reference to Beacon Hill a "cultural system" in the strict sense of the term. Far from making up just a bunch of unrelated sentiments, the values that have their focus in Beacon Hill form an integrated system with its core being an aesthetic-historical-genealogical complex. Needless to say, such an integration is a purely subjective thing and the component ends would lose their togetherness if people ceased holding to the value system in question. . . .

Is there a "social system" on Beacon Hill of greater inclusiveness than individual families, which is organized in terms of the spatially referred values we have been discussing? Is Beacon Hill a *real* community or is it merely a *nominal* one, in the technical sense of these terms? [7]

The problem can be best approached by noting, first, who live on Beacon Hill, and second, how they have become organized. To begin with, the dominant class on the Hill, though not the most numerous—is the old stock Yankee aristocracy. Membership in this class is primarily a matter of birth, and presupposes several generations of upper class forebears in one's family. Despite the displacements following upon the rise of Irish and of non-Bostonian Yankee elements, the old families—the Lowells, Amorys, Frothinghams, Forbeses, Hemenways, Adams', Coolidges, etc.—still retain positions of authority in financial, educational, artistic, and welfare organizations.[8] Among them wealth is not of

[7] *For the establishment and analysis of these concepts see Carle C. Zimmerman,* The Changing Community (*New York: 1938*), *Prologue and chaps. i, vii.*

[8] *Lucius Beebe,* Boston and the Boston Legend (*New York: 1935*), *p. 256.*

primary significance, and there is a goodly number of Beacon Hill elite who are in straitened financial circumstances. The principal function of wealth for them is one of facilitating the actions deemed proper to one of upper class standing.[9] Immediately below this upper stratum of the social pyramid is a sizable population of *nouveaus*—families of respectable qualities and financial affluence, but lacking in proper genealogical qualifications. Together these two strata comprise the "center of gravity" for the values attaching to Beacon Hill.

The upper class thus defined has certain important demographic characteristics which condition the nature of its neighborhood organization. These are as follows: (a) a sex ratio that is unbalanced on the female side; (b) an atypically middle aged population, with a paucity of children; and (c) a large proportion of unmarried women.[10] . . . Only 4.85 per cent of the total population on the Hill is under 15 years of age, compared with 21.38 per cent for Boston as a whole. Equally clear is the preponderance of females at every single age group, the ratio as a whole being 184 women per 100 men. A point not quite so evident without some explanation is the middle age character of the population. To anyone who is familiar with Beacon Hill it will be obvious that the large proportion of persons between 20 and 29 years of age is attributable to the clerical population. Were it not for them the middle age character of the upper class population would be even more evident. . . . Regarding the third demographic characteristic in question there are unfortunately no statistical data available on the marital status of the upper class population of Beacon Hill. There is only the commonplace observation, well testified by direct observations, that "half the aristocratic old maids in Boston live here." [11] Spinsterhood is a phenomenon that typifies upper class Yankee stock in a good many New England communities. . . .

Demographically, then, the dominant group on Beacon Hill is atypically female and middle aged, with a large proportion of childless families and unmarried women. Such a population com-

[9] Cf. *Warner and Lunt, op. cit., pp. 82–83, 98–99.*

[10] *Ibid., pp. 422–423, on the generality of these characteristics in the upper class Yankee stock.*

[11] *Eleanor Early,* And This is Boston! *(Boston: 1938), p. 53.*

position cannot but have its effects upon the nature of neighborhood activities. Perhaps it is not too far fetched to suggest that the
strength of the affect which certain residents have toward the
Hill reflects a sublimation of emotions that have not found their
usual release through marriage and child-rearing. There is a decidedly "feminine" character to organized neighborhood activities on Beacon Hill, if by such a hazy term one means the expectations which generally attach to the woman's role in American
culture. It is something that can hardly be verified by scientific
methods, but which has been painted with artistic subtlety by such
novelists as John Marquand and Anna Farquhar in their stories
about Boston's upper class.[12]

Occupationally the population of Beacon Hill falls into voca-
tions which carry social prestige. . . . The most striking feature
of this make-up is of course the prominence of professional workers on the Hill. A good many of these are lawyers who have
specialized in investment banking, corporation law, and the administration of trusts and estates. Some of them have nearly a full
time job in handling their own inherited investments. All these
positions carry with them authority and prestige and are considered proper callings for upper class men on Beacon Hill and
elsewhere in Boston. No less evident . . . is the negligible proportion of workers on Beacon Hill—whether craftsmen and fore-
men, or operatives and laborers. The only exception to this, and
it is a conspicuous one, is the high proportion of domestic service
workers, almost all women. As indicated earlier in this chapter,
these domestic workers are generally attached to family house-
holds and their residence on Beacon Hill is thus a consequence
of their identification with the upper class.

.   .   .   .

The informal organizations on Beacon Hill center mainly
around kinship ties and visiting relationships. Long inbreeding
within Boston's upper class has led to a complex network of blood
relationships by which each person is related to almost every
other person in the class. These kinship ties go far to determine

[12] See John P. Marquand, The Late George Apley (New York: 1940) or
H. M. Pulham, esquire (Boston: 1941); Anna Farquhar, Her Boston Experiences (Boston: 1900).

one's choice of a mate, one's occupation,[13] the schools one attends, the clubs to which one can gain admittance, and many other aspects of one's life. Needless to say these relationships are not confined to Beacon Hill; this neighborhood is but one locale for "proper" families, and kinship ties extend over the whole Boston metropolitan area. Nonetheless Beacon Hill is the home base for a good many of these families and nearly every member of the upper class will have some relative living on the Hill. Visiting relationships not primarily familial in nature are based upon years of friendship, commonly extending back to childhood. In the past years more so than today they were routinized in the form of afternoon teas, neighbor-clubs, and the like. Even today among some of the older people these observances still hold. Somewhat more formal than the kinship and visiting relationships, but still of a functionally diffuse character, are the exclusive clubs. The Somerset Club, the Union Club, the Puritan Club, and the Algonquin Club are Boston's most exclusive "social" clubs and membership in them is confined to men in upper class families. Again, these organizations go beyond the limited area of Beacon Hill, but nonetheless they are foci for Beacon Hill social interaction and they really do manifest that area's organizational activity.

Of a less routine and intimate nature, but nonetheless comprising informal organizational activities are certain annual ceremonies on Beacon Hill. The principal one of these is [14] the annual Christmas eve candle-lighting and caroling ceremony.

. . . .

Turning to formal organization we find only one association which represents the more specialized interests of Beacon Hill residents as a whole. This is the Beacon Hill Association. Formed on December 5, 1922, the declared object of this organization is

[13] *Consider the expectations which must be imposed upon young men of such families as the Homans' and the Cheevers, who have each had four generations of physicians in their families, the Shattucks, who have had five generations of physicians, and the Porters, who have had physicians in their family ever since the seventeenth century. "Boston Proud of its Surgical Hierarchy," Boston Transcript, July 24, 1930.*

[14] *Or was, until 1940, when the custom was suspended for at least the duration of the war.*

"to keep undesirable business and living conditions from affecting the hill district." [15] Its membership is for the most part confined to property owners on the Hill, and its officers have all been prominent citizens of the neighborhood. The activities of the Association have had profound implications for land use on the Hill. . . .

In addition to the Beacon Hill Association there is the smaller association of Louisburg Square proprietors, consisting of the owners of property abutting Louisburg Square. This association dates from 1844, when the property owners of the Square decided to enlarge and ornament the oval plot in front of their houses and agreed mutually to bear the necessary expenses. Later the association assumed the task of perpetuating the proprietors' collective legal rights to the Square by prohibiting public trespass. In this way it aimed at preventing the establishment of public rights to the Square through uncontested use.[16] The proprietors employ a caretaker to tend the Square and hold annual meetings for the purpose of electing officers. All purchasers of Louisburg Square property are bound by contract to share in the expenses of upkeep and maintenance. A majority vote of those present at any duly summoned meeting is binding upon all the owners.

These organizations, both formal and informal, make of Beacon Hill something more than an aggregate of disparate families. Through them the neighborhood becomes a real community having an identity of its own. . . .

.   .   .   .

The main fact which presents itself is the capacity of Beacon Hill to retain its fashionable reputation and a large share of Boston's upper class families for one and a half centuries, while other fashionable areas have risen to favor and then declined. Beacon Hill was well established as a preferred residential neighborhood by 1805. Today it still has the same preferred character. In the meantime fully six other areas in Boston have been developed as fashionable neighborhoods, have enjoyed favor for a while, and have then declined. Fort Hill, which rose to popularity almost

[15] Boston Transcript, *December 6, 1922.*
[16] *Chamberlain,* Beacon Hill, its Ancient Pastures and Early Mansions, *pp. 191–200.*

contemporaneously with Beacon Hill, had become a slum by 1855. Pemberton square, developed slightly after Beacon Hill, was converted to public and business uses by the Civil War. Temple Place, Colonnade Row, and the Summer-Winter street area, once comprising the largest fashionable district in point of numbers, lasted little more than a generation. The South End's fashionable reputation was of even shorter duration, extending approximately from 1850 to 1865. The Back Bay and Jamaica Plain present a slightly different situation. Both of these neighbor-hoods retain even today some of their fashionable character. Their prestige is waning rapidly however. The Back Bay in particular, though still surpassing in numbers any other single neighborhood, has undergone a steady invasion of apartment buildings, rooming houses, and business establishments which are destroying its aristo-cratic character. Jamaica Plain, on the other hand, has undergone what might be called a succession of elites. While the old stock Yankee elite have been gradually deserting the neighborhood, the "lace curtain" Irish, consisting of professionals, building con-tractors, public officials, and the like, have been replacing them. It is not quite accurate, then, to compare Jamaica Plain's decline with that of the other districts since in all strictness there has been only a change in fashionable occupancy. The fact remains, however, that through all these successions of land use only one neighborhood, namely, Beacon Hill, has consistently retained the kind of land use with which it originally began. In the mean-time the city of Boston has grown entirely around it, a slum directly abuts it to the north, and business has threatened two of its sides. . . .

.   .   .   .

THE BACK BAY. . . . In common usage it extends beyond Massa-chusetts avenue to include Bay State road and even the Fens district. So far as our immediate problem is concerned it has seemed advisable to delineate the Back Bay in terms of the area occupied by families listed in the Boston *Social Register*. For of all the residential quarters in Boston the Back Bay has been gen-erally known as the fashionable district *par excellence*. At one time it was the home of nearly one-half the *Social Registerites* in Boston. Even today, after forty years of decline, the Back Bay accounts for one out of every five entries in the *Social Register. . . .*

Within the Back Bay proper there is a differential valuation of streets which has its origin in the very beginning of the district during the 1860's. According to Boston lore, Beacon street has been occupied by people who have both "family" and money; Marlborough has been occupied by people with "family" but no money; and Commonwealth avenue has been the choice of people with money but no "family." . . .

.   .   .   .

The *Back Bay Ledger and Beacon Hill Times* confidently asserts that: "Without a question people concede that Back Bay is the cultural center of New England." [17] In truth the Back Bay is indeed the seat of a great concatenation of religious, educational, artistic, medical, and other such associations. To begin with, some of the most expensive church buildings in the city of Boston are located there. . . . All of these were built during the latter part of the nineteenth century or the early part of the present century while the Back Bay was at the peak of its aristocratic development. In addition to the churches there are schools, both public and private. . . . Libraries, museums, and auditoriums are located throughout the Back Bay, notably the Boston Public Library, Symphony Hall, the Opera House, the Horticultural Hall, the Museum of Natural History, Museum of Fine Arts, and the Gardner Museum. Finally, though not located in the Back Bay proper but nonetheless connected with it through meaningful association, are the hospitals around Brookline and Longwood avenues. Principal among these are Peter Bent Brigham, Collins Memorial, Huntington Memorial, Beth Israel, and the Children's Hospital.[18]

Intrinsically perhaps there is very little in common between the functions which these different associations perform. But in terms of the values which attach to present-day occupations there is a distinct meaningful congruence between schools, churches, hospitals, and museums. This meaningful congruence arises out

---

[17] Back Bay Ledger and Beacon Hill Times, *February 27, 1941.*

[18] *For an ecological analysis of this Back Bay "cultural" center see Richard E. DuWors, "The Dominant Educational Area of Boston" (MS), 1937.*

of the professional character of the functionaries in such associations. The clergyman, the doctor, the teacher, and the museum supervisor are all persons who have been trained to a high degree of technical competence and they have all been versed in a generalized intellectual tradition.[19] The associations which are staffed by such functionaries partake of the same prestige value that attaches to the professional role in modern society. . . . Today, in the face of waning prestige value, the Back Bay finds itself bolstered up by the presence of distinctly professionalized social systems within its borders. Through this reinforcement it still maintains a semblance of its one-time prestige value. . . .

Nearly twenty per cent of Boston's upper class families continue to live in this one district. Old Boston names like Cabot, Sears, Sprague, Forbes, and Frothingham may still be found on Beacon street, Marlborough street, and Commonwealth avenue. In terms of occupational structure the Back Bay is unmistakably upper class. . . .

There can, however, be no denial that the Back Bay has changed. Today there are less than half as many upper class families in the area as there were forty years ago. The buildings themselves have considerably deteriorated; 14 per cent of them are eighty or more years old, and 68 per cent are forty or more years old.[20] Twenty-six per cent of the dwellings have become multi-family residences or rooming houses and 16 per cent of them are large apartment buildings.[21] These trends reflect the change which tastes in housing and place of residence have undergone during the past fifty years. The late nineteenth century vogue of swell-front or brown-stone front houses extending continuously along tree-lined thoroughfares that lead to the city center has long since been superseded by the vogue of single-family dwellings, with yards, located in "bedroom towns" surrounding the city proper. It is little wonder that upper class families have been deserting the Back Bay and other intown districts (excepting Beacon Hill) and have relocated in fashionable sub-

[19] *These differentia of professionalism have been formulated by Professor Talcott Parsons.*

[20] *The Finance Commission of the City of Boston*, A Study of Certain of the Effects of Decentralization on Boston and Some Neighboring Cities and Towns (*Boston: 1941*), *p. 11.*

[21] *Computed from data in* loc. cit.

urban towns like Newton, Milton, Weston, and remoter communities.

.   .   .   .

THE SOUTH END. One finds in the South End of Boston a population distinguished by its social isolation, its transiency, and its
poverty. . . . The reasons for this state of affairs in the South
End are not hard to find. Life in a rooming house is utterly devoid
of companionship and intimacy. One's fellow tenants are forever
on the move, remaining in one place for a few weeks or months
and then finding a room with better heat or lower rent and
moving away. The constant succession of new roomers makes
social distance and mutual suspicion almost a necessity if one
would not run the risk of theft or personal abuse. The hetero-
geneity of ages, the absence of family identification by which to
"legitimize" one's self, the diversity of ethnic, occupational, and
religious affiliations, and the lack of any "stake" in the local area
—all of these factors prevent any solidarization of personal relationships. Even the landlords and landladies themselves are highly
mobile. Many of them own their homes on a mortgage and are
often unable to meet their obligations. Real estate speculators
have sometimes deliberately "arranged" foreclosures after a land-
lady has paid off a good deal of her mortgage, by steering roomers away from her house or by removing phony roomers that had
been placed there when she made her first payment. Under such
conditions even the landladies constitute an unstable and mobile
element in the South End's population.

The kinds of associations which are attracted to such an area
are even more disintegrative of solidarity. Cheap cafeterias, usually
serving liquor, locate along the main avenues of population flow.
Gambling joints, taverns, variety stores, and other such establishments develop to serve the recreational tastes of the population. In such places one can play the slot machines, buy "numbers," meet women of dubious character, and otherwise engage
in activities that are morally censurable by the scale of values of
the larger society. In the absence of durable personal relationships
there are few sanctions short of legal coercion that may be
brought to bear upon the amoral person. His anonymity and isolation give him an immunity from the moral controls which

operate in "real" communities, such as gossip, ridicule, ostracism, and the like. In the absence of any rewards for proper behavior there is an actual weakening of moral inhibitions and an atrophy of conceptions of right and wrong. Such norms, however well rooted they may have been in individual consciousnesses, tend to deteriorate when the individual is removed from the social context of reward, punishment, and reinforcement in which they were originally defined. It is not surprising then that "the problem of furnished rooms has long been connected with the city problems of vice and immorality." [22]

Let us consider in a little more detail some of the manifestations of this localized anomie. On the whole the South End is one of Boston's major areas of vice and crime. Police squad cars and patrol wagons are ubiquitous features of the South End's landscape. The majority of Boston's "career criminals" live in either the South End or the West End. Petty pilfering, theft from rooms, street brawling, packrolling, narcotic peddling, and prostitution are typical of the illegal activities which characterize the area. These offenses are for the most part by mature men. Juvenile delinquency, while rather high, is not so great as in the West End or even in the North End. . . . Now the unique thing about much of the amoral activity which pervades the South End is that it is engaged in by people who live in other parts of Boston. By virtue of its atomization and anonymity the South End provides a refuge for persons who wish to engage in activities that are legally or morally prohibited in their own communities. This is particularly true of juvenile offenders. Youths who are "looking for a thrill" readily gravitate to the South End where they can escape detection and perhaps pass as adults. . . .

Associational patterns such as these would be inconceivable in a community characterized by solidarity and moral consensus. It is significant that in the North End, where the objective physical setting of the community is far worse than in the South End, violations of morals laws are very few in number. There the identification of Italians with an integrated value system, and the solidarity which such persons have toward local Italian associations, utterly precludes the moral license which characterizes

[22] *Edith Abbott*, The Tenements of Chicago, *1908–1935* (*Chicago: 1936*), p. 324.

the South End. Slum conditions as such are not responsible for amoral activity. Rather it is the socio-economic character of a community—its age and sex composition, its marital status, income level, and population stability—that most tangibly correlates with cultural anomie and its amoral consequences. And this socio-economic make-up is conditioned upon an historically unique structuring of kinship and occupational relations without which there would not even exist a rooming house area with its anonymity, transiency, and poverty.

38   The Problems and Delights of New York City

Many of the problems and joys of life in New York City are shared by the residents of other cities. New Yorkers, however, have long felt that theirs is a unique city. Two views of modern New York are given here: one by the brilliant essayist, E. B. White, long a Manhattan resident, and the other by Robert Moses who has done more to shape the development of the metropolitan New York area than any other man in our day. See Cleveland Rogers and Rebecca Rankin, *New York: The World's Capital City* (New York, 1948), ch. 26.

The census of 1960 gave greater New York City a population of 7,781,984. For a description of the city's newest residents and their problems see Oscar Handlin, *The Newcomers: Negroes and Puerto Ricans in a Changing Metropolis* (Anchor Books, 1962), and Nathan Glazer and D. P. Moynihan, *Beyond the Melting Pot* (Cambridge, Massachusetts, 1963).

THERE ARE ROUGHLY THREE NEW YORKS. There is, first, the New York of the man or woman who was born here, who takes the city for granted and accepts its size and its turbulence as natural and inevitable. Second, there is the New York of the commuter—the city that is devoured by locusts each day and spat out each night. Third, there is the New York of the person who was born somewhere else and came to New York in quest of something. Of these three trembling cities the greatest is the last—the city of final destination, the city that is a goal. It is this third city that accounts for New York's highstrung disposition, its poetical deportment, its dedication to the arts, and its incomparable achievements. Commuters give the city its tidal restlessness; natives give it solidity and continuity; but the settlers give it passion. And whether it is a farmer arriving from Italy to set up a small grocery store in a slum, or a young girl arriving from a small town in Mississippi to escape the indignity of being observed by her neighbors, or a boy arriving from the Corn Belt with a manuscript in his suitcase and a pain in his heart, it makes no difference: each embraces New York with the intense excitement of first love, each absorbs New York with the fresh eyes of an adventurer, each generates heat and light to dwarf the Consolidated Edison Company.

The commuter is the queerest bird of all. The suburb he inhabits has no essential vitality of its own and is a mere roost where he comes at day's end to go to sleep. Except in rare cases, the man who lives in Mamaroneck or Little Neck or Teaneck, and works in New York, discovers nothing much about the city except the time of arrival and departure of trains and buses, and the path to a quick lunch. He is desk-bound, and has never, idly roaming in the gloaming, stumbled suddenly on Belvedere Tower in the Park, seen the ramparts rise sheer from the water of the pond, and the boys along the shore fishing for minnows, girls stretched out negligently on the shelves of the rocks; he has never come suddenly on anything at all in New York as a loiterer, because he has had no time between trains. He has fished in Manhattan's wallet and dug out coins, but has never listened to Manhattan's breathing, never awakened to its morning, never dropped off to sleep in its night. About 400,000 men and women come charging onto the Island each week-day morning, out of the

E. B. WHITE, *Here is New York* (New York, 1949), 17–29. Copyright 1949 by The Curtis Publishing Company. Reprinted with the permission of Harper & Row, Inc.

mouths of tubes and tunnels. Not many among them have ever
spent a drowsy afternoon in the great rustling oaken silence of
the reading room of the Public Library, with the book elevator
(like an old water wheel) spewing out books onto the trays. They
tend their furnaces in Westchester and in Jersey, but have never
seen the furnaces of the Bowery, the fires that burn in oil drums
on zero winter nights. They may work in the financial district
downtown and never see the extravagant plantings of Rocke-
feller Center—the daffodils and grape hyacinths and birches and
the flags trimmed to the wind on a fine morning in spring. Or
they may work in a midtown office and may let a whole year
swing round without sighting Governors Island from the sea
wall. The commuter dies with tremendous mileage to his credit,
but he is no rover. His entrances and exits are more devious than
those in a prairie-dog village; and he calmly plays bridge while
buried in the mud at the bottom of the East River. The Long
Island Rail Road alone carried forty million commuters last year;
but many of them were the same fellow retracing his steps.

The terrain of New York is such that a resident sometimes
travels farther, in the end, than a commuter. Irving Berlin's journey from Cherry Street in the lower East Side to an apartment
uptown was through an alley and was only three or four miles in
length; but it was like going three times around the world.

A poem compresses much in a small space and adds music, thus
heightening its meaning. The city is like poetry: it compresses all
life, all races and breeds, into a small island and adds music and
the accompaniment of internal engines. The island of Manhattan
is without any doubt the greatest human concentrate on earth,
the poem whose magic is comprehensible to millions of permanent
residents but whose full meaning will always remain illusive. At
the feet of the tallest and plushiest offices lie the crummiest slums.
The genteel mysteries housed in the Riverside Church are only a
few blocks from the voodoo charms of Harlem. The merchant
princes, riding to Wall Street in their limousines down the East
River Drive, pass within a few hundred yards of the gypsy kings;
but the princes do not know they are passing kings, and the kings
are not up yet anyway—they live a more leisurely life than the
princes and get drunk more consistently.

New York is nothing like Paris; it is nothing like London; and

it is not Spokane multiplied by sixty, or Detroit multiplied by
four. It is by all odds the loftiest of cities. It even managed to
reach the highest point in the sky at the lowest moment of the
depression. The Empire State Building shot twelve hundred and
fifty feet into the air when it was madness to put out as much as
six inches of new growth. (The building has a mooring mast that
no dirigible has ever tied to; it employs a man to flush toilets in
slack times; it has been hit by an airplane in a fog, struck countless times by lightning, and been jumped off of by so many unhappy people that pedestrians instinctively quicken step when
passing Fifth Avenue and 34th Street.)

Manhattan has been compelled to expand skyward because of
the absence of any other direction in which to grow. This, more
than any other thing, is responsible for its physical majesty. It is
to the nation what the white church spire is to the village—the
visible symbol of aspiration and faith, the white plume saying
that the way is up. The summer traveler swings in over Hell Gate
Bridge and from the window of his sleeping car as it glides above
the pigeon lofts and back yards of Queens looks southwest to
where the morning light first strikes the steel peaks of midtown,
and he sees its upward thrust unmistakable: the great walls and
towers rising, the smoke rising, the heat not yet rising, the hopes
and ferments of so many awakening millions rising—this vigorous spear that presses heaven hard.

It is a miracle that New York works at all. The whole thing is
implausible. Every time the residents brush their teeth, millions of
gallons of water must be drawn from the Catskills and the hills of
Westchester. When a young man in Manhattan writes a letter to
his girl in Brooklyn, the love message gets blown to her through a
pneumatic tube—*pfft*—just like that. The subterranean system
of telephone cables, power lines, steam pipes, gas mains and sewer
pipes is reason enough to abandon the island to the gods and the
weevils. Every time an incision is made in the pavement, the
noisy surgeons expose ganglia that are tangled beyond belief. By
rights New York should have destroyed itself long ago, from
panic or fire or rioting or failure of some vital supply line in its
circulatory system or from some deep labyrinthine short circuit. Long ago the city should have experienced an insoluble
traffic snarl at some impossible bottleneck. It should have perished

of hunger when food lines failed for a few days. It should have been wiped out by a plague starting in its slums or carried in by ships' rats. It should have been overwhelmed by the sea that licks at it on every side. The workers in its myriad cells should have succumbed to nerves, from the fearful pall of smoke-fog that drifts over every few days from Jersey, blotting out all light at noon and leaving the high offices suspended, men groping and depressed, and the sense of world's end. It should have been touched in the head by the August heat and gone off its rocker.

Mass hysteria is a terrible force, yet New Yorkers seem always to escape it by some tiny margin; they sit in stalled subways without claustrophobia, they extricate themselves from panic situations by some lucky wisecrack, they meet confusion and congestion with patience and grit—a sort of perpetual muddling through. Every facility is inadequate—the hospitals and schools and playgrounds are overcrowded, the express highways are feverish, the unimproved highways and bridges are bottlenecks; there is not enough air and not enough light, and there is usually either too much heat or too little. But the city makes up for its hazards and its deficiencies by supplying its citizens with massive doses of a supplementary vitamin—the sense of belonging to something unique, cosmopolitan, mighty and unparalleled.

To an outlander a stay in New York can be and often is a series of small embarrassments and discomforts and disappointments: not understanding the waiter, not being able to distinguish between a sucker joint and a friendly saloon, riding the wrong subway, being slapped down by a bus driver for asking an innocent question, enduring sleepless nights when the street noises fill the bedroom. Tourists make for New York, particularly in summertime—they swarm all over the Statue of Liberty (where many a resident of the town has never set foot), they invade the Automat, visit radio studios, St. Patrick's Cathedral, and they window shop. Mostly they have a pretty good time. But sometimes in New York you run across the disillusioned —a young couple who are obviously visitors, newlyweds perhaps, for whom the bright dream has vanished. The place has been too much for them; they sit languishing in a cheap restaurant over a speechless meal.

The oft-quoted thumbnail sketch of New York is, of course: "It's a wonderful place, but I'd hate to live there." I have an idea that people from villages and small towns, people accustomed to the convenience and the friendliness of neighborhood over-the-fence living, are unaware that life in New York follows the neighborhood pattern. The city is literally a composite of tens of thousands of tiny neighborhood units. There are, of course, the big districts and big units: Chelsea and Murray Hill and Gramercy (which are residential units), Harlem (a racial unit), Greenwich Village (a unit dedicated to the arts and other matters), and there is Radio City (a commercial development), Peter Cooper Village (a housing unit), the Medical Center (a sickness unit) and many other sections each of which has some distinguishing characteristic. But the curious thing about New York is that each large geographical unit is composed of countless small neighborhoods. Each neighborhood is virtually self-sufficient. Usually it is no more than two or three blocks long and a couple of blocks wide. Each area is a city within a city within a city. Thus, no matter where you live in New York, you will find within a block or two a grocery store, a barbershop, a newsstand and shoeshine shack, an ice-coal-and-wood cellar (where you write your order on a pad outside as you walk by), a dry cleaner, a laundry, a delicatessen (beer and sandwiches delivered at any hour to your door), a flower shop, an undertaker's parlor, a movie house, a radio-repair shop, a stationer, a haberdasher, a tailor, a drugstore, a garage, a tearoom, a saloon, a hardware store, a liquor store, a shoe-repair shop. Every block or two, in most residential sections of New York, is a little main street.

UNFORTUNATELY THERE ARE STILL PEOPLE IN OTHER AREAS WHO REGARD NEW YORK CITY NOT AS PART OF THE UNITED STATES, but as a sort of excrescence fastened to our eastern shore and peopled by the less venturesome waves of foreigners who failed

ROBERT MOSES, *Working for the People* (New York, 1956), 74–78, 80–82. Reprinted with the permission of the author. Published by Harper & Row.

to go west to the genuine American frontier. We have had a bad press in the hinterland, and New York has the dubious distinction of leading the nation in exaggerating and dramatizing its deficiencies. . . .

New York and other American municipalities have made the most extraordinary and inexplicable efforts to foul their own nests. We are lucky indeed that discriminating people in other countries see us in truer perspectives. Some of our antics are incomprehensible to others. It is well to attack scandal and crime, but at least equal attention should be given to the many signs of health and idealism in our municipalities.

.   .   .   .

A glance at a map of the greater city will show how relatively small, if not insignificant, is the Great White Way. The core of the city holds many of its greatest attractions. Without it there would be no motivating force, no concentrated high values and therefore no major revenues. But it is a mistake to assume that everything of consequence in New York is within three miles of Grand Central. What is news on the Rialto is gibberish along the Belt Parkway where, far from the frenetic hot spots of midtown, hundreds of thousands of our less advertised citizens keep the even, if not noiseless, tenor of their way.

Here are a few examples of progress in the field of municipal construction which some visitors may overlook: They should note the emerging new neighborhood patterns along the East and Harlem rivers in Manhattan—parks, parkways, housing, the United Nations headquarters, on what was until recently a shambles, reviving adjacent real estate values; the rebuilding of Astoria, across the river; the Triborough Bridge system; the Brooklyn Civic Center; Flushing Meadow Park and its burgeoning environment, with the corridors beyond it extending through Kissena and Cunningham parks to Alley Pond in Queens Borough.

Those interested in the new city that is emerging should note the vast reclamation areas in Queens, Brooklyn and Staten Island, the West Side and Henry Hudson renovations with their widespread repercussions and influences; the gradual reduction of slums in every borough; the salvaging of all of Jamaica Bay and its frontage; the great Soundview, Ferry Point, Whitestone,

Rockaway and Clearview park projects; the many constructive achievements of the Port of New York Authority; the reconstruction of our museums; new schools and hospitals and health centers; the many modern city buildings housing courts, libraries and countless other services.

We would not expect visitors to appreciate our prodigious sewage disposal systems, the pure Delaware upland water supply flowing down by gravity. Our own citizens do not fully appreciate these things or what they represent in the way of hard work on the part of little-known people in the public service. What business, industry, trade and the arts and professions have done within this framework of municipal improvements is most impressive of all.

Local critics who refer mournfully to the exodus of industry from the city talk nonsense. They never see the new plants in the southeast Bronx, trucking in Williamsburgh, and the amazing waterborne commerce of Newtown Creek and the Gowanus Canal. We have had something of a waterfront mess, but it is being cleared up and I doubt if other ambitious ports will draw away our shipping.

We are rebuilding New York, not dispersing and abandoning it. The city spreads into the suburbs, to be sure, and that, within bounds, is what should happen. The process, however, needs no speeding up. It requires no compulsion. It demands no metropolitan supergovernment by ambitious regional planners.

Those of us who have had a hand in these accomplishments are accused by captious and irresponsible mudslingers of failure to work together on a truly metropolitan basis. Committees and commissions are appointed or self-appointed to save us from insularity, narrowness and selfishness. What are the facts?

As an example of voluntary metropolitan cooperation the Port of New York Authority and the Triborough Bridge and Tunnel Authority have laid the groundwork for a vast extension of river crossings intricately meshed with the Federal, state and municipal highway pattern of the entire Atlantic seaboard. Looking up the Hudson from The Cloisters at Fort Tryon Park one may see Fort Washington and Riverside parks, the Henry Hudson Parkway and Bridge, Inwood, Spuyten Duyvil and Riverdale on one side and the New Jersey Palisades and Palisades Parkway on the other, accessible to New York as well as New Jersey, and preserved for all time by a happy combination of private philanthropy, bi-state and municipal action.

Motorists reach Jones Beach over city and state parkways, over lakes and through parks on waterworks property in Nassau County dedicated to the state by the city, and over meadow and town lands given to all the people by townships of Long Island which existed before there was a state or a nation. . . .

.   .   .   .

There is more private generosity in New York than civic spirit. Witness the widespread support of churches, hospitals, charities, welfare and education. There is philanthropy on a huge scale. But the breadwinners, large and small, are bombarded by appeals for myriads of good causes downtown, uptown, in the suburbs, in the slums, appeals in the press, through the mails, over the air. Every approach, charm, shock, lure and persuasion known to fund raising and public relations experts and to advertising salesmen trained in selling cigarettes, detergents, gadgets and nostrums are brought to bear on them. When the targets of these appeals get through selecting the claims they can afford to recognize—over and above fixed obligations and inescapable personal needs—and have tossed out the rest, there is little interest, time, energy and money left for the broader demands of citizenship. We ask the tired businessman to be serious, alert and noble when all he wants is to be relaxed and comfortable.

Among our most doleful domestic critics are representative big bankers and businessmen who solemnly warn that we shall go bust if we do not stop spending. Certainly we must balance our budgets, but economies, however essential, will not keep the total from increasing, because our needs and desires eat up the savings. We must pay taxes, tolls and rentals if we expect more and better services for a growing and ceaselessly demanding population, and if we continue to insist that the good things of life must be fairly distributed. We must work harder, loaf less and stop bellyaching about fear and want.

It is mortifying for New York City officials to have to go to Albany for state aid that is rightfully ours, but it should be even more humiliating to refuse to meet local needs locally and to have distasteful measures, which we ought to swallow without compulsion, ruthlessly rammed down our throats. There will always be disputes between acreage and people, between the big city and the widespread hinterland, between the rural and the urban point of view. We are, however, interdependent here in the Empire State and we should make a virtue of getting along. It is not possible completely to split sovereignty, and home rule, like states' rights, is a relative business. . . .

Next to the dearth of leadership in New York, our greatest handicaps are lack of legitimate pride in our accomplishments, lurid advertising of our deficiencies and difficulties, snide criticism, malicious wisecracking, gossip, controversy for its own sake and sheer ignorance of our own town. I am tired of overnight experts, with a traveling radius of two miles from Times Square, who are barely able to find the television studio where they have the effrontery to lecture on the needs of Canarsie, Mott Haven, Richmond Hill, Inwood and Mariners Harbor; of civic secretaries who throw knives from safe places in the shelter of the wings at human targets out in front on the stage, and of prominent people who lend their names to every cause which sounds grand and impressive, but do not know what they are endorsing or attacking. . . .

Admitting that we have troubles and fall short of perfection, we have done and are doing things here in New York, public, quasi-public and private, on a bigger and better scale than they are done anywhere else in this country or in any other. We have in large measure what the Communists lack and lie about. Our achievements have been phenomenal. It is acknowledged by those not blinded by prejudice. It is the envy of foreign representatives of totalitarianism who come here to scoff and rarely remain to pray.

The trouble is that none of these critics has any idea of what he wants. We must always remember that it is concentration of population which makes possible large department stores and fine shops, financial, management, trade and shipping centers, modern hospitals and clinics, the theater, the opera, the fine arts, the magnets of culture and letters, famous hotels, restaurants and cabarets, continuous athletic and sporting events, conventions and dozens of other human activities which require mass attendance. Without a core of scarce, vertically built, high-value land there is not enough to tax for the operation of city government. This is our dilemma—to keep the urban core active, magnetic and profitable, but not to let it choke us to death with mounting peak loads of traffic and people.

39 Houston's Leadership, 1954

The problems of urban planning in modern America have as much to do with men as with steel, concrete, or brick. Cities are made for people, not for machines. As Stanley Walker (1898–1962), journalist and native Texan, demonstrates through this account of Houston in the 1950's, a city must have responsible and interested leadership if it is to protect and increase its initial commercial or industrial advantages.

On modern Houston, whose population rose in the 1950's from 596,000 to 938,000, see George M. Fuermann, *Houston: Land of the Big Rich* (Garden City, New York, 1951).

THE POWERFUL CHAMBER OF COMMERCE OF HOUSTON, employing the accepted gadgets of the honest statistician, figures that on July 3 [1954] the so-called metropolitan area of Houston reached the 1,000,000 population mark. . . .

There really doesn't seem to be a foreseeable end to the growth of Houston and environs so long as the industries keep on growing and new ones keep coming in. The boosters say—and they may be right—that the 200 or so miles along the Gulf Coast which contains Houston and many other smaller but thriving stops is

STANLEY WALKER, "Houston, Texas: A 'Yes, But—' Town," *New York Times Magazine*, August 1, 1954, 16–36. Copyright by *The New York Times*. Reprinted by permission.

the richest area of its size in the world. Oil and gas, cattle and cotton, sulphur and buried beds of oyster shells, lumber and salt, sea water and rice—these are only some of the principal raw materials. On them rest the railroads, the heavy construction work, the refineries, the chemical plants, and so on.

Well, there she sits, or squats, or sprawls, or festers, or blooms, depending upon how one looks at it. The city is quite vigorous, quite messy, and full of apparent contradictions. Not even its leading residents can agree on what is good about the place and what is wrong with it. . . .

"It's a mining camp," said an old friend of mine from New York as he was catching a plane after two busy days and nights in Houston. "It's a roaring, wild, up-to-date frontier spot, and very high-class." Another man will confide that it is nothing but an old country town that has grown up rather rapidly. Another estimates that, culturally, it is about where New York was sixty or seventy years ago. The charge has been made that the city's affairs are run by a hard-fisted, arrogant oligarchy—rich and often able men who are devoid of any genuine public spirit. It has also been declared that Houston is notable for its well-to-do, civic-minded leaders who will pitch in and give generously of their time and money for the betterment of the city. . . .

In its very early days, more than 100 years ago, in the time of the Texas Republic, Houston must have been one of the most unprepossessing of towns. Laid out by its promoters on Buffalo Bayou, some fifty miles from the Gulf of Mexico, it really seemed to have little economic excuse, and its mud, heat and mosquitos, among other things, made life there far less pleasant than in such more favored towns as Galveston, Austin and San Antonio. The dream of making the bayou a ship channel to the Gulf was nursed for decades; modern Houston really dates from the dredging of the channel, which was finally accomplished forty years ago. As a port, Houston now ranks second in gross tonnage to New York.

But there were many other considerations. For example, the Southern Pacific Railroad, long a main artery for Houston trade, is still Houston's biggest employer. The big oil companies began making their headquarters in Houston. Cotton exporting boomed. And, finally, the big chemical companies began coming in. The economy is not only vast; it is extraordinarily diverse.

. . . The Post said, on the occasion of the 1,000,000-metropolitan-area arrival:

"Population growth, for the mere sake of bigness, would be of little value and might be a bad thing. The cities of China, for example, long have been bursting with people, but the standard of living of the people is so low, there is no happiness for them in being crowded among millions of their fellow men."

Well spoken! Nobody is going to sue on that. Houston has grown, it is rich, and the standard of living is relatively high. But that is not the whole story. Houston (and this, of course, could be said of many other great cities) is a yes-but town. It seems that for almost every obvious advantage there is a disadvantage—sometimes important and sometimes only an annoyance which can be removed. Examples:

The skyline, much of which is the handiwork of Jesse Holman Jones, now 80 years old, is quite clearly a solid and striking sight. But the city has grown formlessly; indeed, every attempt to put into effect a city plan with effective zoning, has been defeated. Unkempt blocks, decayed houses and unsightly parking lots are located among the finest buildings.

There is a pathetic shortage of parks in the main part of the city. . . .

Houston has become a paradise for architects and they have done some fine stuff. The houses in the excellent residential district of River Oaks reflect their work and some of the newer developments are even more magnificent. Private swimming pools are having a great vogue. Air conditioning is widespread both in the business houses and in the better homes. . . . But—Houston is still one of the hottest, muggiest places in America. And its slums, sometimes situated near fancy establishments, are as shocking as the worst of New York or Chicago.

The great bulk of the ordinary citizens of Houston, and most of the well-to-do, might fairly be called "moral" people—at least as righteous as might reasonably be expected. There are many large churches. The more spectacular forms of human misbehavior are frowned upon. Gambling houses have a tough time of it. And yet Houston has been severely plagued in the last few years by gangs of young toughs. The traffic in narcotics seems to be serious. . . .

The clubs of Houston—including the Houston Club, the Bayou, the Tejas, the Ramada, and the new Petroleum on top of the Rice Hotel—are in every way superior to anything that may be encountered in the Southwest. Not even Dallas, which is inclined, and with some reason, to be a bit patronizing toward Houston in all realms where the life more beautiful and abundant is concerned, can approach Houston in the sound luxury of its clubs. Even the food is good, and that is a rare circumstance in Texas, except in a few homes.

Houstonians worry about problems which are possibly of more lasting importance than good food. . . . Several committees made up of both the elder and the younger statesmen of the city are trying to figure out some way of meeting the staggering side costs of rapid growth. . . .

. . . The problem of growth, of the increasing cost of all sorts of public services, is one that bedevils every city. It is, indeed, so serious that in some places the theory has been set forth that there is a law of diminishing returns in the growth of great cities. At the moment, the great mass of Houston's citizens—these are not millionaires, but ordinary folks who have trouble making ends meet—are not in a humor to stand higher taxes or increased bus fares.

The question is often asked outside Houston: What of all these new-rich Houstonians who like to show off? Are they as crazy as we hear? The answer is yes. Some of them are quite impossible. A few are so obnoxious that they would soon be tossed out of any reasonably decent Third Avenue saloon in New York. Others are loudmouths. Others seek publicity by giving silly and extravagant parties.

However, there is not much to be alarmed about. For one thing, the ostentatious boys are very much in the minority, and are not held in very high esteem on their home grounds. They will pass, and their pranks will be forgotten. There is nothing wrong with them except money, ignorance and a desire to express themselves—the same thing that was wrong with Diamond Jim Brady in New York in his day.

There is a great division of opinion in Houston over the probable quality of tomorrow's civic leaders. . . . There is one theory that the new times will always bring forth adequate leadership

—that the new men coming along will be in every way as good as the old, and probably better. The theory is debatable. One thoughtful architect said last week:

"The new ones haven't got it. Don't fool yourself. Houston needs big men and they are not coming along. Pretty fair men, yes, but not big. There are many reasons. The old-timers—men like [Jesse] Jones and Will Clayton and a lot of others—had brains, character, drive and a strange pride in Houston. They were all individualists, which in most cases turned out to be good for Houston. The new ones are corporation men, career men, bank officials, managers of this and that property, members of big law firms and representatives of outside capital. They are push-button men, very good in their way, but they are not pioneers, they are not original thinkers and sometimes it seems that at heart they don't give a damn. I hope I'm mistaken."

Another man, always looking for something to complain about, put his finger on what he said was the fundamental trouble with Houston:

"Let an ordinary man, a man of little schooling and no particular background and no real depth, make a great pile of money over the course of a very few years, and what happens? First, he fancies that it was his own genius that made the money, when it probably was owing to other factors, including luck. But, having granted that he has a touch of genius, this fellow immediately begins to throw his weight around.

"It takes many forms. He may develop a habit of shooting off wires to Senators, Presidents, and even foreign political figures. He organizes and backs groups which are bent on saving the country from something or other. He sees our very vitals threatened—without knowing in the least what these vitals are. . . .

Is it really as bad as all that? It may be questioned. The strange bird thus described is, after all, not peculiar to Houston, or to Texas. The omniscience of the new-rich has been observed over the centuries. It is not new. Like love's old sweet song, it will be with us down to the last gasp of the universe. Viva Houston!

No state has experienced as great an influx of new residents since World War II as California, and no city has grown as phenomenally in recent years as Los Angeles. It has increased by a half million people in each census since 1940, and now has 2,479,015 people. Because of the vast distances within its limits, Los Angeles has become truly a product of our automobile age. There have been many critics of the City of the Angels, including those who protest against what for them is the cultural superficiality of the city or against its idealization of a motorized existence. But in this article by Nathan Glazer, one of our perceptive sociologists, Los Angeles and San Diego and the southern California way of life have a champion.

On the recent history of Los Angeles see Remi Nadeau, *Los Angeles: From Mission to Modern City* (New York, 1960), chs. 17–21.

WHEN I LEFT LOS ANGELES ONE DAY LAST FEBRUARY, after a week in Southern California, the newspaper I picked up at the airport reported that the population of Los Angeles County was now 5,800,000, and that it would reach some unimaginable figure by 1975. I also picked up at the airport a report of the Air Pollution Control, District of the County of Los Angeles, discussing the war against smog, and you could, if you wished,

NATHAN GLAZER, "Notes on Southern California: 'A Reasonable Suggestion as to How Things Can be'?" *Commentary*, 28 (August, 1959), 100–107. Reprinted with the author's permission.

277

put these two things together and ominously conclude that the Southern California boom was coming to an end, strangled by the very things that brought it into being. The balmy weather between the mountains and the sea now helps to create the "atmosphere inversion" that traps the smog-producing irritants. The oil which supplied a good deal of the region's first wealth is now the source of great quantities of the poisonous substances found in the atmosphere. The open space and long beaches suggested a new style of life based on the automobile, and exhaust pipes of automobiles now contribute their share of fumes to the smog. A new city almost without traditions, growing up in the age of the automobile, suggested an urban style that permitted people to live anywhere, and thus prevented the creation of a dense city center which might support a public transportation system and reduce dependence on automobiles.

All these things are so easy to say, and two years ago, after my first trip to Southern California, I would perhaps have said them and stopped there. One's bias in favor of traditional cities —Paris, London, New York—is great, and to see Los Angeles now struggling with its very special problems may afford some malicious satisfaction. But even then, on my earlier visit, there were other things to see which might have modified this too-neat picture of the most American city being destroyed by the most American product. You could (shamefacedly) be exhilarated by the long stretches of white concrete roadway, heavily traveled at a rate of speed and with a precision and articulation in moving together and making turns that was surprising to Eastern eyes. Then there were the wild hills and mountains, almost in the middle of the city, with houses perched on top of them commanding a breathtaking view, and the buildings along Wilshire Boulevard, rather bolder in style and color than you saw in the East, but blending into something that was exciting and perhaps beautiful. One part of Los Angeles reminded you of those desolate stretches of Long Island: long roads, partly developed small-house districts, nondescript business establishments along the roadsides; other parts reminded you of a World's Fair, too extreme in its modernity and shock-impact to be taken seriously. But what separated it from Long Island was that you knew, from the heavier traffic, the brighter and more ingenious neon signs, the richer gardens, that this was not a backwater, something left behind, with a city somewhere in the distance that was the real thing; this was the thing itself. The traffic, and the parking spaces around everything, meant that you could, and did, get to whatever was exciting or important or interesting. And what separated it from a World's Fair was that the sense of hectic movement and activity was here to stay, and people were living in it as a regular thing.

And then you realized: there was so much activity, so much life, so much acceptance of and pleasure in this kind of life, that you could not simply turn up your nose, and rush off to San Francisco—which is certainly prettier and pleasanter, but where there is much less building going on, and where the restaurants vie with each other to achieve a more 1890's look. You at least had to look into Los Angeles, move into the traffic, onto the freeways, head toward the beaches and the mountains, and try to feel what the millions living in Southern California, and the millions more coming, were gaining, and losing.

SAN DIEGO. The city of San Diego is about 120 miles southeast of Los Angeles. It advertises itself as smog-free. It already has more than a half million people (there were only 200,000 in 1940), it is one of the fastest growing cities in the country, and it is, in some ways, more typical of Southern California than Los Angeles. It is perhaps a good place to start with.

It has wonderful beaches, a dry, sunny climate, and a magnificent view of harbors and islands from its main downtown hotel. Hills rise behind the city, but unfortunately they aren't steep enough to provide the views one finds in Los Angeles or the San Francisco bay area. San Diego looks different from other cities and it takes a while to realize that one of the reasons it looks different is that it is rich, but rich in a new and special way. You aren't struck by the splendid houses and hotels, expensive restaurants, and other evidences of wealth—even though it has enough of these. You are struck rather by the fact that it is rich communally. To begin with, San Diego seems to command all the resources needed by a city which must lay out vast sums for the roads and parking places required by a motorized populace. You find magnificent roads paralled by even more magnificent roads; the roadside buildings are handsome drive-ins or elegant motels, decorated with redwood, tropical plants, swimming pools, and set off by ingenious landscaping; the hills are green —thanks to expensive irrigation water; the schools brand-new with all the space in the world; the residential developments have intensively planted, well-kept gardens; there are city parks and state parks and beach parks, all well equipped; and even the used-car lots and automobile salesrooms, generally making the dreariest part of an American city, strike one as neat and clean, with their advertising signs a bit brighter and more imaginative than else-where. Certainly the light contributes to this effect—it is brighter and whiter than elsewhere; certainly one's being a tourist con-tributes to it, too. It is a tourist's reaction to see roads, and road-sides, first. But here it is also a native's reaction—they too see a good deal of the world from a car.

There is this wealth of visible, tangible things. But they are things that everyone, or almost everyone, uses: roads and park-ing space, motels, and drive-ins, small houses and gardens, beaches and parks, schools and government buildings. You wonder if all these roads are necessary; does this fine road need another, finer one alongside it? And if it isn't that necessary, who is paying for it? And then you come to one reason for these communal riches: San Diego is also a great naval base, and Southern California the setting for a great concentration of military bases. The entire region therefore benefits from the lavish expenditures of a wealthy government, in an area—defense—in which expenditure is always freest. So let there be yet another road, going, it ap-pears, nowhere through empty and unusable country—but then one notices that this road is a way of getting to some air base or rocket installation, even though an unnecessarily expensive way of getting there.

The Federal government contributes more than roads to South-ern California. It contributes the water by its irrigation works; it helps to provide cheap electricity with its great dams, and cheap electricity keeps things cleaner, signs brighter, and leads to the widespread phenomenon of stores being lit up all night—all add-ing to the festive air. In the city itself, on a group of islands in a bay, and on the surrounding shores, a great park is being de-veloped—one reads, "By the City of San Diego in cooperation with the Army Corps of Engineers." The servicemen need parks, beaches, seaside facilities for their families—and the government helps pay for at least a good part of it.

Even culture is provided. In Balboa Park, in the middle of San Diego, is a huge complex of exposition buildings, one group in a rich Spanish Colonial style of architecture, another group, more recent, in more modern style. How is it possible for such a city, one asks, simply to maintain all these buildings, with their beautiful landscaping and wonderful gardens? The answer is, that there have been two expositions in San Diego—and the Federal government paid for the buildings and landscaping, or a good part thereof. And so San Diego is endowed with a wealth of facilities: with two large open air theaters (one surrounding a huge organ, one in a natural bowl), a large civic auditorium, a recital hall, buildings for an art gallery, a natural history museum and an anthropological museum, a replica of an Elizabethan theater in which a local group puts on plays, and other facilities too numerous to mention, but all of which seem far, far more than even a city of a half million can use. In any case, it is certainly more than it could have created from its own resources.

The help given by the Federal government is supplemented by private philanthropy. The outdoor organ is the Spreckels organ; one of the largest buildings is Ford Hall; the fine American Indian exhibits in one of the museums bear the name of Scripps, as does the Institute of Oceanography and the Art Gallery and Library of La Jolla, just to the north.

The government and the wealthy have contributed water, roads, institutions, buildings. And now it is all there, part of a concentration of communal wealth that is almost unequaled in the world.

TASTE. When you speak of Southern California taste, you think of the ice-cream parlor in the shape of an ice-cream cone, the hot-dog stand in the shape of a hot dog. But our images are always ten or twenty years behind the reality. A clean, simple line prevails in Southern California, enlivened by color in materials, by tasteful landscaping, and interesting patterns in wood —exuberance is now generally limited to the gardens and the planting. The new building is much better and bolder than the old—as compared with much of the rest of the country, where the new building is often worse than the old. The best buildings tend to be the public ones—the schools and colleges and universities, the motels and shopping centers.

Where, you wonder, did this new California taste come from? There was no tradition to follow. Of course the impact of modern architecture has been enormous, here as elsewhere, and seems to have produced a special local variant. (Compare the Wilshire Boulevard office buildings with the New York office buildings.) But then it dawns on one: the roads must have had something to do with it. They are a dominating experience, the only large common experience that could be responsible for the general upgrading of taste in Southern California. The new roads present not only simple and subtle lines, impressive cross-overs with intriguing concrete support structures and elegant curves, but they present also a clean, uncluttered landscape with continually varied shapes, colors, patterns. There are brown and green hills, there sea-side cliffs, here meadows, there a strange strewing of boulders across hilly country. And on the whole, the way that Southern California is now being built up prevents the landscape from being quite as corrupted by roadside trash as was the case in the 20's and 30's. There are neat if uninspired government installations, sometimes an impressive group of buildings of a great commercial farm, the more exuberant commercial structures. The roads provide quite a different experience and image from those of the first decades of the motor age. They are probably the one uncorrupted expression of a functional-engineering outlook which most Americans regularly experience.

But throughout you are struck by an improvement in taste: it would appear that wealth alone upgrades taste. For if one compares the American roadside of the 20's and 30's with that of the 50's, or with the Mexican roadside just south of the border, you see the effect of professional signs as against crude lettering, of new, smooth surfaces as against patched, broken surfaces put together of clashing materials. Wealth may corrupt taste under certain circumstances, but after a certain point, after all traditional values and proportions have disappeared (as in lower California, and the Southern California of the 20's), wealth serves to upgrade it—somewhat.

There are of course other influences on taste besides the influ-

ence of wealth operating in a society where traditional standards have disappeared. Another influence is the very lack of a
"tradition" (except for the weak Spanish one), which has left
the field wide open to the homemaking and "California living"
magazines. And on these we see the impact of the general rise
of taste in the country, and of the victory of variants of a modern approach in architecture and design. And then another influence perhaps comes from the Japanese gardeners, who are responsible for most of the Southern California gardens. These,
it is true, have at first glance little in common with Japanese gardens: they are based on the intensive cultivation of small plots,
and on the availability of exotic tropical plants—two circumstances which are quite different from those that prevail in Japan.
And yet the general character of these exquisite gardens probably
reflects the good taste of the Japanese.

THE UNIVERSITY. Just north of San Diego, and continuous with
it, along a curving seacoast with mountains looming up behind,
is La Jolla. . . . There are motels and apartment houses on the
side nearer San Diego, and then pretty and expensive houses in
pastel colors on quiet streets, and then a town center with expensive shops, tea-roomy restaurants, a library, a school, an art
museum; palm trees line the streets. You think, the Riveria cannot be nicer: hardly anything on any American coastline compares with it. And yet here the University of California has
bought a tract of land and plans to build a huge new campus that
in time will be as big as Berkeley and the University of California
in Los Angeles, and that may be as distinguished.

This is perhaps the most striking introduction to democracy
in California: that the free state university takes for a new campus (and can afford to take) some of the best and most desirable
land in the state. And this, too, in a state which, because so much
of it is desert, mountain, and agricultural valley, does not really
have a great supply of good residential land. Nevertheless, the
university moves into an exclusive seaside resort and will in time
bring in thousands of poor students—who will certainly change
La Jolla—and thousands of not-so-rich employees and faculty
members—who will change it even more. . . .

LOS ANGELES. You then proceed through Riverside itself, a pleasant town of old trees, white-painted wooden houses. . . . The traffic now begins to get heavier, the roads begin to widen, and you are soon approaching Los Angeles.

Finally you are on an elevated road that carries five lanes of traffic each way, and that approaches other great roads carrying the same incredible load of traffic. To enter Los Angeles on the freeway from the west, and to see the other freeways coming in, crossing over each other, with enormous rivers of cars moving from one artery to another—this is an amazing sight. What wealth has been poured into the Los Angeles freeways! How many hundreds of millions are yet to be spent upon them! From one perspective, this is a huge, misguided undertaking, a great waste of resources which might have been used for an efficient public transportation system. But it also helps make possible a life in which everyone chooses his time to come and his time to go, in which people can swim in the afternoon, work at night, and shop in huge supermarkets in the early morning, in which only a small proportion of the population of a huge metropolitan area ever sees, or has cause to see, the downtown region, in which everything can be done from a car, and in which the New Yorker, to whom a car is a torment, discovers the efficiency of being in a city in which every house, store, institution is surrounded by its own parking space. Here you can conduct your business, go to restaurants and movies, visit friends, on your own schedule. An enormous expanse of space, capital equipment, gasoline is required. But you think too that the world can probably support one great city of this type, and in any case only one country has the resources and the land to carry through such a utopian enterprise. Utopian it is, because a city of this type demands that every adult has his own car—and Los Angeles is not very far from that now. Yet still the traffic moves, and more rapidly than in New York.

But finally you get off the freeway to descend into an endless Brooklyn or Queens: single-family houses, stretching for mile upon mile, with occasional streets devoted to business. But with this difference from Brooklyn or Queens: that here everyone has chosen his way of life, while Brooklyn and Queens have not been chosen, but taken out of necessity. The sense of a chosen city, a desired way of life, a realized wish, is strong. We should not be deceived by the surface resemblance to the endless "bedroom boroughs" of New York and Chicago. Here the bedroom and living room are mixed. The streets with little houses are as busy with traffic as great thoroughfares in the East. This may offend our sense of the proper organization of a city, but in any case the curse of the bedroom is removed when it is not separated from the city by a long ride, at the same hour each day, by subway, trains, or bus. Here the city is scattered all around, as if a bomb had distributed Manhattan south of 59th Street homogeneously throughout Brooklyn, Queens, and the Bronx.

THE PEOPLE. There are of course the old people who have retired, and moved in hundreds of thousands from the Midwest and South. Nathanael West's *The Day of the Locust* described them with horror, and fixes the image of Los Angeles as a place of horror. And yet you don't see these people: they are not on Wilshire Boulevard or in Hollywood, or Beverley Hills, or Westwood, or Fairfax, or in the Valley, or in Boyle Heights, or on Adams and Jefferson Boulevard. Perhaps there are fewer of them than there used to be: they are in any case less mobile and certainly less visible than other parts of the Los Angeles population. More visible are hundreds of thousands of Mexicans, and hundreds of thousands of Negroes. Despite the tight-lipped oldsters from the Midwest and the South, Los Angeles is quite an enlightened city: not as enlightened as San Francisco and New York, but not far behind them.

It is the second largest Jewish city in the country—there are 400,000 Jews or more. There are 40,000 Japanese, more than before the wartime relocation, which uprooted thousands from farms. The old concentration of these groups in downtown Los Angeles has been broken up, by relocation and then by the vast postwar freeway building which has wiped out large areas in the downtown section that were Negro, Mexican, Japanese, and Jewish. This downtown destruction has been combined with vast building on the outskirts: and so the Negroes and Mexicans and Japanese and poor Jews can find fairly good housing (by that I mean—better than in other cities in which they live) that has been left behind by other groups moving out, and we find Negroes, and Mexicans, and Jews, and Japanese, or two or three of these groups, living amicably together in many neighborhoods.

The main Japanese neighborhood has now moved to the west, and stretches for perhaps a mile or so along West Jefferson, and reaches back into surrounding streets. It blends into a Negro neighborhood to the east, and is itself mixed most of the way. You see large and prosperous stores run by Japanese, you see a score of real estate offices—advertising investment property, which seems to be favored by the group. You see a well-designed supermarket with attached one-story offices (a common California arrangement—everyone thus has parking space)—and they contain the offices of a Japanese architect, accountant, lawyer, doctor, dentist. You know too that from this neighborhood and others come great numbers of students for the University of California in Los Angeles—1,000 Japanese attend the university, I was told.

And then there are the young people. So many American cities lose them, so few attract them. Los Angeles is one of those that still attracts them. It is far away, it is different, there are jobs, some of them interesting and glamorous. You suspect that Hollywood's declining predominance in the entertainment industry has been accompanied not only by a rise in its taste, but a rise in the level and character of young people that it and the related entertainment industries attract. You wonder whether Hollywood twenty years ago could have provided the people to support so many little theaters, coffeehouses, and other gathering places for young people of artistic and intellectual bent. In any case, Los Angeles today, with New York and San Francisco, has a "Village"— a place with little theaters (more than one) and coffeehouses, small night clubs in which you hear folk singers, psychoanalytically-wise comedians, flamenco guitarists, and such. Whatever the meaning of all this for the history of culture (and it may be a curse, conceivably), for a city it is fun, and you can hardlly imagine a great city without its bohemia. Los Angeles qualifies; its bohemia is different in quality, perhaps inferior in quality, to that of San Francisco, as that is perhaps inferior to New York's. But its differences also make it interesting. The three bohemias sort out, from the young people coming from the towns and cities of the country, and from these three cities themselves, somewhat different types. Some people, of course, try all three.

Bohemia, too, is democratic: and in a party on the Hollywood hills you will find people who will want to act and people who have actually been seen on the screen, a nightclub chef (his working hours are the same as the entertainers, and he knows them), a jewelry salesman, a psychiatrist from New York for a medical convention, people who are quite indefinable, and a visiting intellectual from New York. The house is an expensive one, but the party is being held in a kind of basement room in which a poor hopeful actor lives, built into the hill, and opening on a garden with a swimming pool, and there is a fine view of the city—for it is winter, and the winds have blown the smog away.

WORK. Los Angeles looks less like a place where people work than any other great city in the world. There are no busy skyscrapers filled with office workers and garment workers, as in New York. The tallest buildings in the city are some downtown government buildings, some elegant hotels, the Prudential Life Insurance Company on Wilshire Boulevard, the Angelus and Mormon temples. There are oil wells and refineries——but they require few workers. The movies and television are main industries, and you do see huge studios—but that is not exactly one's typical image of work. There are factories—but they make things like airplanes and electronic equipment, which require no belching smokestacks. There is no surge of workers into and out of the city—the traffic is dense morning and evening, but it is going both ways, and you can't be sure who is going to the beach, the supermarket, Disneyland, or to work.

Indeed, the gap between work and play in Los Angeles must be narrower than in any other great city. Where do people work in Los Angeles? In supermarkets, in gasoline stations, in parking lots, in the movies, in hotels and motels and restaurants, as gardeners, in offices which have tropical plants and bright cars right outside the door, outdoors as building workers, indoors in bright new factories. And the same universal vehicle, the car, serves work and pleasure interchangeably, and the vast complex of economic activities which serve the car also serve work and pleasure interchangeably.

Life is hard and life is earnest, and there are coal miners and steelworkers and auto workers and textile mill operatives—but not in Los Angeles. There freer styles of work prevail, operating in an urban environment which is more successful in obscuring the sharp division between work and non-work than any other. There are the backyard swimming pools and the beaches, which can be used three-quarters of the year, there is the huge array of service jobs which can be worked at part-time and at odd hours and on odd days, there are all the non-working people who have come with a little money and invested in real estate, and those who have come with nothing but live on pensions. More people act as if they were on vacation (and must feel it, too) than anywhere in the world. There is no way of telling it is Sunday in Los Angeles unless one looks at the calendar.

Los Angeles produces less than any other great city of the things that, from a grim, Protestant way of looking at things, anyone really *needs*. And yet it grows like mad. And those other cities, that supply the country with useful things like coal and steel and cloth and machinery, decline. For Los Angeles, everything has been made easy. The vast investment that is required to maintain 6,000,000 people and 3,000,000 automobiles in the desert seems to require little effort from anyone. The water and the electricity come from hundreds of miles away, and the government helped to pay for it anyway. The oil only has to be taken from the ground. The cars come from Detroit. The roads are paid for by the government, or the gasoline tax. And the complicated engineering effort needed to do these things only requires money and engineers, and there is plenty of both. There is the smog—but that too can be solved by money and engineers. It is hard to see how the machine can stop, and leave these people without water for the gardens, electricity for the bright lights, cars to run around in.

All the rhythms in Los Angeles are different—the daily movement in and out of the city center is hardly greater than other movements, the weekly cycle is scarcely noticeable, the seasonal cycle is different. That dividing line between work and non-work that is at the basis of so much of Western achievement, and misery, loses its sharpness. But perhaps for our society in general work has already done its job, and we can keep things going with much less of it. And if we can, Southern California is not an aberration, but a reasonable suggestion as to how things can be.

Bibliography

GENERAL STUDIES OF AMERICAN URBAN HISTORY

Allen, Robert S. (ed.). *Our Fair City*. New York: Vanguard Press, 1947.

Blake, Nelson M. *Water for the Cities*. Ithaca, New York: Cornell University Press, 1956.

Bridenbaugh, Carl. *Cities in the Wilderness: The First Century of Urban Life in America, 1625–1742*. New York: Alfred A. Knopf, 1955.

————. *Cities in Revolt: Urban Life in America, 1743–1776*. New York: Alfred A. Knopf, 1955.

Dunlap, George A. *The City in the American Novel, 1789–1900*. Philadelphia: University of Pennsylvania Press, 1934.

Glaab, Charles N. *The American City: A Documentary History*. Homewood, Illinois: The Dorsey Press, 1963.

Goldman, Eric F. (ed.) *Historiography and Urbanization: Essays in American History in Honor of W. Stull Holt*. Baltimore: The Johns Hopkins Press, 1941. See especially William Diamond, "On the Dangers of an Urban Interpretation of History," pp. 67–108.

Gottmann, Jean. *Megalopolis: The Urbanized Northeastern Seaboard of the United States*. New York: Twentieth-Century Fund, 1961.

Green, Constance M. *American Cities in the Growth of the Nation*. London: John de Graff, 1957.

Handlin, Oscar. *Immigration as a Factor in American History*. Englewood Cliffs, New Jersey: Prentice-Hall, 1959 (Paperback).

Handlin, Oscar and John Burchard (eds.). *The Historian and the City*. Cambridge: Harvard University Press, 1963.

Hatt, Paul K. and Albert J. Reiss. *Cities and Society: The Revised Reader in Urban Sociology*. New York: The Free Press of Glencoe, 1961.

Holt, W. Stull. "Some Consequences of the Urban Movement in American History," *Pacific Historical Review*, vol. 22 (November 1953), 337–351.

Jacobs, Jane. *The Death and Life of Great American Cities*. New York: Vintage Books, 1963 (Paperback).

Lampard, Eric. "American Historians and the Study of Urbanization," *American Historical Review*, vol. 67 (October 1961), 49–62.

McKelvey, Blake. "American Urban History Today," *American Historical Review*, vol. LVII (July, 1952), 919–929.

———. *American Urbanization, 1860–1915*. New Brunswick, N.J.: Rutgers University Press, 1963.

Mumford, Lewis. *The City in History*. New York: Harcourt, Brace & World, 1961.

Perry, George Sessions. *Cities of America*. New York: Whittlesey House, 1947.

Schlesinger, Arthur M. *Paths to the Present*. New York: The Macmillan Company, 1949. Chapter XI, "The City in American Civilization."

———. *The Rise of the City, 1878–1898*. New York: The Macmillan Company, 1933.

Sjoberg, Gideon. *The Preindustrial City, Past and Present*. Glencoe, Illinois: Free Press, 1960.

Still, Bayrd. "Patterns of Mid-Nineteenth Century Urbanization in the Middle West," *Mississippi Valley Historical Review*, 28 (September, 1941), 187–206.

Strauss, Anselm. *Images of the American City*. New York: Free Press of Glencoe, 1961.

Tunnard, Christopher and Henry Hope Reed, Jr. *American Skyline*. New York: Mentor Books, 1956 (Paperback).

Wade, Richard C. *The Urban Frontier: The Rise of Western Cities, 1790–1830*. Cambridge, Massachusetts: Harvard University Press, 1959.

Weber, Adna Ferrin. *The Growth of Cities in the Nineteenth Century: A Study in Statistics*. Ithaca, New York: Cornell University Press, 1963.

Weimer, David R. *City and Country in America*. New York: Appleton, Century Crofts, 1962 (Paperback).

Wertenbaker, Thomas J. *The Golden Age of Colonial Culture*. Ithaca, New York: Cornell University Press, 1959 (Paperback).

White, Morton and Lucia. *The Intellectual Versus the City: From Thomas Jefferson to Frank Lloyd Wright*. Cambridge: Harvard University Press and the M.I.T. Press, 1962.

Wohl, R. Richard. "Urbanism, Urbanity, and the Historians," *University of Kansas City Review*, vol. XXII (Autumn 1955), 53–61.

Index of Authors

Index of Cities